NUCLEAR ENDGAME

NUCLEAR ENDGAME

THE NEED FOR ENGAGEMENT WITH NORTH KOREA

Jacques L. Fuqua, Jr.

PRAEGER SECURITY INTERNATIONAL
Westport, Connecticut • London

Library of Congress Cataloging-in-Publication Data

Fuqua, Jacques.
Nuclear endgame : the need for engagement with North Korea / Jacques L. Fuqua, Jr.
    p. cm.
    Includes bibliographical references and index.
    ISBN–13: 978–0–275–99074–9 (alk. paper)
    1. United States–Foreign relations–Korea (North)   2. Korea (North)–Foreign
relations–United States.   3. Nuclear weapons–Social aspects–Korea (North)
4. National security–Korea (North)   5. Bush, George W. (George Walker),
1946—Political and social views.   I. Title.
    JZ1480.A57K7   2007
    327.1′747095193–dc22   2007016350

British Library Cataloguing in Publication Data is available.

Library of Congress Catalog Card Number: 2007016350
ISBN-13: 978–0–275–99074–9
ISBN-10: 0–275–99074–5

First published in 2007

Praeger Security International, 88 Post Road West, Westport, CT 06881
An imprint of Greenwood Publishing Group, Inc.
www.praeger.com

Printed in the United States of America

The paper used in this book complies with the
Permanent Paper Standard issued by the National
Information Standards Organization (Z39.48–1984).

10 9 8 7 6 5 4 3 2 1

oclc 123818232

To my wife, Yoshimi, who has been to me like water for a growing tree. And my daughters, Sakura and Miyako, who have served as the source for much of my inspiration in life, so they might know anything is possible.

"I am the object of criticism around the world. But I think that since I am being discussed, then I am on the right track."
—*Kim Jong Il*[1]

Contents

Map of Korean Peninsula. Cartography by Bookcomp, Inc.

Preface

gorae ssaum ae saewoodung tuhjinda
   —In a fight between whales, the back of a shrimp bursts[1]

North Korea remains the enigmatic geopolitical player it has been since its inception in 1948. It continues to threaten regional peace and stability; presents a growing global threat through its propensity to proliferate nuclear weapons technology; and displays behavior that runs counter to accepted international norms. Yet after nearly sixty years of grappling with it, the international community is no closer to solving the North Korea puzzle. The purpose of this book is to provide policy recommendations for the United States and its regional allies to pursue in resolving the nuclear issue, but is premised on a set of assumptions differing from those presently in vogue: (1) that the nuclear issue is not a stand-alone issue and resolution will require a comprehensive approach; (2) because of this, more than just the usual formula of seeking international isolation, imposing economic sanctions and extending promise of economic benefits in exchange for nuclear dismantlement will be required; (3) that no resolution can be achieved without some fundamental understanding of the ideological underpinnings and historical events and relationships that have gone into constructing North Korea's perceptual framework of the geopolitical landscape in which it exists; and (4) that constructively engaging the regime, based on the preceding assumptions, is not tantamount to capitulating to the enemy, rather it forms the basis for strategically maneuvering the United States and its allies into a position of advantage over the regime, which they presently do not enjoy.

This book is divided into two main sections. The first section focuses on the ideological and historical foundations of the North Korean regime, treating the development and importance of the *Juche* ideology; the role of the United States and former Soviet Union in creating a divided peninsula; the regime's historical relationships with China, South Korea and the former Soviet Union; its foreign policy and economic imperatives throughout the last half of the twentieth century; and how these coalesce to mitigate against the success of current U.S. efforts to dismantle the regime's nuclear program. The second section examines the composition of the present North Korean threat: its nuclear, biological, and chemical arsenals; why armed conflict or forced regime change are not viable solutions to the current crisis; and why a comprehensive and aggressive economic strategy offers the best chance for achieving denuclearization in North Korea.

In completing this work, I owe a great debt to a number of colleagues who reviewed drafts of this manuscript and helped to identify areas needing improvement in order to increase its utility: Ambassador Thomas Hubbard, former U.S. ambassador to South Korea; Professor Michael Chambers, Chair of the Political Science department at Indiana State University and associate professor of international relations and comparative and Asian politics; Colonel Mark Franklin, U.S. Army Foreign Area Officer (Northeast Asia); and Mr. John Frank, history teacher at Center Grove High School in Greenwood, IN, and recipient of the 2004 Indiana Governor's Award for Excellence in the Teaching of History. A special thanks to Mrs. Barbara Fuqua, a taskmaster of the English language, who patiently read through several drafts of this manuscript.

Abbreviations

AES	Asymmetric Economic Statecraft
ARF	ASEAN Regional Forum
CBM	Confidence Building Measures
CCP	Chinese Communist Party
CCPSU	Twentieth Congress of the Communist Party of the Soviet Union
CVID	Complete, Verifiable, and Irreversible Dismantlement
DAP	Denuclearization Action Plan
DMZ	Demilitarized Zone
DPRK	Democratic People's Republic of Korea
EU	European Union
FAO	Foreign Area Officer
GDP	Gross Domestic Product
GNP	Gross National Product
HEU	Highly Enriched Uranium
IAEA	International Atomic Energy Agency
IED	Improvised Explosive Devices
ILSA	Iran-Libya Sanctions Act
JANIS	Joint Army-Navy Intelligence Study on Korea
JETRO	Japan External Trade Organization
KEDO	Korean Peninsula Energy Development Organization
KWP	Korean Workers' Party
LWR	Light Water Nuclear Reactors

NBC	Nuclear, Biological and Chemical
NKWP	North Korean Workers' Party
NPT	Nuclear Non-Proliferation Treaty
PDS	Public Distribution System
PPCNK	Provisional People's Committee for North Korea
PRC	People's Republic of China
PSI	Proliferation Security Initiative
SEZ	Special Economic Zone
SKIG	South Korean Interim Government
SKWP	South Korean Workers' Party
SOF	Special Operations Forces
SOTW	Solutions Other than War
UNTCOK	United Nations Temporary Commission on Korea
USSR	Union of Soviet Socialist Republics
WFP	World Food Program
WMD	Weapons of Mass Destruction
WPK	Workers' Party of Korea
WTO	Word Trade Organization

Introduction

U.S. strategy for resolving North Korea's nuclear weapons issue is in need of a paradigmatic shift. The Bush administration's approach over the past six years, on the whole, has proven ineffective for two important reasons. First is the administration's tendency to compartmentalize components of the issue. While it is true that the most immediate threat posed by the regime is through its nuclear weapons program and thus merits attention, the North Korean issue will not be solved through myopic focus on its nuclear program because it is only one piece of a larger whole. What is needed is a comprehensive, long-term and forward-thinking policy that weans North Korea off of its dependence on nuclear weapons as a geopolitical tool. What is meant by "comprehensive" is a strategy that recognizes North Korean nuclear weapons as only symptomatic of a much larger problem that must first be addressed if any resolution is to be achieved. Second has been the lack of clarity with regard to administration strategy and goals; there is little to distinguish one from the other. Complete, verifiable, and irreversible dismantlement (CVID) of the regime's nuclear weapons program has served, for six years, as the cornerstone of the administration's strategy on North Korea. While CVID is viable as a goal, it is not a strategy. It defines a desired end state, not the means for attaining it. Without a clear vision on how best to move forward and to resolve the issue, the administration will likely wind up spending eight years grappling with the North Korean regime and have little to show for it. This, despite the recently concluded Denuclearization Action Plan (DAP), reached within the Six Party Talks venue in February 2007. Although the DAP and the process undertaken to successfully conclude it is an improvement over the administration's previous efforts, it still suffers from a myopic approach to the North Korean nuclear issue, a key characteristic of which is a lack of comprehensiveness. This topic is more fully addressed in the following chapter.

Since its inception in 1948, much has been written about the Democratic People's Republic of Korea, hereinafter referred to as North Korea: from thoughtful analyses rendered by security experts to less insightful and perhaps emotive pontifications and characterizations—axis of evil and outpost of tyranny come immediately to mind. Despite the nearly six-decadelong voluminous treatment of the topic, the world is appreciably no closer to solving the enigma of North Korea than it was when the peninsula was initially divided in the immediate aftermath of WWII. The possible exception to this is the Republic of Korea, hereinafter referred to as South Korea, a point to which I'll return in later chapters. Current events underscore this point. In September 2005 the United States and other members of the Six Party Talks (hereinafter also referred to as the Talks) thought they had reached agreement with North Korea on important dismantlement modalities of its nuclear weapons program. Within only 24 hours, however, differences emerged between the respective U.S. and North Korean positions with regard to the timing of events contained within the agreement. The United States wanted dismantlement activities to precede any discussion of possible provision of light water nuclear reactors. The North Koreans, on the other hand, were more interested in discussing the reactors. Similarly, on July 4, 2006, the world witnessed the launch of seven North Korean missiles, to include the Taepodong-2 missile, much touted by U.S. administration officials as a potential threat to U.S. sovereign territory.[1] This, despite U.S. administration admonishment that test firing the Taepodong-2 would be viewed as a "provocative act."

U.S. policy toward both halves of the Korean peninsula has undergone a fundamental shift since 2001, exacerbated by the events of 9/11, which has neither served well U.S. interests on the peninsula nor in the region. Lukewarm at best to former President Kim Dae-jung's (1998–2003) Sunshine Policy and distancing itself from Clinton-era engagement policies with the North, the Bush administration crafted a policy centered nearly exclusively on nonproliferation of nuclear weapons, which manifested itself in the incessant demand for CVID of North Korea's nuclear weapons program. It has, unfortunately, been devoid of any substantive means for achieving this goal save reliance on Cold War era containment policies, which will be referred to in the aggregate as the Bush doctrine.[2] (It should be noted that both South Korea and China have in the past questioned the viability of such an approach, which they see as the desired end state, but not as the means to an end.) This sort of approach forces one to focus solely on manifest behaviors and consequently overlook potential opportunities to turn the situation to U.S. advantage. Missing is a fundamental understanding of "why" the North Korean regime undertakes such seemingly rash behavior (beyond the rather trite rationale of "they are evil"). Such understanding lies at the heart of innovative and constructive policy development that potentially moves North Korea in a more desirable direction. CVID as a goal is both sound and necessary for the maintenance of regional stability in Asia. Use of Cold War era containment policies, a basic lack of understanding of our North Korean adversary, and confusing policy with goals, however, have undermined any potential progress toward CVID, subjects discussed more fully in Chapter 5.

Events of 9/11 steered U.S.-North Korean policy more definitively in the direction of the global war on terror and by the time of President Bush's State of the Union address on January 29, 2002, North Korea had been inducted into the now infamous axis of evil. Attendant to this designation was a better defined hard-line approach to negotiations with all three nations of the axis, at the center of which emerged a greater disdain for substantive discussion with what were perceived to be rogue nations. Rather, "negotiations" came to be couched in terms of "demands" for acquiescence.

Arguing the merits or shortfalls of the Bush administration's pursuit of the global war on terror and its degree of success is beyond the scope of this book. That there exists the possibility it has diverted the administration's attention away from the North Korean nuclear issue and impacted its efforts at achieving nonproliferation of WMD is, however, an important consideration. A reasonably cogent argument might be made that North Korea's nuclear capability has in fact improved under the Bush administration, thus throwing into question the soundness of its policy pursuits to date. Consider, for example, the following sequence of events. In December 2002 the regime expelled International Atomic Energy Agency personnel assigned to monitor activity at North Korea's nuclear reactors, in part a response to the cessation of heavy fuel oil shipments provided under the Agreed Framework; it reopened a nuclear facility at which were stored 8,000 spent plutonium fuel rods with an estimated yield of five nuclear weapons; it withdrew from the Nuclear Non-Proliferation Treaty (NPT) in January 2003; in July 2006 North Korea launched seven missiles despite U.S. demands that it refrain from doing so; and in October 2006 the regime detonated a nuclear test device. All this occurred in the face of unwavering demands for CVID and the broader Bush doctrine. This mode of engagement simply has not worked.

Other shifts in U.S. policy have taken place along with its emphasis on CVID, the cumulative effect of which has changed the tenor of the Six Party negotiations with the North and significantly impacted the U.S. role in those negotiations. First is the "Sino-fication" of the negotiation process. By this I mean the present U.S. tendency toward strong reliance, or some might argue overreliance, on China to induce North Korea to participate in the Talks and comport itself more in line with international norms, essentially ceding the

U.S. leadership role, in part, to China. Second, has been the U.S. willingness to allow itself and South Korea to take increasingly divergent paths on the North Korea issue—the United States pursuing a more hard-line approach while South Korea seeks broader engagement as a means of persuading the regime to give up pursuit of its nuclear weapons program.

Considering the foregoing, this book seeks to accomplish two important aims. The first is to address the general lack of understanding of North Korea as a geopolitical entity—its history, ideology, and how the regime is likely to respond under certain conditions. As alluded to earlier, a more in-depth understanding of our North Korean adversary would allow the United States to more effectively frame the North Korea issue in its entirety and construct a workable comprehensive policy that ultimately addresses its nuclear weapons program. Yet, this is precisely what the administration has demonstrated a reluctance to do. Such a comprehensive understanding lies at the core of international relations, whether with allies or adversaries; without it most efforts wind up superficial at best, or even counterproductive. Consequently, the first half of this book is devoted to discussing the rise of North Korea as we know it today, from ideological and geopolitical perspectives.

The U.S. Army provides a good example. The Army spends millions of dollars each year training a core group of its officers to become foreign area officers (FAO). These officers devote much of their careers to becoming military statespersons who deal with a host of bilateral politico-military and security issues with foreign governments around the world. They are trained extensively in the target country's language, culture, history, foreign relations, and security issues and their collective contributions to our nation's security are not insignificant. The basis of their accomplishments, however, hinge on understanding the countries and governments with which they work.

The second aim is to develop a workable and more comprehensive framework for engaging North Korea in order to more effectively wean it off its dependence on nuclear weapons as a geopolitical bargaining chip, to which the second half of the book will be devoted. To build an effective foundation for such a construct, the efficacy of various policy options will be explored: armed conflict, regime change, and economic sanctions among them. In the final analysis, the option that offers the greatest chance of success is an aggressive, comprehensive policy approach centering on the regime's soft underbelly—its economy—in what will be referred to as asymmetric economic statecraft (AES). AES seeks to foster greater regime dependence on economic inputs Western nations are in a position to provide, with the goal of slowly eroding the North Korean command economy in lieu of a more market-oriented structure, which in turn can be used as leverage in moving the regime toward complete and permanent denuclearization. Thus, fundamental to the success of AES is the degree of access into North Korea

Western nations can achieve. I suggest ways of achieving greater access in the final chapter of this book. This is, however, not an immediate process; rather it is deliberate and evolutionary in nature.

The basis for any potential success of such an approach, surprisingly, rests within the regime itself. Contrary to popular assertions, the regime is capable of acting pragmatically in furtherance of its own self-interests. Indeed close examination of certain domestic trends and growing economic linkages with South Korea through joint ventures indicates that the regime is exercising a certain degree of pragmatism as it experiments on the periphery of various market reforms.

But in order to use its weak economy to maximum effectiveness, the United States must abandon its compartmentalized approach to the regime's nuclear weapons program in favor of a broader, long-term, flexible policy. Herein lies the road to future success.

1

Debunking the Myth: What's Really Behind the North Korean Nuclear Issue

While we don't think time is on our side, it's not on their side either.
—Christopher Hill, U.S. Assistant Secretary of State for East Asia, during hearings convened by the Senate Foreign Relations Committee

The following section briefly examines some of the more commonly held beliefs and misperceptions regarding the North Korean nuclear weapons program and the negotiations through the Six Party Talks to persuade North Korea to divest itself of nuclear ambitions. This discussion will assist in laying the necessary groundwork for constructing a workable and coherent policy framework for effective engagement of the North Korean regime, offered in later chapters, as the United States and its allies seek the regime's CVID of its nuclear weapons program. The first step in that process is to begin debunking the North Korean myth.

Now that the Denuclearization Action Plan (DAP) is in place can the North Korean nuclear issue be considered resolved?

Simply put, no. News that the North Korean regime had agreed, by signing on to the DAP in the Six Party Talks, to dismantle its nuclear weapons program was greeted with cautious optimism earlier this year; perhaps not without good reason. While the regime agreed to reveal the full extent of its nuclear programs and ultimately dismantle them, the agreement does not address all the possible eventualities and consequently presents some potential sticking points. Following are the major points of the agreement (the entire agreement can be accessed at the U.S. State Department's Web site, http://www.state.gov/r/pa/prs/ps/2007/february/80479.htm):

- That North Korea will shut down and eventually abandon its plutonium-based nuclear program at the Yongbyon facility;
- That the regime will declare all of its nuclear weapons programs, both plutonium- and uranium-based;
- That North Korea will over the next two years be provided the equivalent of one million tons of heavy fuel oil (HFO) in exchange for meeting benchmarks toward dismantlement;
- That both the United States and North Korea will move toward normalization of relations;
- That Japan and North Korea will initiate normalization discussions.

Problematic in this process has been a lack of transparency as to why the regime has agreed to sign on to such an agreement at this point. This is important because it might be a reasonable measure of future behavior with regard to North Korean willingness to comply with the provisions of the DAP. First and foremost for the regime has been its near obsession over $24 million in assets frozen in Banco Delta Asia (Macau) by the United States because of allegations that the institution laundered money from the regime's illicit activities. Under the provisions of the DAP, the United States agreed to remove impediments so that North Korea can regain access to those frozen funds, which was accomplished by mid-March 2007.[1]

The uncertainty now, however, is how supportive the regime will be of the DAP in the coming months now that it has regained access to its financial assets. Hopefully the regime recognizes the good will extended by the United States and will thus feel compelled to comply with DAP provisions. History, however, does not necessarily support such a sanguine outlook. During 1991, for example, North Korea undertook a diplomatic makeover, increasing efforts at rapprochement with Japan. It also agreed to sign on to the nuclear safeguard accord, which permitted International Atomic Energy Agency inspections of its nuclear sites. (The regime agreed only after two U.S. concessions: the United States as well agreed to have its own military installations in South Korea inspected for the presence of nuclear weapons; and, of course, economic inducements from the United States.) Similarly, in 2000, North Korea undertook a broad diplomatic blitzkrieg, establishing diplomatic relations with various Western nations and sending an envoy to Washington, D.C., to discuss with Clinton administration officials ways to move toward peace on the peninsula. This was followed by the visit of then Secretary of State Madeleine Albright to Pyongyang to meet with Kim Jong il. There was even for a short time discussion of a Clinton–Kim meeting. The point here is that a discernible pattern has emerged. The regime has, toward the end of the two preceding U.S. presidential administrations, shown remarkable flexibility in its negotiations, perhaps for the purpose of pocketing as many concessions as possible before their close, only to return to more obstinate behavior in the future. There is no way of telling at this point whether this is presently the case, but the situation does bear close watching.

Another possible reason for North Korea to sign on to the DAP is for the promise of economic assistance. There are indications, for example, that North Korea suffers from yet another food shortage. During the last quarter of 2006, North Korea purchased 15,000 metric tons of rice (one metric ton = 2205 pounds) from China.[2] The timing of these purchases might indicate that North Korea suffered another poor rice harvest in 2006 and is in need of external assistance once again.

Finally, North Korea might have come to the realization that with the ballistic missile launch and nuclear test detonation in 2006 it had overplayed its hand. As is discussed in greater detail later in the book, North Korea regards its nuclear weapons as its sole geopolitical playing card, to be used as a means for extracting economic and other concessions, not for actual employment. If this is the case, now that the nuclear test has been undertaken, there really is no means of increasing pressure on the United States and its allies short of elevating threatening behaviors beyond acceptable levels even for the regime, such as more nuclear tests or actually employing nuclear weapons; in short, the tests were their final option. (Here is where, I believe, China played a major role in curbing North Korean behavior. A nuclearized North Korea represents regional instability and does not comport with Chinese visions of becoming the regional superpower and a global leader. China may have applied pressure sufficient to dissuade North Korea from any further nuclear tests.) One means of creating fodder for negotiations is to identify issues North Korea's adversaries consider important to protect, such as the DAP, and focus future negotiations on its provisions in attempts to wrest additional concessions. History indicates that it is not a matter of if, but when and for what reasons the regime it will return to a more belligerent negotiating position.

What provisions of the DAP might North Korea seek to exploit in future negotiations with the United States and its allies? One area of concern is with the "inducements" contained within the DAP. Under the agreement, North Korea is to be provided one million tons of HFO over the next two years. Under the 1994 Agreed Framework the regime was to receive 4.5 million tons of HFO over a ten-year period. Annual HFO shipments under both agreements amount to the same: 500,000 tons. While in absolute terms both agreements provide the same amount of annual HFO support, in reality the regime signed on to the DAP for fewer inducements. Similarly, under the Agreed Framework there was a promise to provide North Korea two light water nuclear reactors to replace its graphite moderated reactors.

There is no such explicit provision contained within the DAP. Discussions of energy and economic assistance may come later in the process, but it presents a potential problem area as it affords the regime the opportunity to renegotiate terms of the agreement and potentially hold the process hostage for greater concessions. Finally, one must consider why there is a two-year time limit in place for providing HFO. This may be optimism on the part of the Bush administration that denuclearization can be achieved within such a short time frame, although history does not necessarily support such a rosy conclusion. Or it may be that the administration has come to the realization that denuclearization will take much longer than its remaining time in office and hopes only to keep North Korea from becoming yet another flashpoint before the end of 2008—Iraq and Iran have proven to be far more problematic than originally estimated.

The above notwithstanding, there are positive aspects to the DAP, specifically its more forward-looking posture on broader peninsular and regional security issues when contrasted with the Agreed Framework. The DAP provides for the creation of several working groups, one of which has the specific mandate to explore development of a mechanism that will help ensure "Northeast Asia peace and security." It also references the need for a separate forum that should pursue a permanent peace initiative for the Korean peninsula. Although short on details, the DAP at least recognizes the need for broader regional engagement.

North Korea's 2006 missile launch and nuclear detonation were "shows of strength" designed to put the United States and its regional allies on notice that the regime has the capability to strike at any time.

Given the veil of secrecy shrouding the North Korean regime, the world may never know precisely what led to the July 2006 missile test and October nuclear detonation. Popular assessment of course is that they were part of the North's quest to develop its nuclear weapons capability in order to extend the reach of its threat, which in a broad sense is true. The real question, however, is why? The regime understands fully that it is simply no match for the United States, whether measuring its conventional military force or nuclear weapons capability. One can make a variety of characterizations regarding the regime's behavior, but among them would not be the characterization of being "suicidal." What then was the impetus for the missile launch? In the sections and chapters that follow, broader consideration is given to both the genesis of and rationale for North Korea's miscreant behavior, but posited here is another possible reason: a response to external pressure. I have maintained for many years, and continue to do so, that the real threat from the regime is not a purposeful nuclear first strike against any country in the region (to include the United States) because the ramifications of such action would be far too costly. The two real threats the regime poses (besides proliferation of nuclear weapons technology) are: (1) mistakenly launching a missile against a country because of some unforeseen technical problem (for example, if the July 2006 missile launch hadn't gone out of control and landed in the ocean, but rather had landed somewhere on the Japanese mainland); or (2) launching an attack because it feels it has nothing else to lose (see Chapter 5).

An understanding of the regime's ideological development is essential to accurately frame the problem (Chapter 4). *Juche*, very loosely, popularly, and mistakenly defined as self-reliance, provides a clue, but requires that one first understand the concept itself. In fact, much of North Korea's atypical behavior becomes clearer through the *Juche* prism. Chapter 4 offers a detailed definition and explanation of the concept, but for immediate purposes I'll simply define it as meaning "independence of action" rather than "self-reliance," which has a vastly different connotation. In the former, the focus is external to the regime and the behavior is acted out within the context of multiple-party settings, with others being the object of the behavior. The latter, however, is more inwardly focused and in most cases might only tangentially impact other parties. One of *Juche's* major tenets relates to "big power chauvinism," or the avoidance of being unduly influenced by more powerful nations.

When the most recent missile launches are put into this context, one possible rationale for the regime undertaking the launches emerges. In the weeks leading up to the missile test launch, administration officials indicated on numerous occasions that any launch would be "unacceptable" and considered a "provocative act;" in essence, telling the regime to stand down. From the North Korean perspective, it might well have perceived itself as being pushed by a larger power, in this case, the United States. Its response, under these circumstances, was to launch the missile instead of appearing to have been intimidated into not doing so. Recall that the missile sat on the launch pad for several weeks prior to actually being launched. But why then were six other missiles launched after the initial launch? When the Taepoding-2 failed by spiraling out of control, the regime likely felt it then had to save face by successfully launching the other shorter range missiles, all tried, tested, and known to be reliable. The North Korean experience in 1998 with another failed missile launch may have provided the basis for such precautions.

There are, of course, other plausible reasons for the launch, which are detailed throughout this chapter. One possibility is that it was an effort to restart the stalled Talks in such a way as to put the regime in a position of advantage. Another is that it might well have been trying to regain a lost advantage; in this case regaining access to regime funds frozen in an overseas bank by the United States. In order to accomplish this, however, the regime needed to initiate negotiations with the United States. Lessons from its 1998 missile launch may have served as its example. After that missile launch, which overflew Japan's island of Honshu, the United States did come to the negotiating table.

Unfortunately, even the best understanding of the *Juche* concept does not make it a predictive tool or even necessarily a wholly reliable means for explaining all regime transgressions. What it does accomplish, however, is to force a broader and more comprehensive analytical process to be undertaken with regard to the North Korea issue, which hopefully leads to sounder, more coherent, and innovative policy development.

Bush administration officials are prepared to exhaust all diplomatic means in resolving differences with North Korea over its nuclear weapons program.

Moving beyond the daily lead stories in the media and reading between the lines, one might reasonably conclude that the United States is prepared to use a military option if all else fails. While this option does and should remain on the table, realistically the likelihood of such an outcome is virtually nil under present circumstances, leaving the United States with only diplomacy as a viable path toward resolution. There are several reasons for this. First, projected damage assessments from a war on the peninsula are nearly incalculable—the loss of life, property, infrastructure, and national assets would be overwhelming on both sides of the Demilitarized Zone (DMZ). Second, the war in Iraq, which presently demands substantial resources, pales in comparison to the level of commitment that would be required in an armed conflict scenario on the peninsula in terms of time, personnel, equipment, and money. Adding North Korea to existing commitments in Afghanistan and Iraq would further stretch the U.S. military under its current configuration and end strength. Third, under such a conflict scenario, South Korea, Asia's fourth largest economy and the tenth largest economy worldwide, would essentially be sacrificed.[3] Finally, geopolitical considerations mitigate against such a scenario. Given the support provided by China and Russia to North Korea in such multilateral venues as the United Nations, what would their likely reaction be to war on the Korean peninsula, essentially in their own backyards? This approach challenges the cacophony of voices, such as Newt Gingrich, William Perry, and Walter Mondale, who espouse a preemptive strike against North Korean missiles on the launch pad.[4] Vice President Dick Cheney summed up the danger of such an approach quite aptly when he observed that if you fire one missile you better be prepared to fire more. A military solution is not the answer, although military power does play a vital role in successful diplomacy (Chapter 5). In order for diplomatic efforts to have teeth and any reasonable chance of success, U.S. military power must be regarded as an option by North Korea, no matter how remote its potential use (Chapter 4).

President Bush himself acknowledges as much. This is apparent when one juxtaposes the differences in his use of language in the present situation with North Korea to that which he used to frame the situation in Iraq just prior to initiating hostilities. Prior to the Iraq War, he used such language as: "Time has run out"; "Saddam had his chance"; "If we have to go it alone, we will."[5] Compare that approach to the language presently being used: "This is a time for diplomacy"; "We're working it hard"; "Diplomacy takes time"; "You can't do things overnight"; "We have to get a consensus amongst the countries in the region." What lies at the heart of this reversal are three important considerations: (1) North Korea's conventional military capability and its capacity to inflict major damage on South Korea; (2) the regional threat it presents through its ballistic missile program; and (3) its nuclear weapons capability. Iraq simply was not so formidable an adversary. President Bush understands the potential quagmire a Korean peninsula conflict scenario presents (Chapter 5). He pins his legacy on the global war on terror and successfully concluding the war in Iraq; war on the Korean peninsula would likely go a long way toward undermining that legacy.

The aim of the North Korean nuclear weapons program is to develop a credible nuclear threat against the U.S. mainland.

North Korea's nuclear program is designed to function chiefly in four ways: ensuring regime survival; providing negotiating leverage; garnering world attention; and creating divisions between and among members of the world community aligned against it. Uncertainty over the presence of nuclear weapons and the extent to which the program has developed is advantageous to the regime as it helps to keep potential adversaries, particularly the United States, off balance, consequently reducing the likelihood of an attack and preserving the regime. Leverage in negotiations is sought through threatening the development, testing, or use of nuclear weapons, as the world witnessed with the July 4, 2006, missile launches. To what end is this leverage used? It is used primarily for extracting further economic concessions or assistance from the world community or for regaining lost advantages. In this sense, the North's nuclear weapons program can be regarded as an "enabler." As mentioned earlier, one such lost advantage the July 2006 missile launches might have sought to regain was access to the $24 million in assets the United States has frozen in Banco Delta Asia. North Korean deputy ambassador to the United Nations, Han Song Ryol, gave some indication that North Korea would be willing to return to the negotiating table if the United States released these funds.[6] Herein lies one of those potential "missed opportunities," the result of outmoded containment policies alluded to earlier. That was not the first time the North Koreans had expressed a desire to sit down to discuss the issue of its frozen assets—the administration clearly had hit the regime where it hurts. Yet, instead of seeing this as an opportunity to press its advantage, administration officials compartmentalized negotiations, offering no discussion of the assets until the nuclear issue was first settled, in essence pursuing a sequential rather than comprehensive approach (Chapter 4).

Regardless of how one might characterize the North Korean regime's behavior, judging it solely on the merits of its intended purposes, it has been remarkably successful in some areas, although not particularly effective across the board. The regime's bluster and aberrant behavior is designed to refocus U.S. and world attention on North Korea while advancing negotiations with the United States toward a position of advantage for itself. It has at least been successful in refocusing world attention on itself. In the wake of the July 2006 missile launches and October 2006 nuclear detonation, the North Korean nuclear weapons program became the main topic of discussion in the United Nations as the world community tried to decide on an appropriate response; the Bush administration dispatched Christopher Hill to the region to coordinate a common position amongst regional allies; while the U.S. news media replaced the usual headlines on the war in Iraq and domestic political issues with stories about the missile launch, possible sanctions, progress on UN resolutions, and the likelihood of persuading North Korea back to the negotiating table. And as events of early 2007 point out, the North Korean regime was ultimately successful in pushing the Bush administration into changing its theretofore intractable position on no direct negotiations and no economic benefits until full dismantlement was achieved. It, however, lost some tangible short-term benefits in the process when the South Korean government suspended humanitarian assistance until the North Koreans returned to the Six Party Talks.

Closely aligned with the North Korean attention-getting motive is the disruption factor nuclear weapons provide. Despite claims to the contrary, it becomes clear to anyone who regularly follows events on the Korean peninsula that the United States and South Korea, the traditional U.S. ally on the peninsula, are taking diametric approaches with regard to North Korea—the United States a more hard-line approach and South Korea a broader economic and cultural outreach approach. Consider, for example, Seoul's announcement that it will not participate in the interdiction efforts through the Proliferation Security Initiative (PSI), a mechanism through which the United States hopes to enforce the provisions of UN Security Council Resolution 1718 calling for the interdiction of cargo ships suspected of carrying weapons of mass destruction (WMD). South Korea cites its unique circumstances of having North Korea as its neighbor as rationale for abstaining from PSI. South Korea has also been slow to abandon its joint venture projects in North Korea, for example the Kaesong Industrial Park project.

What North Korea's nuclear weapons program is not designed to do is raise the geopolitical stakes to such a level that the only remaining solution would be a military one. Garnering the attention of the United States, and by extension the attention of the world community, remains its goal because the regime sees this as a zero-sum game: attention given to other areas of the world is attention it is not receiving, thus reducing the likelihood of engaging in negotiations that enable it to advance its own position. Over the past several years, U.S. and world attention has very much been consumed with problems in Iraq and Iran's suspected nuclear weapons program. An interesting measure of the "attention factor" is illustrated by the content of President Bush's own State of the Union addresses since 2002. In his 2002 address (axis of evil speech), Bush said the following: "North Korea is a regime arming with missiles and weapons of mass destruction, while starving its citizens." This was offered within the broader context of Iraq and Iran constituting the axis of evil. By 2003, the text devoted to North Korea had expanded to include the following:

> On the Korean Peninsula, an oppressive regime rules a people living in fear and starvation. Throughout the 1990s, the United States relied on a negotiated framework to keep North Korea from gaining nuclear weapons. We now know that that regime was deceiving the world and developing those weapons all along. And today the North Korean regime is using its nuclear program to incite fear and seek concessions. America and the world will not be blackmailed.
>
> America is working with the countries of the region, South Korea, Japan, China, and Russia, to find a peaceful solution and to show the North Korean Government that nuclear weapons will bring only isolation, economic stagnation, and continued hardship. The North Korean regime will find respect in the world and revival for its people only when it turns away from its nuclear ambitions.

Yet, by January 31, 2006, when Bush offered his sixth address, North Korea warranted only passing mention, in contrast to the more extensive coverage of Iraq and Iran:

> At the start of 2006, more than half the people of our world live in democratic nations. And we do not forget the other half—in places like Syria and Burma, Zimbabwe, North Korea, and Iran—because the demands of justice and the peace of this world require their freedom as well.

There are, of course, many problems pressing on any presidency and to devote more than a few minutes in a State of the Union address to any given topic is difficult. But the compelling point here is not how many words were actually devoted to the discussion of North Korea, but how closely the addresses reflected the administration's day-to-day focus. The impasse between North Korea and the United States over the timing of dismantlement and possible provision of light water reactors occurred in September 2005, some four months earlier, and had effectively stalled the Six Party Talks. Added to that, the lion's share of U.S. attention was being devoted to the war in Iraq, Iran's nuclear weapons, mounting domestic political concerns, and 2006 mid-term elections. In short, North Korea-related issues were supplanted by more immediate and higher priority issues. In this regard, the July 2006 missile tests might then be considered weapons of disruption and a means for refocusing U.S. and world attention.

Summarizing, North Korea's nuclear weapons program is designed to do many things: disrupt, distract, garner attention, provide for regime survival, and a means for ensuring negotiating leverage. The one thing it is not designed to do is function as a credible first-strike capability.

Given its poor economy, North Korea can be regarded largely as a paper tiger.

Absolutely not. North Korea remains a dangerous adversary at several levels. First, while its test firing of the Taepodong-2 missile in July 2006 was an unmitigated failure, spiraling out of control some 40 seconds into the launch, it maintains a huge arsenal of short, medium, and intermediate range ballistic missiles along with its nascent, but advancing nuclear program. In addition to this, it also maintains an extensive chemical weapons capability and some amount of biological toxins (Chapter 5). Consequently, it represents a credible regional threat to its neighbors. Additionally, given its proven propensity for worldwide proliferation of nuclear technology and arms transfers, for example to countries like Pakistan, Iran, and Egypt, it represents a global threat as well. North Korea, of course, remains a peninsular threat to South Korea. As well recall that the Six Party Talks, even if successful, address only the regime's growing nuclear program; North and South Korea technically remain at war with each other. While degraded a bit, the North Korean conventional military capability is still a formidable force; with 1.2 million personnel under arms and an extensive conventional weapons arsenal, it constitutes the fourth largest standing military in the world today.[7] Finally, the regime represents a threat to regional stability. Beyond the immediate danger presented by its military and nuclear capabilities, the regime's recalcitrance and manifest behaviors have also destabilized conditions in the region: that the South Korean government is considering a proposal to build a long-range cruise missile to counter the increased threat from the North while Japan considers the constitutionality of preemptive strikes against North Korean missiles serve as just two examples. The regime's destabilizing effect does not dissipate when considering its demise. The idea of a regime and military with no center, with access to nuclear, biological, and chemical arsenals, and hundreds of thousands of North Koreans streaming across the North Korea borders with China and South Korea, is a regional security nightmare (Chapter 5).

A settlement can be negotiated with North Korea that first requires the regime to dismantle its nuclear weapons program and then provides for extending economic carrots and other forms of assistance.

While this has been the position advocated by the United States for six years, the circumstances surrounding North Korea's situation mitigate against a successful outcome under such a scenario. The fundamental reason such a policy has limited probability of success is that North Korea's nuclear program—its plutonium-based nuclear weapons, suspected highly enriched uranium program and ballistic missiles—constitutes its only geopolitical bargaining chip. Without this, the regime perceives it would stand little chance of exercising any leverage within the world community for extracting necessary concessions. Consequently, voluntarily abandoning the program would be tantamount to giving up something for nothing and surrendering itself to the influence of larger powers (Chapter 4). This is precisely what happened during September 2005 when the North Koreans reinterpreted the terms of the so-called agreement to dismantle its weapons program. Given the opacity surrounding domestic affairs within North Korea, it may be a long time before there is any understanding of the motivation behind the regime's willingness to agree to dismantlement followed by its swift reversal of course. The motive may have been to break the long-standing stalemate at the Six Party Talks in order to see what sort of concessions they might wrest from participants under "pressure" to convince the North Koreans to return to the negotiating table. It might also have been a tactic to wear down their adversary.

In the final analysis, however, there is little likelihood that the North will simply negotiate away what it sees as its one remaining geopolitical strength. The nuclear program serves at once as its safety net against what it perceives to be a hostile United States, thus ensuring regime survival; equalizes the relationship between itself, the United States and other Six Party Talk member nations; and, of course, is a means for extracting from concerned nations economic concessions and other forms of assistance. Additionally, North Korea is unlikely to pursue nuclear disarmament when: (1) the U.S. military maintains a presence in South Korea; and (2) maintains its own inventory of nuclear weapons. From the North Korean perspective, denuclearization not only offers nothing to them, but they also lose an important advantage. Under the present scenario the current stalemate is likely to continue for the foreseeable future. The conundrum the United States and other countries confront is how to address this reality in order to move North Korea and its threatening policies toward more acceptable behavior.

The most likely avenue is through application of aggressive and comprehensive economic strategies that require the regime to reprioritize economic and security imperatives, devoting its meager resources to the former rather than the latter (Chapter 7). If the United States and its regional allies pursue a strategy of engagement focusing on economic linkages rather than isolation and economic sanctions, much of the rationale cited above for the regime's maintenance of nuclear weapons is removed.

Given that North Korea's stated aim is to govern the entire peninsula under communist rule, the United States and South Korea naturally share similar policies with regard to resolving the nuclear issue.

This is actually a two-part issue. While it is true that for many decades the North's aim was to extend its control over South Korea by fomenting a socialist revolution that would promote unrest and enable absorption of the South by the regime, this goal was abandoned somewhere during the late 1980s and early 1990s in favor of a more pressing need: regime survival. The transition from socialist aggressor to socialist survivor was brought about by the rapidly changing geopolitical landscape of the period. First was the growth of democratic governance in South Korea that began to take root during the 1980s. By 1988, the country experienced its first peaceful and constitutional transition of power since its inception in 1948 with the ascension of Roh Tae Woo to the presidency (1988–1993). His successor, Kim Young Sam (1993–1998) was the first civilian rule in the country since 1961. This led to greater stability in the South and presented fewer potential opportunities to take advantage of social and labor unrest. Second, there was the South Korean leadership's abandonment of its long-standing, staunchly anti-communist approach to the world beginning with the Roh administration, which ultimately had a devastating impact on North Korea. Through his policy of *Nordpolitik*, Roh began outreach efforts to the communist bloc of nations, which ultimately brought about rapprochement with some of North Korea's strongest allies: the former Soviet Union (1990), China (1992), Poland and Hungary (1989). Added to this was the fall of East Germany in 1990, another strong socialist ally. Finally, in 1994 the death of Kim Il Sung, the only leader North Korea had known to that point, forced North Korea to confront challenges on both domestic and international fronts. The regime had to consider, perhaps for the first time, its own mortality. As a result, it cast about looking for a means of ensuring its own continued existence by keeping at bay external intrusion and influence. The method upon which it ultimately decided was a nuclear weapons deterrent (Chapter 3).

Perhaps the success of German reunification and the breakup of the former Soviet Union have influenced South Korean government officials to pursue the goal of peninsular reunification with an increasingly vigorous outreach policy toward North Korea. This approach reached a zenith with former President Kim Dae-jung's (1998–2003) Sunshine Policy and President Roh Moo-hyun's (2003-present) continued outreach efforts. The South Korean government has opted for stability through outreach, avoiding a hard-line approach. Fundamentally, the policy is a sound one, although in execution it tends to be light on demands for reciprocity from the North Korean regime, which in the end, I believe, impacts its ultimate effectiveness. In this regard, Seoul's policy pursuits tend to be more closely aligned with the Chinese and Russian "go slow" approach and less so with that of the United States and Japan, both of which have supported a harder-line policy in the past. In fact, in a 2006 New Year's survey commissioned by the *Korea Times* and *Hankook Ilbo*, 36.5 percent of respondents indicated that South Korea's most important relationship is with China, up from 24 percent who indicated China was the most important relationship in October 2004. Conversely, those who considered the relationship with the United States as most important comprised 48 percent of respondents, down from 53 percent a year earlier.[8]

The perception in growing segments of the general population of South Koreans follows a somewhat similar trend. For them, because North Korea has transitioned from aggressor to survivor, it no longer represents the imminent danger it once did. Consequently, they see unification of the peninsula as an inevitable outcome of this transition. Consider for example the Korea Gallup Poll taken in August 2005 that measured attitudes of respondents born during 1980–1989.[9] In the poll, 65.9 percent indicated that they would support North Korea in a war with the United States; 21.8 percent felt Korea must support the traditional alliance with the United States; the remainder weren't sure.[10] Admittedly, the poll was administered in an antiseptic environment—respondents may have answered differently under a genuine threat of war, yet the general trend is one of which U.S. government officials might want to take heed. As the generation that experienced the Korean War and its aftermath dies off, the complexion of peninsular issues, perceptions, and attitudes will change markedly. This is not a caution without some basis. Recall that the division of the Korean peninsula, which the United States originally regarded as temporary, has lasted for three generations and South Korean enmity of its northern neighbor has given way to ever-expanding economic, humanitarian, commercial, and cultural ties.

Another example of the divergence in U.S. and South Korean perceptions of North Korea can be gleaned from how negotiations proceeded in developing a "coordinated" response to last year's missile launch. In addition to joint U.S. and Japanese efforts to push through a UN Security Council resolution calling for sanctions against North Korea that met with stiff resistance, Cheong Wa Dae (Blue House, South Korea's equivalent of the U.S. White House) spokesman, Jung Tae-ho, chastised Japan for considering a preemptive strike against North Korea's missiles, characterizing consideration of such an approach as "rash and thoughtless." Disturbing in this exchange was the Blue House characterization of Japan's consideration of such action as not against North Korea, but against the "peninsula."[11]

The official language is telling because it at once defines an emerging relationship between the two halves of the peninsula and "Korea's" position vis-à-vis other sovereign nations. This should be a red flag for the U.S. administration as it portends a shift in South Korean perceptions and policy that prioritizes its own approach to peace and reconciliation on the peninsula over the more traditional U.S.-South Korean approach, which in the end may not accord with broader U.S. interests. Such a shift became yet more noticeable in the wake of the October nuclear detonation. South Korea has elected not to participate in PSI activities in the vicinity of the Korean peninsula despite U.S. officials strongly urging Seoul to do so.

Given the long history of strong bilateral relations between the United States and South Korea, there is consonance with respect to their policy positions.

The foregoing examples point to a broader problem in U.S.-South Korean relations: that each country is taking an increasingly divergent path in seeking resolution of the North Korean issue. Much debate has ensued in the years following the introduction of Kim Dae-jung's Sunshine Policy emphasizing South Korea's softer approach with the North, centering on economic outreach in comparison to the more hard-line approach favored by the United States. While philosophically both nations agree that a denuclearized Korea is necessary for regional peace and stability, in concrete terms the two approaches have not been mutually supportive. As long as South Korea (and China) provides a support net for North Korea, the U.S. goal for CVID will likely not be achieved. Consider, for example, that the combined food aid provided to North Korea by China and South Korea in 2005 amounted to 85 percent of all such foreign assistance received.[12] Also consider the extensive economic outreach being undertaken by Seoul: expanding the joint Mt. Kumgang tourist resort project, undertaken by Hyundai Asan and the North Korean government and operating since 1998; South Korea's leading fixed line telephone provider, KT, signed an outsourcing contract with a North Korean institute to develop sophisticated software programs during July 2006; and South Korea's continued support of the joint North-South industrial complex project being undertaken at Kaesong, North Korea, despite U.S. objections.

The North Korean regime may have overplayed its hand with South Korea and ironically helped to close the gap between U.S. and South Korean policy. In the wake of the July 2006 missile launches, South Korea suspended humanitarian assistance to the North until it agrees to return to the Six Party Talks. This differs, of course, from a sanction but has similar impact when one considers that Seoul provided 36 percent of all the food aid received by North Korea in 2005 as well as 60,000 tons of coal during winter 2005–2006.[13]

Overall, however, the trend is not favorable for our bilateral relations with South Korea. Underscoring this point is the recent U.S. decision to speed handover to the South Korean government of wartime control over its military forces, currently commanded by a U.S. four-star general under Combined Forces Command; peacetime control of South Korean forces was relinquished in 1994. Originally scheduled to occur in 2012, the United States has unilaterally moved up that timetable to 2009. Rationale for the decision was provided by a U.S. defense official who preferred to remain anonymous—improved capability of South Korean forces; the growing pro-Pyongyang posture assumed by the South Korean government; and a more pronounced anti-U.S. position of South Korean leaders.[14]

Direct U.S. engagement with the North Korean regime would be counter-productive and such an opportunity should only be afforded after the regime undertakes denuclearization.

With the recent successful conclusion of the DAP, the United States has finally moved toward direct negotiations with the North Korean regime, abandoning its insistence on CVID before any discussion of economic assistance can occur. An unwillingness to negotiate with what were considered rogue regimes, however, has been a long-standing U.S. position, adhered to by most U.S. administrations; it took the current administration six years to conclude that such an approach is not effective. The rationale supporting such a policy was at its core based on both moral and pragmatic arguments. Morally, U.S. administrations have found it offensive to negotiate with regimes and governments that operate contrary to the value set recognized by Americans. From a pragmatic standpoint, the current administration contended negotiating with rogue nations weakened the U.S. position, strengthened our adversaries, and in the final analysis "rewarded bad behavior," thus reinforcing the very behavior we sought to modify. Notable exceptions to this approach were undertaken during the Clinton administration: first, during the negotiations that yielded the 1994 Agreed Framework, which called for North Korea to abandon its plutonium-based nuclear program in return for two light water nuclear reactors; and second, at the end of the Clinton administration when Secretary of State Madeline Albright made a trip to Pyongyang in October 2000 to meet with Kim Jong Il. In her assessment of the regime, Secretary Albright surmised that Kim was anxious for some recognition from the United States through negotiation and diplomatic relations.[15]

While successive U.S. administrations have found some measure of ra-
tionalized solace in this "don't go there" approach, it suffers from one
shortcoming—it has proved largely ineffective. After nearly forty-seven
years, despite best efforts, Fidel Castro remains a thorn in the side of the
United States; Iraq fell into a similar category; and Iran presents a growing
nuclear menace with its weapons program. And after nearly sixty years, such
an approach has not rendered the North Korean threat harmless; rather it
has grown from a peninsular threat to one that directly menaces the region
with its nuclear weapons program and the world with its propensity to proliferate nuclear weapons technology.[16] Thus, as the geopolitical stakes have
risen, failure to engage rogue regimes has led to greater negative results,
particularly in the case of North Korea: the nuclear crisis of 1993–1994;
the missile launches of 1998 and 2006; and the recent nuclear detonation
illustrate this. Additionally, as much energy is expended after the fact to
maintain the status quo as might be expended in developing innovative and
comprehensive approaches to engage the North on terms more favorable
to the United States and its allies. In the end, with this type of approach
one is always fighting the most recent transgression and seldom winds up
advancing discussions.

U.S. officials have recently reaffirmed their commitment to the diplomatic process through the DAP proceedings and agreement, which offers
some measure of reassurance. The objective of diplomacy is to find a path
forward, through negotiation and compromise, between or among disagree-
ing parties. Under the earlier Bush Doctrine, which one hopes is a relic of
the past, diplomacy had come to mean discussion in order to achieve prede-
termined and nonnegotiable outcomes. U.S. disdain for dealing with rogue
regimes notwithstanding, the point of engaging Pyongyang in diplomacy is
to find a way past the impasse of North Korea's nuclear weapons program
and bring its aberrant behavior in line with accepted norms. Cloistering U.S.
policy on the moral ground of contempt for engaging regimes will hardly
accomplish that.

There are advantages to engaging the North. Most immediately, active
dialogue, referred to herein as "constructive engagement," maintains open
lines of communication without which opacity further clouds an already
unclear situation, obscuring any potential path forward. In this regard, the
Bush administration at least deserves credit for engaging in and sticking
with the Six Party Talks despite their long record of unfruitful discussions.
This venue, however, does have its drawbacks as the present mandate limits
discussions solely to dismantlement of the North's nuclear program, in effect
reducing the scope of any negotiations. This approach has proved largely
ineffective because, as mentioned earlier, it treats only the symptoms of a
much larger problem, a shortcoming that remains even with the DAP. The
symptom it seeks to treat is what the North perceives as its only card to play
within the context of regional geopolitics. The multilateral framework is an

important one, but requires modification so that it permits discussion of a broader range of issues influencing the regime's nuclear program.

In his article, "Rationale for Enhanced Engagement of North Korea: After the Perry Policy Review," Victor Cha cites several other reasons to pursue expanded engagement with North Korea. First, it is the best way of building a coalition that is able to dispense punishment at some later date should it be required. Although he doesn't refer specifically to the Six Party Talks by name because the article was written four years prior to its creation, the idea has merit. Some U.S. policymakers, however, consider such an approach counterproductive because it may limit U.S. unilateral options. Second, Cha points out that engagement, rather than strengthening a rogue regime, can actually produce dissension within leadership circles, because unlike a policy of containment, engagement provides little with which to stoke the fires of nationalism. Finally, Cha points out that North Korea, much like other rogue regimes, must open itself up in today's global and economic security environment. In the process, it becomes necessary to surrender itself to uncontrollable forces that introduce change in the way the regime operates.

This final point is the key and in accord with the premise of this book: that a paradigmatic shift in U.S. and allied policy is required if the issue of North Korea's nuclear program, indeed its entire arsenal of WMD and its aberrant behavior in general, is ever to be resolved. At the heart of such a policy is a long-term view, combined with constructive, comprehensive, and innovative (to the extent it recognizes that the Cold War containment paradigm has outlived its usefulness) thinking (Chapter 5).

China is an ally in the effort to get North Korea to denuclearize and represents the best opportunity for coaxing the North Korean regime to give up its nuclear weapons program.

Again, yes and no. To the extent that China wants to maintain stability on its border with North Korea and within the region, this is true. Chinese leadership is focused on becoming the preeminent power in East Asia and a major global player and sees maintaining stable conditions in the region as an antecedent to these goals. A nuclearized North Korea, however, fosters instability and in the Chinese perception, undermines its vision of preeminence. Not only because it might do something dangerous and reckless with the weapons, but because it could well lead to other destabilizing conditions, such as the nuclearization of Japan. So in that regard, China is allied with the United States and other countries in the region in not wanting to see a fully developed North Korean nuclear weapons program.

China and the United States, however, did not share a common vision with regard to the modalities for achieving denuclearization in North Korea until early 2007 when the United States began genuinely pursuing a course of constructive engagement. China regards past U.S. measures, particularly the imposition of sanctions, as harsh, risky, and likely to elicit undesired behavior from North Korea—North Korea tends to behave poorly when it perceives external pressure is being exerted against it. Again, what China fears most is instability. Sanctions could spark destabilizing domestic conditions in North Korea that, in the worst case, could cause the regime to implode. An imploded North Korea with hundreds of thousands of its citizens streaming across the Chinese-North Korean border would generally cause widespread destabilization within the region and China directly. Then of course there remains the question of what happens to its WMD under such a scenario.

How deeply do the differences run between the United States and China on this issue? Again, consider the diplomatic machinations undertaken by the UN Security Council in the wake of North Korea's missile launches and the opposing positions taken by the United States and China: the United States and Japan sought imposition of sanctions under UN Charter Chapter VII against North Korea, while China threatened to veto any resolution that included sanctions.[17] In the end, the resolution passed by the Security Council was a watered down version devoid of sanctions that was far from the stern response promised by U.S. administration officials, in effect giving North Korea a "pass" on not one, but seven missile launches.[18]

This points to a growing weakness in U.S. policy: Sino-fication of the U.S. policy process, that is, its overreliance on China to resolve North Korea-related issues. To be sure, China has had an expanding role in negotiations over North Korea since initiation of formal discussions with the regime through the Four Party Talks, which began in 1997 and included the United States, China, South Korea, and North Korea. The difference between 1997 and the present is more a matter of degree of reliance on China. Where previously China had been regarded as an important participant among the four countries involved in the discussions, China is presently regarded as the primary means through which to reach the regime and advance the Six Party Talks. Any viewer following the diplomatic efforts in the aftermath of the North Korea missile launch was treated to a litany of official U.S. statements that called on China to begin exercising its influence with North Korea in order to get the regime back to the negotiating table, a refrain sung off and on over the past several years by U.S. administration officials. The genesis of such thinking likely comes from the decades-long Sino-North Korean relationship, which has included ideological as well as extensive bilateral trade, cultural and, at least through the 1960s, military ties. While it is accurate to say that North Korea has had close ties (at times closer than at others) with China, it is not accurate to say that North Korea has always followed the counsel of either China or the former Soviet Union even during the period when these countries served as its major benefactors. What more accurately describes North Korea's relationship with the two communist giants is that while the regime was prepared to accept the tangible benefits of being allied with both countries, it was not prepared to surrender to either what it regarded as its independence of action (Chapter 4).

Equally important to consider, however, are broader U.S. and Chinese motives with regard to the North Korea problem and how they work against a more closely aligned U.S.-Sino approach to its resolution. Since the events of 9/11, the United States has been guided in large measure by its global war on terror. North Korea, a member of Bush's axis of evil, is a major target of that war, particularly with its propensity to proliferate WMD and development of a nuclear weapons capability the U.S. administration claims threatens U.S. sovereign territory.

The Chinese are less concerned with the global war on terror—their interests lie in maintaining regional stability in order to create a stronger economy and build its military to become the preeminent regional power and a global leader. Consequently, North Korea, for reasons cited earlier, cannot be allowed to fall, hence China's extensive trade and economic support of the regime. For example, in addition to the food aid provided to North Korea cited earlier, Chinese investment in the North Korean economy during 2004 reached $50 million (U.S.); for 2005, this figure nearly doubled. Compare this to the 2003 figures of $1.1 million in Chinese investments.[19] Similarly, the trade volume between the two countries reached $1.5 billion, an amount which comprises approximately 48 percent of North Korea's total foreign trade volume.[20]

This doesn't mean China turns a blind eye to the regime's miscreant behavior. As North Korea's behavior has edged closer to destabilizing the region, China has been more willing to apply pressure. Consider, for example, that in the wake of the July missile launches China actually voted, for the first time, in support of UN Security Council resolution censuring the regime rather than abstaining from the proceedings; this sent a clear message to the regime regarding its behavior. It can also be surmised that China has been instrumental in reigning in the regime in the wake of the October nuclear detonation. Initially, there were reports that the regime contemplated follow-on nuclear testing; soon thereafter the regime announced it had no plans for further testing. This was closely followed by China's commencement of discussions between the United States and North Korea in Beijing, which helped to bring the regime back to the Six Party Talks in 2007.

Thus, while it is accurate to portray China and the United States as sharing a common goal in achieving a denuclearized North Korea, the two countries have vastly different motives for achieving this goal that ultimately impact how they define their respective national interests. In the end, China is a strategic competitor; it is not a "friend" and will pursue peninsula issues within the context of its own interests, not those of the United States.

Once North Korea enters into an agreement to dismantle its nuclear weapons program, the "heavy lifting" of dismantlement will have been completed.

Simply put, the regime is neither trustworthy nor, as history has demonstrated, is it necessarily bound by agreements into which it enters. In fact, the record of negotiations is replete with examples of the regime agreeing to be bound by certain parameters and then either pursuing policies that run counter to those promises or simply trying to renegotiate the terms of the agreement to something more favorable. Consequently, agreements are less a mutually agreed to conclusion, but rather often represent a single step among several steps subsequent to a negotiated agreement. Recall how the regime sought to renegotiate the agreement reached during the Six Party Talks to dismantle its nuclear weapons program; this was followed by the events of 2006, demands for releasing its frozen bank assets in Macau, and successful conclusion of the DAP. Similarly, after signing the 1994 Agreed Framework and agreeing to its terms, by January 1995 the regime sought greater economic benefits and refused to permit South Korea to build the two light water nuclear reactors, which were the centerpiece of the agreement.[21]

This is the dilemma that has confronted successive U.S. administrations since the advent of the regime's nuclear weapons program: how to negotiate with a regime that simply refuses to be bound by proper negotiating decorum and how to force it to submit.

What then is the road ahead?

The means for moving forward with discussions of North Korea's denuclearization, while not necessarily clearly defined, does have certain path markers that perhaps identify what courses not to take. Armed conflict in pursuit of denuclearizing the regime is a nonstarter; it would be too costly in terms of human lives, and in terms of the devastation it would bring on both countries' infrastructures and on the regional economy. Sanctions, while a popular standard, have historically demonstrated a lack of any real success. This is particularly true in the case of North Korea. With Chinese and South Korean support, both of which consider a collapsed North Korea a greater immediate regional hazard than one pursuing nuclear aims, sanctions are wholly without meaning. (Chinese and South Korean trade and economic programs with North Korea are worth nearly $1.5 billion annually.) While the Bush Doctrine has, for the past six years, had glimmers of success, when considered in its entirety, has rendered disappointing results. The road ahead will require a much more flexible, innovative, and comprehensive approach to influence North Korea's aberrant behavior and more effectively guide it in a desired direction. The course the community of nations has followed—one which infuses highly fungible humanitarian assistance and support into a nontransparent environment on the one hand while demanding compliance with denuclearization initiatives on the other—has been equally ineffective.

North Korea must, in the end, be induced to function with a normal economy, devoid of handouts and concessions. Doing so will require the regime to divert production, capital, and economic resources from abnormal reliance on its nuclear weapons program to building and maintaining a more normal economy (Chapter 7). The first step in this process will necessitate change in the underlying premises on which U.S. policy is based. The short-term discomfort of working with a regime U.S. policymakers find morally reprehensible can be offset by the long-term gains of greater security stability in the region. Critics will contend that such a course aids in perpetuating an odious regime and strengthens its nuclear hand. I contend that six years of current U.S. policy has already accomplished that—the regime has withdrawn from the NPT; it now has access to needed plutonium and potentially uranium for its nuclear weapons program, all with no international monitoring; it has launched a test missile in defiance of the world's superpower; and has detonated a nuclear blast. Along the way, U.S. and South Korean policy pursuits have taken increasingly divergent paths, despite official contestations to the contrary.

Part I

Ideological Foundations

2

Juche: The Centrality of Existence

> ...our Party has made every effort to establish Juche in opposition to dogmatism and flunkeyism. Juche in ideology, independence in politics, self-reliance in the economy and self-defense in national defense... If one fails to establish Juche in the ideological and political spheres, he will be unable to display any initiative because his faculty of independent thinking is paralyzed.[1]
>
> —Kim Il Sung

It is time for a paradigmatic shift in thinking with regard to North Korea and its nuclear weapons program because, despite best efforts, change will not be sudden, cataclysmic, or revolutionary, nor should it be. It will not occur by some sudden stroke of negotiating genius at the bargaining table that garners North Korean acquiescence to demands to abandon its nuclear program. Nor will it occur through forced regime change, either peacefully or through other means. Given the various stakeholders in the region—the United States, the People's Republic of China (PRC), South Korea, Japan, and Russia—and the ways in which they define, and are redefining, their respective self-interests, anything short of a peacefully negotiated settlement could prove disastrous for the region as a whole. As the United States assesses policy options for North Korea's nuclear weapons program, it must do so within the broader context of East Asian security. Evolving roles and relationships in the region, particularly with regard to U.S. relations with PRC, South Korea, and Russia, portend shifts that could well transcend older Cold War allegiances and divisions.

Such change will not occur overnight, but rather through a slow and deliberate process. Bringing North Korea out of its self-imposed isolation will occur by forcing it to redefine its priorities and national interests away from nuclear weapons and threats of potential military options toward broader economic and diplomatic engagement in the global community. Such action should seek to increase North Korean interdependence with, vice its current dependence on, humanitarian handouts from other nations. On its face, this argument may appear counterintuitive, but by moving away from a model that provides continued and near unfettered humanitarian assistance and toward a development model requiring increased domestic inputs into the North Korean economy, the regime will be forced to reallocate resources into nonmilitary sectors of the economy. In short, what is needed is a model that forces North Korea to become a more normal nation, not one that relies on global assistance to keep its society afloat while siphoning its own resources into its nuclear and military programs.

The United States and its regional allies have treated the North Korean nuclear issue with a surprising degree of disconnectedness to which short-term immediate solutions can be affixed through offers of economic inducements or threats of sanctions. Additionally, while all have made North Korea's nuclear weapons program their respective focal points and the centerpiece of the Six Party Talks, each also has peripheral agenda items that, in the best case, serve as potential obstacles to negotiations with the North Korean regime and undermine their collective efforts: the United States continues to raise human rights issues; Japan focuses on resolving residual issues over North Korea's abduction of Japanese citizens during the 1970s and 1980s; South Korea pursues an expanded program of economic rapprochement under a millennial version of the Sunshine policy; while the PRC functions as the regime's guarantor within the broader community of nations. This is a scenario that plays to the advantage of North Korea. Pursuit of such diverse interests and divergent approaches detracts from the singularity of purpose required to resolve the nuclear issue and provides the North Korean regime the grist to protract discussions over its nuclear weapons programs. This is not meant to diminish the significance of any of these other issues, but introducing them while negotiating over the North's nuclear weapons program allows the regime to shift the focus of discussions. And the longer North Korea is able to shift the focus of discussions, the better able it is to wait out any U.S. administration. Since North Korea's establishment in 1948, there have been eleven different U.S. administrations and we make preparations for a twelfth in 2008; North Korea has had only two leaders—Kim Il Sung and Kim Jong Il—father and son. As a result, one could argue that there has been more coherence in its policy pursuits with the global community than there has been in U.S. ability to develop a coherent policy approach amongst its regional allies toward North Korea.

Resolution lies in long-term solutions marked by evolutionary changes in the North Korean regime's management of its economy and internal governmental processes, changes that cannot be reversed on a whim and that withstand North Korea's hallmark unpredictable negotiating style. The United States and its allies will be better served by moving toward a more strategic policy perspective that recognizes the multifarious and interconnected dimensions of the North Korean nuclear issue—applying short-term fixes to problems requiring long-term solutions nets, at best, only short-term gains and long-term frustration. A long-term comprehensive view, patience, consistency across U.S. administrations, plausible objectives, and a willingness to use "2X4 diplomacy," in effect applying a big stick when necessary, should serve as the cornerstone of a coherent North Korea policy.

None of this, however, will help to develop a policy that yields greater success than that achieved to date unless there is an accompanying shift in thinking that recognizes the importance of first better understanding the North Korean adversary—how he thinks and why he reacts as he does. An equally important consideration is what comprises the foundation of his unpredictable nature. Without such understanding, fixes to the nuclear issue will remain, at best, superficially focused on economic inducements, sanctions, and humanitarian aid.

The first point with which we must come to grips is what makes the North Korean regime "tick"—what forms the basis of its thinking and actions? The answer lies in the core ideological element of the North Korean regime and the society it has created—*Juche*—the center of its existence.

THE EVOLUTION OF *JUCHE*

Any discussion of the manifest behaviors of nations presupposes recognition that each has at its disposal, to differing degrees, certain implements of statecraft to carry out its foreign policy objectives—economic, military, diplomatic, and technological. How each of these is ultimately employed, to what degree and level of success, and whether employed positively or negatively, is contingent upon three factors: the level to which each implement has been developed; the commitment to use it; and the impact of external factors on that domestic commitment. The Iran-Libya Sanctions Act (ILSA) passed by the United States in 1996 serves as a good case in point as it illustrates how, despite its ability and commitment to punish those who cooperated economically with Iran, U.S. diplomacy ultimately failed to win international support for the measure owing to the external forces aligned against it.

The Republican takeover of both the House of Representatives and Senate in January 1995 augured a period of greater pressure on the Clinton administration to take action against Iran as a result of its alleged support for terrorist bombing activities against Israel; additionally, there was growing concern that Iran was acquiring components necessary in the manufacture of weapons of mass destruction (WMD). This, in combination with strong Jewish lobbying efforts on Capitol Hill netted the ILSA, Libya having been added to the bill by Senator Ted Kennedy for its role in the Lockerbie bombing incident.[2] The stated purpose of the bill, which also included language for secondary sanctions against foreign companies investing in Iran's oil industry, was to deny Iran access to the monetary resources necessary to finance international terrorism and its WMD program by limiting its ability to sell natural gas and oil.

European Union (EU) reaction was both swift and decisive, adopting legislation that essentially provided for its own sanctions against companies complying with the ILSA; the EU also threatened to bring action against the United States in the World Trade Organization (WTO).[3] As a result, the United States was forced to approve waivers for French companies investing in Iran's petroleum industry and never sought action against Turkey, which penned its own agreement with Iran for construction of a gas pipeline.[4] With the Clinton administration granting a growing number of waivers, proponents of the law feared the bill might lose all of its teeth and consequently began taking a less aggressive posture with regard to pressing the administration in its implementation of the law—external dynamics impacted the domestic situation. So, although the United States had both the requisite statecraft implements and domestic political commitment and momentum to pass the ILSA, these failed to translate into effective action, causing the United States to fall short in its diplomacy to "sell" the economic sanctions contained within the bill. This, of course, is just one example. The other implements of statecraft—military and technology—are equally subject to such vagaries.

North Korea too has at its disposal these implements of statecraft, some to a greater degree than others. Because of a confluence of past internal and external circumstances such as floods and crop failures during the early and mid-1990s and loss of its chief ideological partners and technological and economic benefactors, the Soviet Union (to political disintegration in 1991) and the PRC (to greater pursuit of market-oriented economic reforms and foreign investment that began under the leadership of Deng Xiaoping), North Korea presently finds itself with only three functional implements—military, diplomatic, and to a lesser degree, nuclear weapons-related technology. Further, its self-imposed isolation, loss of like Marxist-Leninist ideological partners within the former socialist bloc of nations, present economic straits, the technological superiority of the ROK-U.S. bilateral alliance aligned against it along its southern border and, of course, its pervasive doctrine of *Juche*, have impacted North Korean leaders' collective view of the world over the years and consequently how the nation employs its three functional implements of statecraft, which can best be described as "brinksmanship diplomacy."

Successive U.S. presidential administrations have been forced to deal with the North Korea question in one form or another since the mid-twentieth century, each in differing forms and with varying degrees of success. Truman was forced to confront the regime during the Korean War (1950–1953); Johnson during the North's military build-up under the aegis of Soviet assistance in the 1960s[5]; Clinton's attempt to head off a nuclear crisis on the Korean peninsula by signing on to the 1994 Agreed Framework; and Bush's attempt to reverse course on what he saw as Clinton administration coddling of North Korea by taking a hard-line approach to the North's nuclear weapons program. Despite how the threat has metamorphosed since the signing of the Korean Armistice (1953)—from conventional warfare, to a China and Soviet supported North Korea, to vitriolic propaganda to the present standoff over the regime's nuclear program—there is a common thread that has run throughout—*Juche*—and it has become the basis of North Korea's existence.

Typically, *Juche* is treated as a single component of a larger whole—as part of a broader pattern of North Korean behavior, or perhaps more accurately, misbehavior. I take a slightly different tact in this book as I believe that *Juche* lies at the heart of most of what North Korea does or does not do and has for decades. Consequently, if one fails to understand *Juche*—what it is, its importance to North Korea, how it evolved, and its application—one fails to understand a primary interlocutor in the battle to control the proliferation of nuclear weapons.

THE *JUCHE* CONSTRUCT

North Korea's manifest behaviors toward the outside world have been characterized in various ways—occasionally crazy, sometimes vitriolic, to a greater extent unreliable, and ofttimes vexing. The Bush (43 administration's further characterizations of Kim Jong Il as a "pygmy" and the regime as an "outpost of tyranny," while perhaps appealing to a domestic audience, do little to advance substantive understanding of the basis for North Korea's behavior, and more importantly, how to proceed in effective policy formulation based on that understanding. Without developing some meaningful context for why North Korea perceives the world as it does and how, based on its perceptions, it then engages with the outside world, U.S.-North Korea policy will remain, at best, fractured and incoherent with minimal likelihood of developing a well articulated policy that offers some measure of success.

Juche is the single most important concept with which one must come to terms when considering the manifest behaviors of North Korea, as much of its inexplicable behavior becomes more easily understood when analyzed through its prism. Broadly speaking, *Juche* has been defined as meaning "self-reliance." While self-reliance is an integral aspect of *Juche*, this definition fails to explain the totality of all that it embodies. *Juche* is more accurately described as autonomous self-identity, which has an enabling independence of action that in its ideal state renders North Korea insusceptible to, or at the very least mitigates the undesirable external influences of larger powers, particularly the United States, and to a lesser degree the PRC. The concepts of "independence of action" and "big power influence" are keys to understanding both *Juche's* conceptual framework and application.

Despite labels to the contrary (including my own), *Juche* has metamorphosed into much more than a concept over the decades, evolving from its initial conceptual framework to ideology to doctrine to codification in the form of *Kim Il Sungism*, resembling more of a religion-like belief system. *Juche* has been crafted for application to both domestic and foreign policy issues so it is at once a political framework and implement as well as a philosophy for daily life. *Juche* has functioned as a tool for ousting Kim Il Sung's domestic political opponents; achieving political consolidation; galvanizing the masses in North Korea, exhorting them to support the regime while simultaneously depriving them of basic human rights and sustenance; and most importantly, controlling the behavior of North Korean society as a whole. It also serves as the core of its foreign policy, first in adroitly handling relationships with its two feuding communist benefactors, the PRC and the former USSR, throughout most of the latter half of the twentieth century, and presently, the United States and other members of the Six Party Talks with regard to its nuclear weapons program. In short, *Juche* pervades the whole of North Korean society and serves as the source of collective and individual self-identity.

To derive a sense of the fundamental nature of *Juche* in North Korean society one need look no further than its two basic governing documents: the *Charter of the Workers' Party of Korea* and the *Constitution of the Democratic People's Republic of Korea*. Consider for example, the opening statement of the *Charter of the Workers' Party of Korea*: "The Workers' Party of Korea (WPK) is the *Juche*-type, revolutionary Marxist-Leninist party created by the great leader Comrade Kim Il Sung."[6] It further states that "The WPK strives to strengthen the ideological unity of its entire body on the basis of the *Juche* ideology."[7] Similarly, the *Constitution of the Democratic People's Republic of Korea* in Article 3 notes:

> The Democratic People's Republic of Korea makes Juche ideology a revolutionary ideology with a people-centered view of the world that aims towards the realization of the independence of the masses, the guiding principle of its actions.[8]

At least in terms of relative importance accorded to political belief systems, it would not be overstating the case to say that *Juche* is to North Korea what democracy and independence are to the United States—both are ideals inculcated into respective citizenries at the political, social, and cultural levels. Examples of how important such ideals can be are not far from hand. Consider our own zealous defense of the Bill of Rights, particularly Article One which ensures freedom of speech, religion, press, and assembly; and Article Two that protects the right of citizens to bear arms. This is not to argue qualitative similarities between the U.S. and North Korean systems of government, but merely to point out that commitment to each can be zealous.

At this point it might be worth considering the major doctrinal determinants of *Juche's* autonomous spirit, which include the following: independence, pragmatism, flexibility, equality, and nationalism. *Juche* was ideologically aligned with Marxism-Leninism during its formative years for purposes of building Kim Il Sung's legitimacy, facilitating political consolidation, and because of Kim's strong ideological ties with the Soviets. However, very early on, Kim sought to maintain a comfortable buffer between North Korea and the Soviets and Chinese to ensure that an ideologically independent North Korea would be free to develop its own brand of communism. *Juche* was first formally mentioned in a speech delivered to KWP propaganda and agitation workers on December 28, 1955, during which Kim set forth the importance of *Juche* to the North Korean style of communism.[9]

> What is Juche in our Party's ideological work? What are we doing? We are not engaged in any other country's revolution, but solely in the Korean revolution. Devotion to the Korean revolution is Juche in the ideological work of our Party...When we study the history of the Communist Party of the Soviet Union, the history of the Chinese Revolution, or the universal truth of Marxism-Leninism, it is entirely for the purpose of correctly carrying out our own revolution.[10]

Similarly, Kim propounded the importance of maintaining an *independent posture* vis-à-vis the Soviet Union and PRC, as he did in a lecture given in Indonesia in 1965.[11]

> The establishment of Juche means holding fast to the principle of solving for oneself all the problems of the revolution and construction in conformity with the actual conditions at home, and mainly by one's own efforts...This is an independent stand, discarding dependence on others, displaying the spirit of self-reliance and solving one's own affairs on one's own responsibility under all circumstances.[12]

Despite his staunch advocacy for maintaining an ideologically independent North Korea, Kim also pursued a pragmatic approach to relations with both the Soviet Union and the PRC, working assiduously to avoid irretrievably alienating either benefactor.

> ...all communists worthy of the name have always defended the Soviet Union. We search in vain for a historical example of a person who became a genuine Communist while, simultaneously opposing the Soviet Union. He who opposed the Soviet Union invariably either inflicted damage to the revolution or betrayed the interests of his people. Such is the lesson of history.[13]

From Kim's perspective then, North Korean success hinged on some measure of alignment with other socialist nations, particularly the Soviet Union and PRC, while simultaneously keeping them at arm's length—*flexibility* was important for ensuring Kim could take advantage of opportunities with either benefactor as they arose irrespective of the differences that existed between the two communist giants. Additionally, his pragmatism espoused never straying too far from the core material support potentially garnered from either in the form of economic, technological, or military assistance, provided independence, in the ideological and political sense, was maintained. I'll refer to this practice as *pragmatic alignments*, which called for sometimes supporting the Soviets, sometimes the Chinese, while at other times taking a position of alignment with neither.

Pragmatic alignments proved a useful tactic as Kim maneuvered the tricky waters of international politics with the PRC and Soviet Union during the 1960s, and one at which he demonstrated some acuity. Consider, for example, that North Korea concluded a defense treaty with the Soviet Union on July 6, 1961; only five days later North Korea concluded a similar pact with the PRC. This was during a time when there were visible strains in the relationship between the PRC and the Soviet Union. Another example of pragmatic alignments was North Korea's sudden rapprochement with the Soviets beginning in 1965 after several years of closer alignment with the PRC (1962–1964), a period which itself had been preceded by North Korea being more closely aligned with the Soviets than the Chinese. Why the switch back to the Soviet Union in 1965? : In a word, economics. Contrasted with earlier periods, the PRC was no longer in a position to offer North Korea the type of economic aid it required, still recovering from Mao's failed policies under the Great Leap Forward. The Soviets, however, were in a position to offer assistance, particularly military aid, and strengthening North Korea's military posture was the key to Kim's ultimate goal of reunifying the Korean peninsula under his leadership.

Quantitatively, rapprochement with Moscow netted Kim much needed military armaments in the form of MiG aircraft, bombers, air defense facilities, tanks, submarines, and ships.[14]

During the period of postwar rehabilitation our country received from fraternal countries economic and technical aid amounting to some 500 million rubles (550 million dollars). This, of course, was of great help. But in those days we put main emphasis on enlisting the efforts of our people... We by no means... advocate building socialism in isolation. What we do reject is the big-power chauvinistic tendency to restrain the independent and comprehensive development of the economy of other countries... [15]

At the heart of Kim's aversion to "big-power chauvinism" is the determinant of *equality*, which was and remains critical to how the North Korean regime perceives threats from the world around it and how it forms foreign policy decisions in relation to them. While its genesis can be traced back to Kim's concern over undue Chinese and Soviet influence in North Korea's domestic affairs, aversion to big-power chauvinism continues unabated under Kim Jong Il as well. The North Korean view of the world is aptly summarized in the Korean proverb that sees itself as a shrimp amongst whales, the whales being China, the Russian Federation (the former Soviet Union), Japan, and the United States, coincidentally four of the five countries (the fifth being South Korea) with which it presently negotiates issues related to its nuclear weapons program through the venue of the Six Party Talks. The notion of equality has been central to both Kim Il Sung and his son, Kim Jong Il, although the countries with which parity has been sought differ; the former sought parity with the former Soviet Union and the PRC, while the latter seeks it with the United States. As the elder Kim surmised, in order for North Korea to thrive it was necessary to ensure that its relations with other countries were conducted on an equal footing, not from a position of subordination; freedom of action and flexibility, through pragmatic alliances, helped lay the groundwork for parity in its relationships with larger countries. Similarly, Kim Jong Il seeks to ensure regime survival by simultaneously extracting aid from the world community while keeping it at arm's length so as to maintain independence in the handling of domestic issues, foreign policy, and military development, thus achieving what North Korea considers parity with other nations.

Ironically, while the venue of the Six Party Talks is a necessary and useful structure for ensuring some measure of engagement with the North, its own perceived status of "shrimp" versus multiple "whales" potentially undermines the long-term success of this venue. Although the United States has stridently maintained that the Six Party Talks venue is the only one through which it will undertake negotiations with the regime, the fact that four of the participating members to the Talks fall within the parameters of the regime's characterization of "big power chauvinists" will likely continue to impede progress. Thus, the one venue that has successfully brought North Korea to the negotiating table in a multilateral setting is the same one that cuts to the heart of the greatest North Korean sensitivity—its own self-perception vis-à-vis larger countries.

Examples of how the determinants of *Juche* play themselves out in international politics abound. Consider the example of the joint statement reached by all parties during the 5th round of the Six Party Talks (November 2005) that calls for North Korean dismantlement of all its nuclear weapons programs and, in exchange, allows for discussion of the provision of light water nuclear reactors at "some appropriate time in the future." Less than 24 hours later, North Korea reinterpreted this statement to provide terms more favorable to its own self-interests. When this action is viewed through the prism of *Juche's* determinants of independence, flexibility, and equality, it should not have come as a surprise. From the purely North Korean perspective, the agreement is tantamount to giving something for nothing and subjects them to big-power chauvinism—undue influence from larger powers—thereby delimiting its own freedom of action. Understanding your interlocutor's framework is paramount.

The final determinant, *nationalism*, finds its genesis in the centuries-old inability of Koreans to be masters of their own collective destiny, at various times in its history experiencing invasions from the Chinese mainland, Japan, and western nations, all impinging Korean sovereignty.

This strong sense of nationalism, which lies at the heart of a North Korean autonomous self-identity in terms of foreign policy, economic development, and military strength, is a concept that actually operates on both sides of the Demilitarized Zone (DMZ) and is born of North and South Korean shared history of living for centuries as a shrimp among various regional whales. Consequently, it would be misleading to discuss the importance of Korean nationalism only within the context of North Korea. In fact, the idea and term of *Juche*, while commonly thought of as unique to the North Korean regime's brand of communism, has been espoused by South Korean leaders as well during the past half century. Consider Park Chung Hee's (former president of South Korea, 1961–1979) self-proclaimed importance of *Juche* to South Korea:

> In order to carry out a great renovation movement in search of political liberty, economic self-reliance and social harmony and stability, we must first of all wage a spiritual revolution on the individual level. Every citizen must inculcate in himself an independent chuch'e (*Juche*) consciousness, firmly establish the spirit of self-reliance and self-help whereby one becomes the master of one's own destiny, and achieve the correct spiritual posture of national self identity.

Park's own definition of *Juche* further evolved to include the additional element of self-defense, and grew to be seen as important not only for domestic development, but development vis-à-vis "big power relations" as well.[16] Nor is this a theme relegated to the distant past. Consider South Korean President Roh Moo Hyun's comments during a September 2005 speech delivered at the United Nations during which he eschewed the undue influence of major world powers, exhorting the world body to avoid "great power politics."[17]

As this notion evolved on either side of the DMZ, there were superficial similarities between them. For example, both used the term and idea as a means for creating a uniquely Korean framework of governance—Kim for a unique brand of communism, Park for a peculiarly Korean style of democracy. Both sought solutions that took into account the special circumstances of their respective halves of the Korean peninsula.[18] Similarly, both concepts came to embrace not only the implements of statecraft, but also the individual citizen, as well as each nation's standing in relation to larger countries. Despite the similarities, however, what cannot be overlooked is the major difference in how each has employed *Juche*. For Park, and subsequent South Korean leaders, it has served as a rallying cry or political slogan, for Kim and the North Korean leadership it became an implement of governance and a way of life for the whole of North Korean society.[19]

In the end, understanding *Juche* and its determinants does not serve as an instrument for infallibly predicting the unpredictable nature and brinksmanship behavior of North Korea. The operative word remains "unpredictability" when discussing the behavior of the North Korean regime. But what greater understanding does afford is the opportunity to move beyond trite sound bites and superficial treatment of North Korea-related issues and fuller recognition of what one is dealing with—the regime's perceptions of the world, how it is likely to respond to those perceptions, and what conditions are present that will likely elicit productive or counterproductive behaviors—in short, it provides a construct for understanding the North Korean interlocutor, a first step toward developing more viable policy options, or at the very least, mitigating formulation of counterproductive ones. But how has *Juche*, both as a political philosophy and implement, been applied to North Korea's broader engagement with the outside world via its own set of statecraft implements?

THE *JUCHE* CONSTRUCT: NORTH KOREA'S IMPLEMENTS OF STATECRAFT

Recall that each nation has at its disposal certain implements of statecraft for carrying out relationships with other nations—military, economic, diplomatic, and technological. North Korea, as discussed, is no exception. As *Juche* evolved over time it came to identify three integral areas requiring application of autonomous action, which conceptually, function as North Korea's corollaries to implements of statecraft: *Chaju*, independence in politics, which should be construed as both foreign and domestic policy; *Charip*, self-reliance in the economy; and *Chawi*, military self-reliance.[20]

> ...the Government of the Republic will implement with all consistency the line of independence, self-sustenance, and self-defense to consolidate the political independence of the country (chaju), build up more solidly the foundations of an independent national economy capable of insuring the complete unification, independence, and prosperity of our nation (charip) and increasing the country's defense capabilities, so as to safeguard the security of the fatherland reliably by our own force (chawi), by splendidly embodying our Party's idea of Juche in all fields.[21]

Juxtaposed against the implements of statecraft introduced earlier in the chapter, one could say then that it is *chaju* and *chawi* that have coalesced to create North Korea's brinksmanship diplomacy.

Under the *Juche* construct, any consideration of attaining *chaju* requires eschewal of big-power chauvinism—minimizing the influence of larger nations. Grace Lee points out, however, that minimizing the influence of larger nations has, in practical terms, come to mean not cooperating with them as this might somehow impinge on "national independence and sovereignty...consequently leading to the failure of the socialist revolution in Korea."[22] So while implements of statecraft typically help define the method of engagement for most countries, in North Korea's case it has an almost antithetical result by constructing barriers to expanded engagement as a means of self-preservation. This becomes an important consideration when developing policy options for engaging North Korea. Consider the lack of past success of the U.S. policy of demanding CVID of North Korea's nuclear weapons program—not only were negotiations stalled, but the regime launched several missiles and detonated a nuclear test explosion. Understanding how your opponent thinks and how best to engage him is critical.

Chaju also embodies such ideas as equality among states; the right of national self-determination; and the rejection of subjugation—some of the more important elements of *Juche's* "equality" determinant. Ironically, while *chaju* provides for such rights at the national level in North Korea's relations with other nations, it does not translate into rights accorded its own citizenry vis-à-vis the KWP. Rather, *chaju* in foreign policy has as its domestic corollary application as a tool for achieving domestic political consolidation and maintaining political control. Under its auspices, both Kim Il Sung and Kim Jong Il have used it as a means to galvanize, unify, and maintain the support of the people for themselves and the KWP.

Charip is a particularly interesting mix of the two Kims' vision of the ideal and a pragmatic approach toward engaging with the world, a recognized necessity on the part of the regime since the country's inception.

Economic self-reliance has served as the regime's objective since the 1950s, although achieved with varying degrees of success. Kim Il Sung, a supporter of Stalinism, originally envisioned achievement of economic independence through the development of heavy industry.[23] When the former Soviet Union disparaged such an approach for North Korea, believing that light industry was a course more suitable for the regime to follow, the relationship between the two countries cooled and Kim aligned himself more closely with Mao and his economic policies. Of particular interest to Kim was China's Great Leap Forward, which led to development of a similar program in North Korea known as *Chollima*.[24] (*Chollima* is a legendary horse said to be able to travel 400 km a day.) Despite its ultimate failure to achieve the economic autarky Kim Il Sung originally envisioned, *Chollima*'s objectives for providing the foundations of economic self-reliance remain an important cornerstone of regime policy. The (North) Korean Central News Agency reported, for example, that as the country prepares to celebrate the 50th anniversary of the movement in December 2006, there has been steady progress under the slogan "Charge ahead at the speed of Chollima!"[25] Reality, of course, does not support such enthusiastic rhetoric.

A review of the World Food Program's (WFP) statistics of food aid delivered to recipient countries underscores the regime's continued adherence to pragmatic policies. During the period 1996–2005 North Korea received the greatest amount of aid among all recipient countries of the world, accepting over 10.1 million tons of food assistance.[26]

From the North Korean perspective there is no ideological incongruity between the goal of economic self-reliance and accepting outside economic assistance, a pattern characteristic of its economic policies since the country's inception. In a speech delivered in Indonesia in 1965 Kim Il Sung pointed out:

> . . . we fully recognize the importance of international support and encouragement, and consider foreign aid a necessity . . . self-reliance should be given primary importance; support and encouragement from outside should be regarded as secondary . . . We have thus, on the principle of self-reliance, laid the solid foundations of an independent national economy.[27]

Of the three integral areas of *Juche* cited in the preceding passage, *chawi* forms the basis for success of the other statecraft implements, *chaju* and *charip*, because both Kims believe a strong military provides the foundation for all power: without a strong military to defend the nation there is no basis for its ideals of political independence, economic self-reliance, or the ultimate communization of North Korea.[28] Developing a strong military became a priority for Kim Il Sung as the result of several key events: the South Korean military coup of May 1961, which catapulted Park Chung Hee into power; Soviet acquiescence to the United States during the Cuban missile crisis; and the cooling of Soviet-North Korean relations all served as important contributing factors to the development of this line of *Juche*. It has remained a constant theme for the North Korean regime over the decades, hence its continued emphasis on military preparedness, to include nuclear weapons, and why current U.S. guarantees for its security fall on deaf ears within the North Korean regime.

> ... today the (North) Korean people have turned out in the general onward march toward a new victory ... through intensified revolutionary upsurge of Songun (military first).[29]

In addition to the three fundamental areas of *chawi*, *chaju*, and *charip* identified by Kim Il Sung, other implements of statecraft have emerged over the course of time to help reinforce *Juche*. As a matter of necessity, technology has come to play a greater role in sustaining *Juche*, albeit on a comparatively limited scale, and only so far as it contributes to the success of *Juche* as discussed above. Technology, for the purpose of increasing the quality of life of its citizenry, has not been high on the regime's list of priorities and what little does exist is subject to the vagaries of how the regime perceives technology as a threat to broader national security. In an article written by Brent Choi of the Joongang Daily, he cites that in April 2005 Kim Jong Il ordered 90 percent of the country's international phone lines to be cut in an effort to reduce information leaks out of the country. Similarly, the regime reportedly confiscated 20,000 cell phones in the wake of the explosion at the rail station in Ryongchon in April 2004; it believed cell phone usage accounted for the leaked news of the incident.[30]

North Korean technological advancements have focused largely on two areas: domestic technological developments, particularly in the areas of agriculture and light industry, and military application. As pointed out earlier, economic self-reliance remains a key objective for the regime, the greatest obstacle to which has been the country's inability to feed its citizens for over a decade, hence the prioritization of agricultural advancement. Light industry has also become a focal point as the joint venture projects with South Korean firms in the DMZ border city of Kaesong illustrate. By far, however, the preponderance of regime resources used for purposes of technological advancement has gone into its military, which since the early 1990s has prioritized the development of nuclear weapons and ballistic missiles.

Finally, I would argue that North Korea, because of its willingness to operate outside the pale of accepted international norms to the extent that it does, possesses an additional statecraft implement that most nations do not—*audacity*—doing the least expected thing at a time of its opponent's greatest perceived vulnerability in order to put the adversary at a psychological disadvantage. Audacity is typically associated with armed conflict—the speed, surprise, and combat power with which one engages the enemy. Given the centrality of the regime's *songun* program to its foreign policy, the foundation that *chawi* (military self-reliance) provides within the *Juche* construct, and the unpredictability for which it has become renowned, this is precisely what the North Korean regime is doing—audaciously fighting a war, by other means, with brinksmanship diplomacy as its weapon of choice. Curiously, in many respects, North Korea's current policy of engagement with the world is the inverse of von Clausewitz's strategic thinking on armed conflict, which contends that "war is a continuation of 'policy'—or of 'politics'—by other means." For North Korea, international politics associated with negotiations to dismantle its nuclear weapons program is war by political means. Thus, the mindset with which North Korea approaches discussions of its nuclear dismantlement fundamentally differs from its U.S. interlocutor. The United States approaches negotiations within a western framework of debate, compromise, and resolution. North Korea, however, perceives negotiations as war by other means under which compromise is a tool of last resort through which one capitulates to his adversary. Understanding your adversary is essential.

JUCHE AND ITS HISTORICAL UNDERPINNINGS

Juche, by design, was less revolutionary than evolutionary. When the concept was first formally introduced in 1955 by Kim Il Sung, there was little collective understanding of either its ideological parameters or application. The KWP leadership's consternation over the concept proved politically advantageous to Kim for two reasons. First, with undefined parameters, the concept of *Juche* could be applied to just about anything and in any way Kim found politically expedient. Second, his political adversaries found it problematic to successfully oppose a concept about which they understood little; the safest course was to acquiesce. Consequently, using it as both an ideological and political implement, Kim successfully crafted a philosophy that has survived into the new century, which is not necessarily a positive outcome. That the society upon which *Juche* is imposed shows indisputable signs of stress is without question: an impoverished citizenry; because of its isolation, a nation in dire economic straits that has required massive infusions of international aid to survive; a rogue nation that operates outside the pale of international norms with regard to WMD, human rights, drug trafficking, and counterfeiting, along with a host of other activities. Yet, it survives against decades-long prognostication to the contrary.

Up to this point, the scope and dimensions of *Juche* have been treated, but what remains to be discussed is what provided its genesis—what allowed for the birth of *Juche* and its subsequent nurturing? That the basic idea of *Juche*, as discussed in the preceding section, exists on both sides of the DMZ with shared elements of self-reliance and an aversion to the influence of larger countries, albeit with very different applications, point to the common history shared by North and South Korea.[31]

Although Korea's history of suffering foreign incursion dates back as far as 109 B.C., establishment of the Koryo Dynasty (935–1392) serves as a turning point with respect to the characteristics of those incursions. Prior to this period, incursions were generally reciprocal in nature as Korea, that is the various smaller kingdoms that ultimately came to comprise Korea, was as likely to encroach on the territory of its neighbors as it was to have its own territory encroached upon.[32] With the rise of Koryo, however, Korea became more the object foreign incursions; it seldom initiated them. As a result, Korea developed unique coping mechanisms to ensure its survival amid much stronger neighbors in order to avoid total subjugation, in effect, early implements of statecraft: *sadae* and *mohwa sasang*. *Sadae* was the practice of "serving the great;" *mohwa sasang* that of emulating China. In practical terms this came to mean that Korea, as a smaller and more vulnerable nation, ensured its survival by simultaneously aligning itself with purveyors of power in the region, most particularly the dynasties of China, and serving their interests, as dictated by current conditions.[33] These approaches become particularly prevalent with the onset of the Koryo Dynasty.

While the first attempt to subjugate Korea came in 109 B.C. at the hands of the Han Empire, it was during the period of the three kingdoms (seventh century) when the Korean peninsula was controlled by Paekche in the southwest, Silla in the southeast and Koguryo, the largest, in central and northern Korea, that the record of historically significant incursions begin.[34] Emergence of the Tang Dynasty in China (618–907) ushered in a period of hostilities against the three kingdoms, particularly Koguryo in the north. After several unsuccessful attempts to bring Koguryo under its domination, Tang Chinese forces aligned themselves with Silla and undertook offensives against both Paekche and Koguryo; Paekche fell while Koguryo continued its resistance until 667 after which it fell as well. The Tang then brought Paekche and Koguryo under its administrative control and attempted to assert dominion over Silla as well. Military confrontation under such a scenario was, of course, inevitable. Tang forces, however, suffered a reversal of fortune. Not only did it fail in its efforts to subjugate Silla, but it also lost control over both Paekche and Koguryo in the process; Silla regained control of previously lost Paekche and Koguryo territory as far north as the Taedong River. Silla's victory not only forestalled Tang domination of the peninsula, but also unified a good portion of it under Silla for a period. Silla, however, was unsuccessful in regaining all territory lost to Tang China as the broad area of Manchuria which had formerly been under Koguryo control remained in Tang hands.[35]

With the fall of Silla and ascendancy of the Koryo Dynasty, a more lasting and stable unification of the Korean peninsula was achieved, although

Koryo too was beset by foreign incursions from the north (Manchuria), initially by the Khitan, which proved largely unsuccessful, and subsequently by the Jurchen, which established the Ch'in state and proved more formidable. In 1125 the Jurchen began to move southward confronting Koryo and demanding that it recognize the suzerainty of the Ch'in over Koryo territory, to which Koryo ultimately capitulated. By 1202, however, the Ch'in themselves came under siege from another rising power on the Asian mainland, the Mongols, who overtook the Ch'in and in turn sought domination over Koryo. By 1273 Koryo had been fully subjugated by the Mongols, becoming a tributary state of its empire. It was under this arrangement that Koryo supported the Mongol's two failed attempts to invade Japan in 1274 and 1281. The Mongols, however, were only one threat with which the Koryo had to contend. Koryo was also confronted by *waka*, Japanese pirates, who raided the coastland areas and the Red Turbans out of China who sought control of its northern territory. During the early years of the Yi Dynasty (1392–1910), Korea undertook military expeditions to regain lands lost in the north to Jurchens and Mongols, successfully reclaiming lands as far north as the Yalu and Tumen rivers, which stand as Korea's borders today.[36]

The Japanese, under Hideyoshi Toyotomi, first invaded Korea in 1592, sweeping across the whole of the country. A combination of Admiral Yi's now famous "turtle ships" and intervention by a 50,000 strong Chinese Ming army pushed the Japanese back and the Chinese recaptured Pyongyang. As a result, the Japanese entered into negotiations for settlement, which were on track until the Japanese demanded that some portion of Korean territory be ceded to them. Negotiations broke off as a result and Japan renewed its attacks in 1597, but against a better prepared Korea further bolstered by Chinese forces. The protracted fighting ended in 1598 with the death of Hideyoshi.

With the ascendance of the Ching in China, Korea was again attacked by a foreign power, in 1627 and 1636, with demands that Korea recognize Ching dominance, which it ultimately did via a suzerain-vassal relationship that lasted until the rise of Japanese dominance in East Asia in the late nineteenth century.[37]

The nineteenth century introduced new potential adversaries to the whole of East Asia—western powers. Japan, China, and Korea, while essentially confronted with the same threat, faired very different fates. Japan ultimately became a colonial power; China was divided among western powers into spheres of influence, and in some cases, colonies; and Korea, after being wrested from Chinese suzerainty, itself became a colony of Japan by the early twentieth century. Korea, much like the other nations of East Asia, was forced open for the purpose of increased commercial interaction. Despite its attempts to fend off such overtures, by 1882 and the signing of the Treaty of Chemulpo, a commercial treaty with the United States, Korea had been opened, much as Japan and China had already been, through the imposition of unequal treaties.

It was also during this period that Japan, which had also been subjected to the imposition of unequal treaties for the purpose of expanded commercial ties, decided it needed to recast itself along the lines of western powers if it was to avoid being carved up like China. Korea again became the object of Japan's attention as it sought to emulate the West. In 1875, Japan dispatched several ships off the coast of Korea ostensibly to survey the waters near Kanghwa Island; in reality it was an attempt to manufacture an incident with the Koreans. Korean shore batteries responded to the incursion by firing on the ship, to which the Japanese responded by dispatching six war ships, ultimately forcing the Koreans to capitulate and compelling them to sign with Japan an unequal treaty of its own, the Treaty of Kanghwa (1876), one of the important terms of which was to recognize Korea as an independent nation, breaking its centuries-old ties with China. This served only to embolden Japan with regard to the issue of Korea. With Japan's defeat of the Chinese in the first Sino-Japanese war of 1894–1895, the Chinese were forced to renounce any claims to Korea. Thus Korea increasingly fell under Japanese control, becoming a protectorate in 1905 and, with its annexation in 1910, a Japanese colonial possession until the end of WWII in 1945.

SUMMARY

Juche, which in its ideal form determinedly pursues autonomous action across a full spectrum of policy decisions, has for decades, and continues to be, the core of North Korean existence. It has served as a tool for domestic political consolidation as well as an implement of foreign policy. In pursuit of *Juche's* ideal state, an independent military posture plays a central role as it lays the foundation for independent political and economic policies—*chaju, charip*, and *chawi* constitute the regime's implements of statecraft, the unifying theme of which is independence. Independence, however, is not synonymous with self-reliance; they remain very different concepts, although both are integral to *Juche*. Self-reliance, particularly with regard to North Korea's economy, recognizes the pragmatism of accepting external assistance while moving toward the ideal of a self-reliant state; independence of action, however, is never subservient to nor does it exist under external influence. Such a scenario works to North Korea's advantage because the "carrots" put before the regime, in the form of economic benefits, and to a lesser degree humanitarian assistance, to induce desired behavior have been of such a nature that they can be "pocketed" with little offered in the way of any meaningful quid pro quo.

The regime has an established history of accepting external economic assistance without modifying its own policies; it is a pattern steeled in decades of Cold War experience. By offering or threatening to withhold such assistance, a point on which the United States and regional countries have not achieved consistency, the issue of economic assistance and its effectiveness as an implement, becomes a distracter, not the intended means to an end. Further, to the extent disagreement exists among the countries involved in the Six Party Talks, it divides and undercuts the strength of a unified position, a typical North Korean negotiating tactic. One of two consequences is likely to result. In a best case scenario North Korea deprives its negotiating partners of a unified position, thus stalling negotiations; in a worst case scenario it leads to its negotiating partners pursuing discordant courses of action, in effect working at odds with one another. Consider the alignment of nations participating in the Six Party Talks. Over time, the U.S. and Japanese positions have taken harder-line approaches with the regime while Chinese and South Korean positions have followed a path of broader economic engagement in an attempt to maintain regional stability. Whether one position is superior to the other is a discussion undertaken in later chapters; of immediate concern is that such circumstances deprive participants to the Talks of a unified position, thus making negotiations more problematic. Humanitarian assistance programs further complicate the problem. These programs have characteristically been lacking in transparency, making them potentially subject to a high degree of fungibility, with food or other assistance winding up in unintended sectors of the economy such as the military or among the political elite.

North Korea's economy, since the early 1990s, has functioned as an abnormal one—external assistance, along with its illicit activities, has kept North Korean society afloat while many of its own resources have gone into supporting its policy of *songun*, which includes both conventional forces and its nuclear weapons program. A strategic policy that compels the regime to recast its economic policies toward greater normalcy, requiring it to shift resources currently earmarked for *songun* into other sectors of the economy, will be the key to achieving modification in the regime's behavior. Consequently, programs that focus on controlled economic development rather than economic and humanitarian assistance will be important in bringing about such a shift.

3

Historical Foundations: Creation of a Rogue Regime

No division of a nation in the present world is so astonishing in its origin as the division of Korea; none is so unrelated to conditions or sentiments within the nation itself at the time the division was effected; none is to this day so unexplained; in none does blunder and planning oversight appear to have played so large a role. Finally, there is no division for which the U.S. government bears so heavy a share of the responsibility as it bears for the division of Korea.

—Gregory Henderson, Former U.S. Foreign Service Officer and noted Korea scholar (1974)

THE MAKING OF A DIVIDED NATION

Japan's occupation of the countries and islands of East and Southeast Asia during the first half of the twentieth century monumentally impacted their political and economic systems, societies, and cultures, particularly in the wake of its Greater East Asia Co-prosperity Sphere, perhaps less for what the Sphere actually accomplished than for what the Japanese military authorities felt free to do under its conceptual rubric.[1] Among those countries that suffered under Japanese colonialism, of course, was Korea, a colonial possession during the period 1910–1945. Ironically, if one considers the course of events on the Korean peninsula since 1945 and Korea's liberation, the manner in which liberation was affected by the Allies has proved as problematic for Korea as was its status within the Japanese colonial empire.

It was the result of decisions made during the last years of WWII in planning for the defeat of Japan, its ultimate surrender, and the disposition of the fruits gained through its territorial aggrandizement, that Korea became as we know it today—a nation divided—which has had repercussions for the world ever since.

By early in the twentieth century the U.S. geopolitical perspective had relegated Korea to a secondary status; a means to greater U.S. strategic ends that merited only tangential consideration. Consider, for example, that as early as 1905, under the Taft-Katsura Memorandum, an agreement in principle between the United States and Japan, the two nations recognized each other's respective interests in Asia—Japan recognized American paramount interests in the Philippine Islands while the United States agreed to recognize Japanese suzerainty on the Korean peninsula. So it remained throughout nearly the whole of the first half of the twentieth century as Korea's status as a Japanese colonial possession warranted little else. To the extent that Korea was ever a geopolitical consideration, even during WWII, U.S. strategic and operational planners thought of it only in relation to Japan, China, and at the end of the war, the Soviet Union.

Two meetings took place during the course of WWII that would prove to be watersheds with respect to Korea's future: the Cairo Conference (1943) and the Potsdam Conference (1945). The Cairo Conference, held in Cairo, Egypt, on November 22–26, 1943 between Franklin Roosevelt, Winston Churchill and Chiang Kai-shek, addressed the Allied position regarding postwar Asia, and was articulated in the Cairo Declaration (November 27, 1943). In addition to declaring that Japan would lose sovereignty over all territory it had seized since 1914 and asserting that territory lost by China would be restored, the following was provided regarding Korea:

> Japan will also be expelled from all other territories which she has taken by violence and greed. The aforesaid three great powers, mindful of the enslavement of the people of Korea, are determined that in due course Korea shall become free and independent.

The terms agreed upon in the Cairo Declaration were confirmed in the Potsdam Protocol, August 1, 1945 (Annex II, Section 3 (b) 8):

> The terms of the Cairo Declaration shall be carried out and Japanese sovereignty shall be limited to the islands of Honshu, Hokkaido, Kyushu, Shikoku and such minor islands as we determine.

As is sometimes the case, disagreement hinges on a matter of a few words. The words "in due course" of the Cairo Declaration provide such an example. The Korean people believed, as noted Korea historian Andrew Nahm contends, that this meant "when Korea was liberated from Japan."[2]

This idea was propagated by the Korean provisional government located in Chungking, China since 1919. Anxious to provide good news to Koreans living under Japanese colonial rule, members of the provisional government chose to translate the "in due course" clause of the Declaration as "immediately" or "within a few days."[3] Thousands of copies of the translated version were then made and distributed throughout the Korean peninsula.[4] That this was the prevailing view among Koreans is borne out by the fact that when U.S. occupation forces landed in Inchon, Korea in September 1945, subsequent to Japanese surrender a month earlier, they were greeted by members of a hastily established Korean provisional government.

Conversely, Donald W. Boose, Jr., writing in *Parameters*, the U.S. Army War College Quarterly, argues that some sort of trusteeship in Korea had always been considered part of the Korea equation as participants to the Cairo Conference had discussed such an arrangement, which was further discussed between Roosevelt, Churchill, and Stalin during the Teheran Conference (1943), and then again subsequently in May 1945 during a meeting between U.S. Special Representative Harry Hopkins and Stalin.[5] The actual modalities of such a trusteeship were never concluded or officially announced, which may have contributed to consternation on the part of Koreans, but that such stewardship was central to the Allies peninsula solution is well documented.

Two events would further complicate any planning for postcolonial Korea: the Soviet Union's entrance into the war against Japan and Japan's unexpected surrender to the Allies. Planning for Operation Downfall, the invasion of Japan's home islands, was still underway when Japan unexpectedly began seeking a peaceful means for withdrawing from and ending hostilities in the Pacific, the result of the two atomic bombings at Hiroshima and Nagasaki.[6] Japan surrendered on August 14, 1945.[7]

With the Soviets' official declaration of war against Japan on August 8, 1945 they quickly moved forces onto the Korean peninsula; by August 10 the Soviets had moved into the northeastern cities of Chongjin and Nanam. The United States feared Soviet forces were in a position to press their advantage and potentially occupy the entire peninsula, something the United States would be powerless to stop as the closest U.S. forces in proximity to the peninsula were located on Okinawa. Compounding this issue was the fact that the units making preparation for the invasion and occupation of mainland Japan had priority for movement and would have used nearly all available transportation assets in the theater.[8] Thus, even if U.S. authorities had decided to dispatch troops from Okinawa in support of contingencies on the peninsula, they couldn't have undertaken such a move until after the planned operations in Japan had been successfully concluded. Consequently, U.S. planners decided that a formal plan was needed that clearly demarcated the two nations' respective spheres of influence, an important consideration of which was to ensure its acceptability to the Soviets as the United States was in no position to immediately challenge them.

Hence, U.S. Army planners Colonel Charles H. Bonesteel and his assistant Colonel Dean Rusk (later to become Secretary of State under Kennedy and Johnson), working through and under the direction of the State, War, Navy Coordinating Committee, sought to quickly develop a plan that bisected the peninsula in such a way that took into account the following: (1) the dividing line was drawn far enough south to appease the Soviets; (2) U.S. interests were recognized, specifically that the American occupation zone included Seoul, the capital; Kaesong, a culturally important site; and prisoner of war camps located outside of Seoul; and (3) that the boundary did not appear to be politically derived.[9] As Bonesteel described it in his correspondence with Boose dated April 14, 1973:

> A first matter for choice was whether the line should serve Korean provincial boundaries or be a more non-political designator. The Allies, at the summit conferences, had agreed that Korea would be removed from Japanese hegemony and in due course become again an independent nation. However there was considerable vagueness in how this formula would be carried out and it was felt that every effort should be made to avoid the implication that the line for surrender had any political connotation in regard to the evolution of an independent Korea. Thus the choice of a parallel of latitude over the perhaps more recognizable provincial boundaries.

In the end, the Soviets agreed to such a partition.[10]

Although neither Bonesteel nor Rusk was aware of it, their selection of the 38th parallel as the peninsula's dividing line offers a little historical serendipity. The Soviets had sought their own sphere of influence in Korea as early as the late nineteenth century and had, since that time, considered a division along the 39th parallel acceptable. In fact, the Soviets contended that Ito Hirobumi, a noted Japanese statesman, had been on his way to Moscow to discuss the matter in 1909 when he was assassinated in Harbin, China. Given that such a division was something to which the Soviets had been historically amenable, Stalin actually agreed, in principle, to some division of the peninsula as early as February 1945 during the Yalta Conference.[11]

As a practical matter, the bisecting line was roughly equidistant from Korea's northern and southern borders but left the preponderant resources in the southern portion: 21,000,000 of Korea's population of 30,000,000 would live in the southern half of the peninsula; 12 of its 20 major cities lay south of the 38th parallel; and the American zone included the agriculturally rich farmlands and light industrial facilities (in 1940 what was to become South Korea produced nearly three-quarters of the peninsula's light industrial and processed goods).[12] Conversely, the Soviet occupation zone contained more of the peninsula's land mass, 55 percent (48,240 square miles) to the American occupation zone's 45 percent (37,060 square miles); the northern occupation zone was home to most of Korea's heavy industry; and from the Soviet perspective they gained access to two important ports, Wonsan and Chongjin.[13]

The impetus for all this activity, of course, was Japan's surrender to the Allies, but in order to make arrangements for accepting surrender, the United States and its allies had to establish a mechanism through which Japanese military forces and colonial officials throughout Asia could do so. What emerged from the process was General Order 1, which in part reads:

> The senior Japanese commanders, and all ground, sea, air and auxiliary forces within . . . Korea north of 38 degrees north latitude . . . shall surrender to the commander in chief Soviet Forces in the Far East . . . all ground, sea, air and auxiliary forces in . . . Korea south of 38 north latitude . . . shall surrender to commander in chief US Army Forces in the Pacific.[14]

Thus, with General Order 1, Korea's occupation zones were affected and, for the United States, the hasty planning that characterized preparations for occupied Korea presaged the many problems that would plague its military government in southern Korea until 1948 and the creation of a sovereign South Korea, the Republic of Korea.

CHARACTER OF THE OCCUPATION

U.S. and Soviet occupation forces had four primary missions on the Korean peninsula. The first was to accept the surrender of Japanese military forces and colonial officials, ensuring their demobilization and repatriation; second, to disassemble the colonial governmental and administrative apparatus in Korea; third, to create a functional governing apparatus to replace the dismantled colonial apparatus. Both sides, however, failed in the fourth, final, and arguably most important mission: to establish a trusteeship over the whole of the peninsula with the ultimate goal of removing the division between the two halves of the country and restoring sovereignty to a reunited Korea.

While both powers were guilty of making poor occupation policy decisions that impacted the reunification of the two halves of the peninsula, the root cause of failure rested primarily in the implicit agendas that both the United States and Soviets operated under, agendas that would only harden as the broader Cold War between the two countries took shape, and which ultimately proved to be at odds with the goal of a reunified peninsula. For the Soviets, this meant "Sovietizing" northern Korea with the aim of bringing it into the larger sphere of Soviet Bloc nations. For the United States, southern Korea became a battleground for containing the spread of communism in general and denying the Soviets influence in southern Korea in particular.

What ultimately came to be played out on the Korean peninsula then was a reflection of the broader Cold War in which the United States and Soviets had become embroiled. This scenario was further complicated by the fact that the explicit tasks and implicit agendas of U.S. and Soviet occupation forces were undertaken against the backdrop of a confused and rapidly changing domestic political landscape on both sides of the 38th parallel.

The conditions within the northern and southern occupation zones were representative of fractured post-WWII U.S.-Soviet relations; the policies, methods of implementation, and degrees of effectiveness within the Soviet northern and U.S. southern zones differed markedly. A juxtaposition of U.S. and Soviet policy pursuits provides a useful context. One significant difference between the two occupation zones was the presence of an overall strategy in the northern region, that of Sovietizing the population, its administrative machinery, and its governing apparatus. The United States, on the other hand, was for a time devoid of any coherent strategy within its southern occupation zone, save perhaps that of holding the line. The policy implementation structures created within each zone also differed, at least superficially, and in this case appearances were important. U.S. occupation forces developed a more visible governing apparatus through creation of its military government, which at least structurally, more closely resembled the colonial government it replaced; the Soviets chose to create a façade of self-determination from behind which they were able to control much of northern Korea's society. Another important difference was the manner in which each of the occupation authorities handled dismantlement of the Japanese colonial government. The Soviets undertook an across-the-board removal of all colonial elements, while the United States initially sought to maintain the colonial structure in order to provide for a smoother transition. Another key difference was how each of the powers permitted the local populations to pursue self-determination. The United States attempted to create an American style democracy but in the process alienated significant portions of the southern population. This can be attributed to several reasons: the lack of any real strategy for its occupation zone; policy mismanagement; and what turned out to be a natural inclination toward strongly conservative elements in Korean politics at the expense of the more liberal ones, causing discord between them. The Soviets, on the other hand, chose to Sovietize the northern region through the use of locals in order to give the appearance of Korean self-determination, although the end result resembled nothing of the sort. The cumulative result of these differing approaches was greater political polarization within the U.S. region. In fact, polarization and political discontent also existed within the northern occupation zone, however, Soviet style "democracy" did not countenance political dissidence; political miscreants were either forced into submission through various means or they were forced to flee to the southern occupation zone, but were in any case expunged from northern Korea.

"IN DUE COURSE": FAILURE OF OCCUPATION POLICY

Political Failure

The U.S. and Soviet plan, or at their least agreement in principle, was to ultimately return complete sovereignty of the Korean peninsula back to the Korean people "in due course." Inherent within this charge was the task of establishing the required working relationships between the two occupation authorities in order to facilitate the necessary economic and political cooperation between the two halves of the peninsula.

An intermediate step toward that end emerged from the Foreign Ministers' Conference held in December 1945 in Moscow attended by the United States, Great Britain and the Soviet Union, and through which the Moscow Agreement was concluded. At the behest of the United States and its representative to the meeting, Secretary of State James F. Byrnes, the foreign ministers of Great Britain and the Soviet Union agreed that steps should be taken sooner rather than later to remove the line bisecting Korea and the military occupation zones administering the two halves of Korea, thus reunifying the peninsula. Several key provisions comprised the Moscow Agreement, but its centerpiece was the establishment of a Joint Commission on which representatives of the United States and the Soviet Union would serve. Generally speaking, the Commission's mandate was to oversee the processes of economic and political reunification, which included the following: (1) determining the modalities for forming a provisional Korean democratic government, which in turn would oversee development of industry, transportation, and agriculture on the peninsula; (2) together these two bodies would work out the parameters for creating a five-year four-power trusteeship that would include the United States, Soviet Union, Great Britain and China; and (3) to immediately convene a meeting of the Joint Commission to coordinate the actions of the two spheres of occupation.[15]

While the Joint Commission served as its centerpiece, it was the trusteeship provision that proved to be the insurmountable obstacle to progress under the Agreement. That segments of the Korean population, for example the nationalists, would staunchly oppose such an arrangement isn't particularly surprising. That it was the Soviets, and by proxy their communist protégés, who were strongly in favor of the trusteeship deserves further consideration because on its face such a position appears counterintuitive. Bradley K. Martin proffers in his book, *Under the Loving Care of the Fatherly Leader*, the following rationale for the Soviet's position. The trusteeship would have provided the Soviets more time to try and consolidate their communist followers in the U.S. southern zone of occupation. Another theory, also covered in Martin's book, posited by Dutch scholar Eric van Rhee, is that the Soviets were focused on gaining more time to firmly establish a communist satellite state within their occupation zone.[16] While both theories are certainly plausible, there is another possible explanation. Considered within the broader context of the Cold War and the ideological battle being waged against the United States, the Soviets may have considered southern Korea as a new front and seen the trusteeship as an opportunity for legitimate access to the southern U.S. occupation zone with the goal of fomenting discontent in order to convert all of Korea into a Soviet Bloc nation.

Had the provisions of the Moscow Agreement ever been implemented, they might have successfully created an undivided Korea. While the Commission was successful in establishing guidelines for such things as ground and water transportation between the two zones, mail exchange, and radio frequencies, it was less effective in establishing a provisional government.[17] The problem from the very beginning was the Joint Commission itself and the inability of U.S. and Soviet representatives to successfully coordinate and negotiate between themselves the modalities of their agreement, the root cause of which was mutual lack of trust and a preoccupation with their own respective spheres of interest. Acrimony came to characterize their relationship from the outset. For example, disagreement erupted during the Joint Commission's very first meeting centering on a single clause: "In preparing their proposals the Commission shall consult with the Korean democratic parties and social organizations."[18] The sticking point was which Korean organizations would be deemed "acceptable" to either side. The Soviets wanted to exclude as ineligible any group or representative who had ever expressed criticism of the trusteeship, which was a euphemistic reference to the Nationalists. Similarly, the Soviets contended U.S. representatives to the Commission precluded participation of some major democratic organizations in southern Korea (communists) while simultaneously supporting participation of a group that had opposed the Moscow Agreement and its provisions for trusteeship (nationalists).[19] Not surprisingly, U.S. representatives opposed the Soviet position on the grounds that it would deny the right to free speech.[20] In substance, their respective positions violated neither the spirit nor intent of the Moscow Agreement.[21] Unfortunately, these disagreements continued throughout summer 1947 and in the end assured the failure of occupation authorities to reunite the peninsula.

Although the Soviet position on which Koreans should be consulted in the process of reunifying the peninsula technically comported with the Moscow Agreement, the United States had good reason to generally regard Soviet activities with some circumspection. From commencement of the first meeting of the Joint Commission in mid-January 1946, Soviet efforts can accurately be characterized as working to maintain the division of the peninsula rather than its reunification. As indicated by General Shtykov, Lieutenant General Hodge's Soviet counterpart in the northern occupation zone, on the eve of his departure from Seoul in 1946: " . . . the main reason the Soviet delegation insisted on barring certain persons from consultation is that Russia is . . . interested in establishing in Korea a provisional democratic government which would be loyal to the Soviet Union."[22]

Finally, the United States reached the conclusion that continued attempts to negotiate through the Joint Commission would likely continue to yield fruitless results. Consequently, the United States proposed to the United Nations, through the General Assembly, that it assume responsibility for disposition of the Korea issue.[23] Despite staunch Soviet opposition to the plan, the UN General Assembly, in September 1947, voted to consider the U.S. proposal. In a resolution passed on November 14, 1947, the UN General Assembly essentially established new parameters for resolving the Korea issue, to include: abandoning the idea of the four-party trusteeship; committing to a course of self-determination for the Korean peninsula; conducting free elections as the means to assuring self-determination; creation of a UN body, the UN Temporary Commission on Korea (UNTCOK), to oversee the election process; and removal of occupation forces.[24] Specifically, the resolution provided:

> Inasmuch as the Korean question . . . is primarily a matter for the Korean people itself and concerns its freedom and independence; and recognizing this question cannot be correctly and fairly resolved without the participation of representatives of the indigenous population: The General Assembly, resolves that elected representatives of the Korean people be invited to take part in the consideration of the question; . . . that the Korean representatives are in fact duly elected by the Korean people . . . there be forthwith established a United Nations Temporary Commission on Korea . . . to travel, observe and consult throughout Korea . . . that the national independence of ' Korea should be re-established and all occupying forces then be withdrawn at the earliest practicable date . . .

Despite UN attempts to persuade the Soviet Union to the contrary, Soviet officials in northern Korea refused to permit UNTCOK officials to conduct elections, which ultimately compelled the UN to hold separate elections in southern Korea.

The period immediately preceding elections in the south were anything but uneventful, with the attempted assassination of Seoul's police chief and eruption of several armed rebellions. This notwithstanding, nearly 90 percent of 8 million eligible voters in the south registered to vote in the 10 May election to select representatives for the national assembly.[25] Despite election day violence, the election process went smoothly, which UNTCOK certified the following month. Democratic processes were instituted quickly thereafter as the new National Assembly convened at the end of May and elected Syngman Rhee as its new chairman; enacted a new constitution in June; and later that month elected Sygnman Rhee as president. Finally, the

National Assembly created the Republic of Korea (South Korea) on August 15, 1948, as a separate and sovereign nation.

On the northern side of the peninsula UN sponsored and monitored elections, as a result of Soviet opposition, were not undertaken. In response to elections in the now established Republic of Korea, however, the Supreme People's Assembly convened in September1948, ratifying a constitution and electing as its premier Kim Il Sung. In October 1948, the Soviet Union and other nations of the communist bloc officially recognized the creation of the Democratic People's Republic of Korea (DPRK).

The conduct of elections on both sides of the 38th parallel sealed the fate of Korea and signaled the failure of former WWII allies to bring about unification and sovereignty on the peninsula.

Economic Failure

Overall failure of the respective U.S. and Soviet occupation policies to reunite Korea was not only the result of political failure, it also represented a failure in bringing about the necessary economic linkages between the two halves of the peninsula. Under the terms of the Moscow Agreement, U.S. and Soviet occupation forces, working through the Joint Commission, were to pursue economic reunification of Korea as a precursor to political reunification. This was necessary because the bizonal division of the peninsula exacerbated weaknesses created under Japan's colonial system. Under the system, there emerged in Korea a regional specialization of production between northern and southern Korea, with the former specializing in heavy industrial capacity and the latter in agricultural and consumption industries.[26] Far from being eliminated under occupation policy, such vestiges of colonial Korea were further reinforced under allied occupation as there was little trade across the 38th parallel.

Korea had for centuries been a chiefly agricultural society, a trend that continued under Japanese colonization; roughly 73 percent of all households were so employed during the Japanese occupation period.[27] It was logical that Japan would avail itself of the agricultural resources of its new colonial possession, particularly in light of growing Japanese domestic concern over its own rice production. Consequently, beginning in 1921, the Japanese undertook a concerted effort to increase rice production in Korea for the purposes of exporting it to Japan. Production was increased by 3 million *koku*,[28] from 14.9 million *koku* to 17.9 million *koku* during 1920–1935, 9 million *koku* of which was exported to Japan.[29] When rice was no longer a priority commodity for the Japanese domestic economy, light and consumption industries came to prevail in southern Korea.[30]

Industrialization of the northern zone didn't become a priority until several years later, the genesis of which was the Manchurian Incident, which put the Japanese economy on a semiwar footing, thus stimulating the economy and business investment in research and development.[31,32] Prior to that time, there had been little to induce Japanese business investment in the area because the quality of Korea's brown coal, iron ore, and other minerals was considered inferior. With the introduction of hydroelectric power and advances in chemical processes, the theretofore inferior minerals could be processed to an acceptable quality, thereby increasing their utility and importance to the Japanese war-time economy.[33]

The impact of Japan's activity on the Korean economy during its period of colonial dominance remained intact after its surrender to the Allied Powers in August 1945. In effect, its legacy left an agricultural southern region and an industrial northern region. The notable difference between Japanese and allied occupation, however, was that Japan's colonial government created an interdependent economy where both halves contributed to the functioning of the whole, thus regional specialization proved an economically viable model. Under the allied occupation, however, each half of the peninsula was forced to function independent of the other, leaving each with problematic deficiencies. Consequently, the preponderance of southern industries relied on raw materials and production capacity located in the north, which included most of the fertilizer and chemical plants, electric power, and gas deposits.[34] These conditions were in part responsible for the rice shortage experienced in southern Korea during spring 1946.[35,36] A converse situation existed north of the 38th parallel, the greatest deficiency being in its agricultural production capacity. While northern farmers grew such produce as sorghum and soybeans, these were grown primarily for export; oats and millet were used as animal feed; and the amount of corn and buckwheat produced was inconsequential in relation to its needs.[37]

Had economic rapprochement been achieved by U.S. and Soviet occupation authorities, it might have served as sufficient impetus for greater political rapprochement; whether it would have led to reunification and how quickly remains an open question. Korea was beset by significant obstacles: disagreement between the populations of both occupation zones as to the future of Korea; disagreement among the southern population over the issue of trusteeship; significant political stratification within the southern zone; and divergent policy pursuits by both occupation authorities. These circumstances must be considered within the broader context of world events: Korea came to represent the larger Cold War being waged between the two occupying powers, to which, in the end, it would ultimately fall victim.

In the end, it was a convergence of historical lessons learned by the Korean people through efforts to subjugate them, their unfulfilled expectations after liberation from the Japanese colonial authority, and unsuccessful political and economic occupation policies that came to lay the groundwork for the situation on the Korean peninsula as the world knows it today. The following two chapters will examine how these seemingly distant events of over half a century ago have impacted the geopolitical landscape of the Korean peninsula and East Asia over the past sixty years.

4

Triangular Relationships: North Korea, China, and the Former Soviet Union

It does not matter whether we eat our meal with the right hand or the left, whether you use a spoon or chopsticks at the table. No matter how you eat, it is all the same insofar as food is put into your mouth, isn't it?[1]

—Kim Il Sung's speech to the Party Propaganda and Agitation Workers, December 28, 1955, offering thoughts on internal Party squabbles over whether to align with the Soviets or Chinese

North Korea's advance toward statehood and the rise of Kim Il Sung as its first leader can generally be traced through three stages: the Soviet satellite period (1945–1948); the consolidation period (1949–1958); and the sovereignty period (1959–present). The sovereignty period can be further divided through characterization of North Korea's threat posture: prenuclear and nuclear, which can be dated from the early 1990s.

The Soviet Union served as the impetus for much of the political activity in North Korea during the satellite stage, which was characterized by the imposition of Soviet-style socialism; the elimination of potential suitors to political power in the North; the North's realization of statehood; and Kim's installation as leader of North Korea, the Soviet clear choice. The consolidation phase was characterized by Kim's expansion of his own power and substantial weakening of Soviet and Chinese influence within the country while eliminating vestiges of domestic political competition. The final stage, the sovereignty period, can generally be described as the period during which Kim created a foreign policy independent of either China or the Soviet Union; developed a North Korean styled communism; and redoubled his efforts to bring about reunification of the peninsula under communist control through threats, acts of terrorism, and violence against South Korea, and largely belligerent engagement with the United States and South Korea.

Despite the fact that there was no organized political or religious resistance to Soviet occupation or comparatively little flagrant opposition against Moscow's policies, there nonetheless existed a field of other significant players within northern politics, a number of whom were indeed potential suitors for political power. At this point it might be useful to remind the reader that the political landscape of postcolonial Korea was anything but clear-cut; communists were not relegated to the northern zone nor were nationalists found only in the southern zone. Koreans of all political persuasions lived throughout the peninsula and arbitrary imposition of the dividing line along the 38th parallel, along with U.S. and Soviet occupation mandates within their respective zones, only served to further consternate an already confused state of affairs. Consequently the postcolonial period within both zones was characterized by domestic political consolidation, a process that occurred sometimes through natural evolution of the political process and sometimes through less natural means like assassination.

There were essentially five different groups that potentially vied for political power within the Soviet occupation zone: the Yenan faction (Chinese-supported), domestic communists, the Soviet Koreans, domestic nationalists, and the Kapsan faction. It is worth noting that typically only the first four groups are identified as vying for power in northern Korea, with the Kapsan faction usually being excluded. It is, however, important to identify this group as a separate entity because the Kapsan faction was led back into northern Korea by Kim Il Sung upon his return from the Soviet Union; although they supported communist ideology, their platform differed from that of domestic communists and Yenan factions. The Kapsan faction was more closely aligned with Soviet doctrine and in the eyes of the Soviets not all communists were created equal.

The Kapsan faction had waged a guerilla-style campaign against the Japanese in Manchuria during the early part of WWII, but spent the last years of the conflict within Soviet borders. Sometime during the first half of the 1940s Kim and his followers, fleeing from the Japanese, made their way into the extreme southern portion of the Soviet Far East, the Maritime Province, where they eventually joined the Soviet Army's 88th Special Independent Sniper Brigade, a unit comprised of Chinese, Korean, and Soviets of Korean descent.[2] Kim was commissioned as a captain and put in command of one of the brigade's battalions. The mission of the brigade was twofold. Its short-term mission was to conduct reconnaissance against Japanese military units in Korea and Manchuria. Its long-term mission was to establish Soviet-style communist parties in both China and Korea.[3]

Among the other significant groups in the Soviet occupation zone were the Soviet-Koreans, introduced in the preceding section, who the Soviets brought with them to assist in enforcing occupation policy; serve as the Soviet mouthpiece in policy development; and function as their "eyes and ears" on the ground. This group was, however, less a potential political suitor than it was a tool for Soviet occupation authorities. They had in fact been selected precisely for their loyalty to the Soviet Union as they remained members of the Soviet Communist Party and would come to form the nexus of what was regarded as the "Soviet faction" in the years following the creation of the Democratic People's Republic of Korea. This group would ultimately be expunged under Kim's purge of foreign influence within North Korea.

A group that would come to represent the "Chinese faction" in North Korea was comprised of those Koreans who fought against the Japanese alongside the Chinese; this group was known as the "Yenan faction," which too would ultimately be purged by Kim.

There were also, as one might expect, Korean nationalists, those who were not necessarily aligned with any group politically but who were ardently in favor of a Korean society and government, for and by Koreans, based on the principles of self-determination and devoid of any outside control or influence. Finally, there were the indigenous Korean communists who, despite Japanese efforts to quash their activities, proved resilient enough to maintain an underground presence in Korea throughout the colonial period.

With the existence of such a potentially destabilizing array of groups vying for political power immediately after Soviet arrival, the Soviets were concerned with how their presence might negatively impact plans for Sovietizing the northern occupation zone. Through a combination of merging some groups, eliminating others, assassination, and collaborating with unlikely partners for the sake of expediency, they proceeded with their plans for building a Soviet Bloc nation. One means employed toward this end was a measure known as the "united front" tactic, which provided the Soviets with the necessary, albeit temporary, buffer for consolidating a power base comprised of Koreans loyal to Moscow and its vision for the north.[4] Such an approach was necessary in the Soviet's northern occupation zone because the preponderant communist strength in the immediate aftermath of occupation was actually located within the southern zone.[5] Thus, in an attempt to solidify their position and diffuse any potential backlash as a result of occupation, the Soviets undertook such a united front with Korean nationalists, led by Cho Man-sik, a very popular Christian nationalist leader who advocated Korean independence through self-sufficiency, particularly economic and educational self-sufficiency.[6] Perhaps because of his popularity, his predisposition toward nonviolence, or because he provided access to a potentially problematic segment of the Korean population, the Soviets concluded it would benefit their aims to work with Cho and his followers.

Another reason the Soviets might have found Cho a convenient expedient is that by the time of their arrival in northern Korea, the Japanese Governor General had already turned over power to Cho and his nationalist followers after their surrender. Cho as well concluded that despite disagreement with their occupation policies and methods, working with Soviet occupation authorities would be politically expedient. As a result, the Soviets appointed Cho as head of the Provisional Political Committee followed by an appointment as head of the Five Provinces Administration Bureau.[7] This tactic of forming a united front with the nationalists, however, proved short-lived and of limited effectiveness in the Soviet's dealings with the northern nationalist element as their fundamental disagreements were both deep and irreconcilable.

The tenuous relationship between the two became irretrievably fractured by December 1945 with the announcement of plans for the four-nation trusteeship provided for under the Moscow Agreement: Cho was not at all amenable to an arrangement that he perceived as merely replacing the Japanese colonial authority with a colonial authority of Soviet making.[8] Consequently, he denounced the trusteeship decision, something the Soviets were not prepared to countenance. In response, the Soviets convened a meeting of the Five Provinces Administration Bureau during which support for the trusteeship was announced and in response to which Cho resigned as the Bureau's head; he was later arrested in January 1946 after which he simply disappeared and was never heard from again.[9] Soviet experience with Cho effectively ended any efforts at a united front with the nationalists and from that point they pursued a policy of using communists to fill important positions within the newly established government. Many nationalists, understanding the shift in political winds, began heading southward into the U.S. occupation zone.

The domestic communist party also experienced internal upheaval, with its own leader, Hyon Chun-hyok, meeting a fate similar to Cho Man-sik's. Hyon, although communist by political persuasion, was not of the ilk that supported peasant uprisings to bring about a Korean Revolution. Rather, he believed that the first order of business was to establish functionality and credibility for a new Korean nation, an end he believed required some measure of cooperation between and among political parties. Hyon had in fact attempted a partnership with Cho at one time.

Perhaps there was concern that such a political alignment would prove too strong or popular to overcome in Sovietizing the northern zone; or that Hyon's ideas of communism did not comport with Soviet communist ideals; or that Hyon did not appear ideologically malleable enough for Soviet purposes; or that it was Kim Il Sung and not Hyon who the Soviets wanted in a position of leadership. In any case, Hyon was assassinated on September 28, 1945—fewer than sixty days after the Soviets arrived in northern Korea.[10] The message sent by his murder was clear—there was no room for political freedom within the northern occupation zone and leadership within the North Korean Communist Party was not up for grabs. The Soviets had specific designs for the domestic communist party, which ultimately came to center on Kim Il Sung.

If the experience of the nationalists and domestic communists serves as an example of how ruthlessly the Soviets were prepared to undertake their transformation of northern Korea into a Soviet bloc nation, then the Yenan faction is an example of how deftly they were able to merge political parties in support of broader Sovietization of the area. Operating under the banner of the New People's Party (NPP), the Yenan faction enjoyed increasing support among northern Korean intellectuals, causing concern among the communists. Unable to outflank them politically, the North Korean Communist Party decided that merging the two parties would be a more effective course and subsequently joined with the NPP to form the North Korean Workers' Party (NKWP).[11] Of course, in reality it was less a merger than it was absorption of the NPP. This served well the aims of the Communist Party because it added to the ranks of its peasants the NPP's intellectuals. The merger of these two parties underscores an important point alluded to earlier. For the Soviets, and later by extension Kim, there could be no coexistence among the various factions of the communist party operating in northern Korea; they were mutually exclusive.

Kim Il Sung arrived in northern Korea not long after the Soviets; the Soviets arrived in August 1945 and Kim the following month. It was not until a month later that he made his first public appearance at a specially organized rally held on October 14, 1945, at which he was introduced to the citizens of northern Korea as a national hero.[12] It is worth noting that Kim, while known to the Soviets, was much less known among Koreans. Kim could likely not have ascended to his position of power within northern Korea and the NKWP without the solid backing of the Soviets.

There were several reasons for Kim's rise to power. First, through some combination of his self-cast image as a national Korean hero from his days as an anti-Japanese guerilla fighter in Manchuria and the result of his training and service with the 88th Special Independent Sniper Brigade, Kim had distinguished himself in the eyes of the Soviets who clearly had plans to make special use of him. From their perspective, he was regarded as trustworthy: he had proven himself loyal to the Soviet cause during his years in the Soviet Union. Second, there were few other contenders acceptable to the Soviets for assuming the mantle of leadership in northern Korea; the leader of the domestic communists, Pak Hon-yong, was headquartered in Seoul. And as mentioned earlier, Hyon had been assassinated and Cho served merely as a political expediency. Third, Pak was pursuing his own united front with nationalists under the rubric of the Korean People's Republic whose reach, Pak contended, was peninsula-wide.[13] This in effect competed with the Soviet's alliance with Cho. Pak's efforts were also independent of

Soviet oversight, not an acceptable solution toward Sovieting the north, so consequently Kim proved the most acceptable, and accessible, choice.

The Soviets undertook several initiatives that promoted Kim as the Koreans' rightful leader, permitted him to strengthen his own political power base and ensured effective political consolidation (or expunging) of disparate and potentially destabilizing political entities within the Soviet occupation zone. In late 1945 he was selected as first secretary of the North Korean Central Bureau of the Korean Communist Party.[14] In support of his new position, his followers were appointed to strategically important positions within the emerging governmental structure. His arrival in Korea was also heralded by the Soviets as a monumental event—the return of a national hero. And with creation of the PPCNK in February 1946, Kim was selected as its chairman.

By August 1948 an election was conducted within the northern zone to create the Supreme People's Assembly which, at least in name, was a representative body of the Korean people, the representatives to which were elected by citizens 18 years and older. By mandate, the Assembly's representatives originally represented citizens in both the northern and southern halves of the peninsula. Functionally, however, it provided a veneer of participatory and representational governance for citizens within the northern occupation zone while endorsing the dictates of the North Korean Communist Party.[15] One of its first acts was to recognize the creation and existence of the Democratic People's Republic of Korea (September 9, 1948); ratify the new nation's constitution (September 3, 1948); and select as its first leader Kim Il Sung. With the Supreme People's Assembly's approval of Kim's selection of cabinet officials on September 10, Kim's first phase of political consolidation had been completed. The following year, the NKWP and SKWP merged to form the Korean Workers' Party (KWP) with a membership of over 790,000 members; it became the preeminent political organization in newly formed North Korea and Kim Il Sung ascended to the position of General Secretary.[16]

POLITICAL CONSOLIDATION CONTINUES: THE TEN-YEAR PURGE

Kim's ascension to North Korea's premiership, while solidifying his political base, did not signal the end of rivalries or potential political suitors. Kim remained ever vigilant against possible usurpers of his political power and authority. His efforts between the years 1948–1958 centered on three groups in particular: the South Korean Workers' Party; the Yenan faction; and the Soviet-Koreans. It was Kim's success at undertaking the purging of these groups that provided him with near absolute power and paved the way for the creation of North Korea's cult-like political system. Impetus for further political consolidation came about as a result of two events: the Korean War and Nikita Khrushchev's crusade during the Twentieth

Congress of the Communist Party of the Soviet Union (CCPSU), which sought to de-Stalinize Soviet communism, directly leading to the August Incident in North Korea.[17]

Until intervention by the Chinese People's Volunteer Army, North Korea suffered humiliating military defeats during the Korean War; Chinese assistance kept the North Koreans from being routed, but did not secure realization of Kim's vision of a reunified peninsula under communist rule. Responsibility for the setbacks experienced during the war had to be shifted away from Kim if he was to remain unchallenged as the nation's premier. Consequently, during a meeting of the KWP's Central Committee in December 1950, General Mu Chong, commander of the Second Corps, was charged with "propagation of a defeatist mood" and "insubordination."[18] That someone other than Kim needed to bear the brunt of responsibility for North Korea's reversal of fortunes was almost a forgone conclusion, but selection of Mu Chong as the scapegoat reveals that political consolidation was still underway. Mu Chong was the leader of the Yenan faction and enjoyed a good deal of prestige amongst not only its members, but in China as well, as he was a veteran of the Long March and established and integrated the artillery capability for the Communist Chinese Eighth Route Army.[19] Given Mu Chong's stature and that it was now only the Chinese who stood between North Korea and annihilation, Kim likely saw him as a political threat. In any case, as a result of Kim's accusations he was purged in December 1950; Chinese intervention spared his life and Mu Chong lived the remainder of his life in China.[20]

The Soviet-Koreans fared no better in Kim's internal "cleansing" of the party. In the following year their leader, Ho Ka-i, too was accused of malfeasance. He opted for suicide in 1953 to avoid standing public trial against the accusations.[21] The result of both the Ho Ka-i and Mu Chong purges was to severely weaken their respective organizations, although their respective memberships remained intact. Given the efforts the Soviets had undertaken in North Korea during 1945–1948 and the military armaments and materiel they provided during the Korean War, this was particularly troubling for them.

Hostilities associated with the Korean War ended with the signing of the Military Armistice (July 1953). As a result, Kim was able to turn his full attention to completing his political purges; the one remaining potential suitor to power was the South Korean Workers' Party. Kim assailed its leader, Pak Hon-yong and his followers of spying for U.S. forces during the war and denounced them for planning to overthrow the North Korean government. Pak was executed in December 1955 and with his death the domestic communist faction (as opposed to Kim's Kapsan faction) ceased to function as a viable political entity. Pak's removal further solidified Kim's hold over North Korean politics and society.[22]

Although these events helped Kim further strengthen his political base, it was the August Incident that removed any remaining potential political threat to his position. The genesis of the August Incident is found in the CCPSU, held February 14–25, 1956. During the proceedings, Khrushchev convened a "secret meeting" at which he denounced Stalin and his cult style of leadership. That portion of the meeting relegated to assailing Stalin was actually held February 24–25, 1956 and opened with Khrushchev offering the following remarks:

> Comrades! In the Party Central Committee's report at the 20th Congress and in a number of speeches by delegates to the Congress...quite a lot has been said about the cult of the individual and about its harmful consequences. After Stalin's death, the Central Committee began to implement a policy of explaining concisely and consistently that it is impermissible and foreign to the spirit of Marxism-Leninism to elevate one person, to transform him into a superman possessing supernatural characteristics, akin to those of a god. Such a man supposedly knows everything, sees everything, thinks for everyone, can do anything, is infallible in his behavior.

While Khrushchev's remarks were directed at Stalin's reign of terror in the Soviet Union, their context was uncomfortably applicable to Kim and Mao as both had established domestic cult leadership styles of governance in North Korea and China, respectively.

Taking as their cue the proceedings of the secret meeting, the leaders of the Yenan and Soviet-Korean factions within the KWP attempted to foment revolt against Kim's leadership while he was out of the country touring the Soviet Union and Eastern Europe for two months trying to secure development assistance. During Kim's absence, the leadership of the two factions wrote articles denouncing Kim's personality cult and failure to meet the challenges set forth in Khrushchev's remarks during the CCPSU; he was also accused of failing to meet the needs of the people by focusing too much on development of heavy industry. During the August 1956 meeting of the KWP (hence the name August Incident), the leaders of the Yenan and Soviet-Korean factions verbally attacked Kim over what they considered to be grave abuses of power. In the end, however, Kim prevailed—his position and supporters were too firmly entrenched to be removed. Consequently, Kim undertook a purge of both factions beginning with their leadership, stripping the leadership and their followers of their rank and titles and expelling them from the party.[23] This represented the last attempt to challenge Kim's position within the KWP. After successfully putting down this revolt, Kim effectively operated without challenge.

PYONGYANG'S RELATIONS WITH MOSCOW AND BEIJING: THE 1950S

To fully understand North Korea and its development after its inception in 1948, one must also understand its relationship with the former Soviet

Union and China, as well as the ideological struggle that existed between the two communist giants. It was through a unique combination of the military and economic assistance provided by both nations to North Korea and their own polemics over the future course of socialism that contributed to shaping the new nation.

As noted in the previous section, Pyongyang's relationship with the Soviet Union and China during the decade of the 1950s came to be directly defined by the Korean War and the proceedings of the CCPSU. The end result of these events was not cataclysmic, but rather was instrumental in laying the foundation for gradually increased discord between the Soviet Union and China and establishing the modes of interaction North Korea would come to employ with both. These two events also caused a "see-saw" effect over time in the level of influence each nation exercised with North Korea. China had exercised little meaningful influence in the country prior to the Korean War because of its preoccupation with its own revolutionary consolidation of Chinese territory, at the time focused on Taiwan and Tibet. As a result of the Korean War, however, China came to be regarded by the North Koreans as a loyal socialist nation because of the assistance the Chinese rendered. On the other hand, the Soviets, as a result of their direct intervention in North Korean affairs during the occupation period, enjoyed a greater advantage in this regard before the Korean War, but eventually suffered diminished stature as a result of it.

Both nations provided support to the North Koreans during the Korean War. The major difference between the two lies in the type of support provided by each: the Chinese provided, amongst other things, soldiers to assist in the fighting when North Korean military units were effectively decimated, to the tune of approximately 300,000 men and $2 billion in loans (received from the Soviet Union) to underwrite the cost of the war; the Soviets provided the means to wage war—war materiel, advisors and some fighter pilots—but offered no direct intervention in support of North Korea.[24] To Kim Il Sung and the North Koreans this was a profoundly important difference because the war, from their perspective, was one fought for Korean liberation and independence for which the Chinese had spilled their own blood. In fact Chinese intervention had been predicated upon the widely touted campaign of "Resist America, Aid Korea."[25] Soviet efforts, on the other hand, came to be regarded as mercenary and the Soviet Union came to be derisively known as a "merchant of death."[26]

In a pragmatic sense, any support of the Korean War by either the Soviet Union or China was driven less by a fervently shared sense of socialist destiny than by the pragmatism of geopolitics. The Chinese, for example, wrestled with several concerns not the least of which was Soviet intentions regarding Manchuria. The Chinese feared that any failure on their part to act decisively against a growing American presence in North Korea once UN forces crossed north of the 38th parallel would invite Soviet intervention via Manchuria under the pretext of friendship and assistance through the terms of the Sino-Soviet Treaty of Friendship, Alliance and Mutual Assistance (February 1950).[27] The terms of the agreement would have provided the Soviets needed justification for reoccupying the area: that each side would come to the aid of the other in the event of attack from Japan or one of its allies.[28] (Although the Soviet Union and China concluded their agreement, at the time of the signing strains in their relationship had already begun to emerge.)[29] Japan provided major basing and transshipment operations for the United States during the Korean War. China also became increasingly concerned with both the immediate and long-term geostrategic implications of the war as it related to domestic security. As the war progressed, Mao came to believe that North Korean military units had overextended themselves and thus would unlikely achieve their goal of reunifying the peninsula.[30] Consequently, he began considering the ramifications of massive U.S. intervention in Korea on the Chinese domestic situation.[31] China was likely also uncomfortable with the prospect of an immediate American presence on its border and what that might portend for China in the long-term should North Korea fall to UN forces; essentially reverse application of the *Domino Theory*.[32] Finally, earlier Chinese preoccupation with the liberation of Taiwan was put in abeyance by the Truman Statement of June 27, 1950, that included Taiwan within the defensive sphere of the region, effectively freeing up Chinese soldiers and war materiel that could then be used to assist the North Korean war effort.[33] China was not, at that point, strong enough to militarily engage the United States over the Taiwan issue and opted to put plans to invade Taiwan on hold.[34]

Conversely, the Soviets calculated their lack of intervention in broader geopolitical terms. Attempting to take advantage of the western powers' entanglement in hostilities on the Korean peninsula, the Soviets saw this as an opportunity to make headway in the broader Cold War being waged globally, particularly on the European continent. Stalin also saw the war as a means of "taming" the recalcitrant Chinese leader, something he had had difficulty doing, by encouraging increased Chinese dependence on Soviet support of the war, especially through the extension of loans.[35] From Khrushchev's point of view, this, in turn, would help the Soviets consolidate their position within the region.

The impact of the CCPSU and its proceedings, particularly on North Korea and China, shouldn't be underestimated as two key issues were brought forth that potentially had long-term ramifications: (1) Stalin's legacy to communism; and (2) through what means the Soviet Union, and the rest of the communist bloc countries, would seek to undertake future engagement with Western powers.[36] Through this single event, Khrushchev sought to redefine the future of communism not only within the Soviet Union but throughout the socialist world while also defining how the socialist world would pursue foreign policy aims with its ideologically antithetical competitors in the West. Despite then what many have referred to as his plenteous failings, Khrushchev at least demonstrated the vision necessary to use the Congress as the means to setting a bold new course for the socialist world.

Khrushchev's secret speech, which heralded in a period of severe reproof of Stalin's policies, had immediate implications for both North Korea and China. As discussed in the preceding section, Khrushchev used the secret proceedings to castigate the "cult of the individual" through an anti-Stalinist diatribe; a direct link could be drawn to both Mao and Kim as theirs were regimes founded upon Stalinist principles and cult leadership.[37] In the case of North Korea, there were certainly those within the KWP who drew the connection, leading to the August Incident which sought to remove Kim from power because of his Stalin-esque transgressions. This was from Kim's perspective a rather uncomfortable position to occupy as he was in no position to either discount or ignore Khrushchev's contentions, but he needed to assure his own continued supremacy in domestic politics. He maintained his supremacy by not only using the immediate tact of purging those responsible for fomenting the August Incident, but also through innovatively and limitedly construing the meaning of the cult of the individual to internal party politics and only insofar as it sought to upset the existing status quo. Thus, any attempt to oust Kim and his leadership was deemed tantamount to advancing the cult of the individual.[38]

Khrushchev introduced another concept during the CCPSU proceedings that too ultimately proved distasteful to North Korea and China, that of peaceful coexistence with Western powers. The North Koreans and through later intervention, China, had just waged a war against what they regarded as imperialist intrusion of sovereign Korean territory, the main protagonist of which was the United States. Neither North Korea nor China was particularly amenable to the notion of peacefully coexisting with the United States, especially as it maintained a presence in the southern half of the peninsula. Although dissatisfaction with this policy did not immediately surface, it did feed the discontent attendant to the Cuban missile crisis a few years later.

Major events of the 1950s helped to forge closer ideological alignment between North Korea and China. This was not a situation of mutual exclusivity with regard to North Korea's continued support of the Soviet Union as both communist giants were wooed for their contributions to North Korea—the Soviet Union for its creation of the nation and China for its sacrifices during the war. Thus, while simultaneously showing support for most Soviet policies, North Korea also demonstrated similar support of Chinese ideological and policy pursuits. An example of such support of China's policies can be found in the Sino-Indian border dispute that took place during the late summer of 1959. This is both an insightful and telling case not only because it illustrates how the North Koreans skirted contentious issues between the Soviet Union and China, but also because it offers a glimpse into the evolving pattern of engagement North Korea would pursue to keep both communist nations appeased and supportive of North Korean policy pursuits.

When the border dispute broke out between India and China as a result of China's territorial incursions into Indian sovereign territory in the Kashmir and Jammu regions, the Soviet Union was less than supportive of China's position, choosing to remain neutral. (This would become yet another important contributing factor to the deteriorating relationship between the Soviet Union and China.) North Korea, on the other hand, opted to offer full support of Chinese efforts by expressing "complete solidarity with the justifiable position of the PRC [in the] Sino-Indian territorial question [which was] part of an Asia-wide anti-Communist and anti-Chinese campaign conducted by the U.S. imperialists."[39] Such a position had something for everyone: it supported the Chinese in their territorial struggle with India while castigating U.S. imperialism as anticommunist, which would appease the Soviets.

Another important example of North Korea's expanding support and emulation of China was implementation of its own Chollima Undong (Flying Horse Movement), which was, at its core, a mirror image of Mao's Great Leap Forward. The goal of each was to increase small-scale industrialization in order to advance economic development, the most distinguishing feature of which was the exclusive reliance on massive inputs of manpower to achieve economic goals rather than increased technology or more efficient work methodologies. Particularly interesting was North Korea's effort under this program to increase production of pig iron. Local blast furnaces were established across the country to produce crude iron that could later be refined for the production of other goods. Firsthand accounts of the Great Leap Forward also document the thousands of local furnaces that were constructed for the purpose of melting down farm implements, metal gates and kitchen utensils for later reuse.[40]

Beyond ideological compatibility or an extended sense of gratitude for past support, there was a more functional reason for North Korea to remain in the good graces of the Soviet Union and China, namely economic support and assistance. In the case of China, not only did members of their volunteer military force provide much needed fighting strength during the war, they played a key role in postwar reconstruction efforts in North Korea. According to some sources, the Chinese volunteers helped construct bridges, dikes, reservoirs, and repair damaged roads, railways, and houses.[41] China also made more direct monetary contributions in support of North Korea's economic welfare, which included waiving "all supplies given and expenses incurred" related to the Korean War.[42] It also included providing a $317 million (U.S.) grant for the purchase of such items as agricultural tools, building materials, grains, and a host of other necessities under the auspices of the Treaty for Economic and Cultural Cooperation.[43] As a result of this increased economic interaction, China's trade with North Korea, as a percentage of the latter's total trade volume, increased over 200 percent to 27.3 percent by 1957.[44]

External economic assistance was also provided to North Korea by the Soviet Union and its Eastern European socialist bloc nations. In fact, North Korea received some grants simultaneously from both the Soviet Union and China. For example, during the life cycle of the $320 million (U.S.) grant received from China (1954–1957), North Korea also received a $250 million (U.S.) grant from the Soviet Union, which was further increased by another $75 million (U.S.) in 1956. Soviet socialist bloc countries (East Germany, Poland, Czechoslovakia, Hungary, Romania and Bulgaria) also contributed some additional $298 million (U.S.).[45]

This was the basic pattern established by the Korean War and the proceedings of the Twentieth Congress. Neither yielded immediate rifts within the socialist camp, yet both laid the groundwork for future discontent as represented by the major Sino-Soviet rift that would become apparent to the world during the 1960s. Regardless of how North Korea perceived the results of the War and the Congress, there was little outward manifestation of its dissatisfaction. Whether the result of the Soviet Union's leadership position within the communist bloc nations, its economic assistance, or out of recognition that North Korea was born of Soviet efforts, Kim and the KWP continued outward support of Soviet policies. For example, the KWP, together with China, gave the proverbial head nod to the October 1956 Soviet declaration that internal relations amongst socialist countries be governed by equal rights. Similarly, in 1957 Kim and a contingent of KWP delegates attended the 40th anniversary of the October Revolution during which Kim lauded the Soviet Union's advancements over the years and proclaimed, " . . . the Korean people stand shoulder to shoulder with the Soviet people and will do the same forever."[46] In fact, the Treaty for Economic and Cultural Cooperation reached between the Chinese and North Koreans was negotiated with the assistance of the Soviets.[47]

While overall relations appeared placid and based on a certain socialist camaraderie, seeds of discontent had already been sown. For Mao and China, the 1950s had surfaced important ideological differences between themselves and the Soviets: the cult of the individual concept; the Soviet lack of commitment to the Korean War; and the Soviet's cool response to the Sino-Indian border issue. They would be unable to paper over these continuing and growing differences during the next decade. For the North Koreans, three important realities emerged. First, that both the Soviets and Chinese had something to offer North Korea and in order to maximize gains they'd need to avoid alienating either communist country. Second, because of their growing rift, the Soviet Union and China could be played off against one another. Finally, that despite its dependence upon the economic assistance of both countries, North Korea needed to pursue a course of political independence in order to avoid unwanted external influence, a topic covered at length in Chapter 2. The value of these lessons goes well beyond their historical significance—they provide an insight into the North Korean mindset with regard to how they approach current negotiations over its nuclear weapons program. Finding the proverbial "crack" in an otherwise unified position in order to play one party off against another; pocketing concessions with no offer of a quid pro quo; and above all else, maintaining its recalcitrance in the face of world condemnation of its actions—in essence what it perceives as its independence—all hallmarks of its behavior, find their genesis in the Cold War relations between and among communist bloc nations and the *juche* philosophy.

THE DECADE OF THE SIXTIES: THE SCHISM GROWS

Generally speaking, the 1960s begin and end in roughly the same place although the journey was anything but uneventful; relations between North Korea, the Soviet Union, and China experienced quite an upheaval. The first half of the decade proved pivotal in terms of how relationships developed between and among the nations of the socialist bloc. Unlike the preceding decade, differences during this period were no longer masked in order to present a picture of socialist solidarity; rifts had clearly emerged. By 1963 there existed widespread polarization among the communist nations, with countries generally falling into either the pro-Soviet or pro-Chinese camps; this was the backdrop against which the relationships between North Korea, the Soviet Union, and China ebbed and flowed. From 1960 the rift between China and the Soviet, for example, became one less of ideological differences and one more of substance. The impetus for this more open parting of the ways between the two communist giants was China's open rejection of Khrushchev's vision for peaceful coexistence with the West and creation of its own road toward socialism that was at odds with the Soviet model. From about 1962 onward, North Korea, while not completely severing ties with the Soviets, aligned itself much more discernibly with the Chinese on those issues over which the Soviets and Chinese found themselves at odds, leading to a commensurate decrease in bilateral interaction with the Soviets, but increased ties with China. The two events most directly affecting Soviet-North Korean relations were the Cuban missile crisis and the January 1963 East German Party congress. By 1965 and Khrushchev's removal from power, however, North Korean alignments again shifted and an air of rapprochement settled over the Soviet-North Korean relationship, accompanied by North Korea commensurately distancing itself from China.

If the decade was characterized by increasing interaction between North Korea and China, it was also a period during which the seeds of disagreement between the Soviets and Chinese sown during the 1950s began bearing fruit. One of the major reasons for this was Mao's proffering in 1958 of an alternative means for achieving socialism in Asia. His concept, the nexus of which focused on expanded collectivization and creation of communes, light industry, and the Great Leap Forward, differed markedly from the Soviet's heavy industrial development model. It was not, however, only the idea of an alternative route to socialism that affected relations with the Soviet Union. There was inherent in the Chinese concept of collectivization a direct rebuke of Khrushchev's anti-Stalinist policy; Stalin was the architect of the Soviet Union's first experiments with collectivization in the latter half of the 1920s, one of the many points raised by Khrushchev in his secret speech during the Twentieth Congress.[48] While the Soviets did not immediately regard Mao's vision as a threat, by the 1960s it had become another major contributing factor to the decline in Sino-Soviet relations. Growing Soviet dissatisfaction with the Chinese occurred because Chinese efforts came to be seen as a challenge to Soviet leadership within the communist bloc nations. The Chinese challenge was not limited to Asia. From the Soviet perspective it extended into Europe as well as Albania supported Chinese policy almost unwaveringly.[49]

Subsequent to China's challenge of the Soviet blueprint for socialism, an article was published in the April 16, 1960 edition of *Hung Chi* entitled, "Long Live Leninism!," which rejected as revisionist the entire premise of Khrushchev's vision for peaceful coexistence with the West as enunciated during the Twentieth Congress.[50] What the Chinese proffered instead was the idea that war was inherent to imperialism and that as long as imperialism existed, so too would war. Following this line of thinking, it was then unrealistic to postulate that peaceful coexistence could be undertaken with countries regarded as being imperialistic.

We believe in the absolute correctness of Lenin's thinking: War is an in-evitable outcome of systems of exploitation and the source of modern wars is the imperialist system.[51]

The real crux of this article was in its potential practical application—the U.S. remained, at least in the eyes of the Chinese and North Koreans, the leader of imperialist nations. War with the United States then was inevitable, a conclusion the Soviets were unprepared to countenance. The Soviets had considered Chinese actions with regard to the Sino-Indian border dispute only a year earlier as reckless; the Chinese doctrine of the inevitability of war, particularly as it related to the United States, hardly fared a different judgment.

The North Korean response to the CCP article, which in itself is telling, was muted. North Korean leadership was walking the proverbial tightrope between China and the Soviet Union to ensure healthy bilateral ties with each, and not without good reason. April 1960 was also a time of tumult in South Korea as its staunchly conservative anticommunist leader and first president, Dr. Syngman Rhee, was forced to resign, the result of growing popular discontent with his policies, which manifested themselves in student riots.[52] Rhee's was replaced by two very short-lived administrations (Ho Chong, April-July 1960 and Chang Myon, August 1960-May 1961), the latter ultimately falling to the military coup of Park Chung Hee in May 1961.[53]

The new "military government" in South Korea, which also fostered strong anticommunist policy positions, clearly caused anxiety within North Korean leadership circles given that hostilities associated with the Korean War had ended only eight years earlier. Kim felt the need to assure North Korea of the support of both communist benefactors. In fact, Kim considered the coup's genesis the direct result of U.S. meddling in South Korean affairs.[54] Consequently, by July 6, 1961, Kim had negotiated with the Soviets the Treaty of Friendship, Cooperation and Mutual Assistance which provided in part for the mutual defense of each nation should either come under attack from another nation or coalition of nations; the coalition of nations was an unveiled concern Kim had to a possible repeat of the employment of a United Nations coalition like the one that nearly decimated the North during the Korean War. True to what was becoming the modus operandi of North Korean foreign policy, Kim signed a similar treaty on July 11, 1961, with the Chinese. The rationale for signing two treaties is readily apparent. First, Kim did not want to alienate one communist guarantor over the other—both had been treated equally. Second, it provided North Korea greater assurance that at least one of the two communist giants would come to its aid in the event of renewed hostilities; Kim sought to avoid another scenario under which the Soviets would provide the means for war without actually committing troops as it had during the Korean War.

Eruption of the Cuban missile crisis in 1962 and its ultimate outcome would profoundly impact North Korea's relations with the Soviets and further exacerbate the rift between the Soviets and Chinese.[55] For North Korea and China, the crisis represented the quintessential confrontation of socialism and imperialism, of good (socialism) versus evil (imperialism). It was the opportunity for socialist nations to demonstrate to the world their strength, solidarity, and supremacy over imperialist nations. Mass rallies were conducted in North Korea in support of Cuba and its citizens while the Rodong Sinmun spewed forth pro-Cuban and anti-U.S. editorial commentary.[56, 57] Consequently, when the Soviets backed down in the face of U.S. resolve, it was a major blow to both the North Koreans and Chinese and Soviet prestige suffered immensely as a result. Attacks against the policy of peaceful coexistence grew and fueled the intensity of dissatisfaction with Khrushchev and Soviet policies. The missile crisis represents the commencement of the period during which the nadir of Soviet relations with both North Korea and China was reached.

Events like the Cuban missile crisis and the reactions they elicited among members of the communist bloc nations facilitated greater polarization amongst communist countries and forced them to declare their allegiances with either China or the Soviet Union. Among them, of course, was North Korea. The existence and impact of such divided alliances became clear during the various European communist party congresses convened in the immediate aftermath of the missile crisis. North Korea's growing allegiance with China earned it the enmity of most communist European nations, with the single exception of Albania. Representative of this deterioration in relations was the ostracization of North Korea at the East German Party Congress in January 1963 during which it was not accorded the opportunity to make customary speeches nor to meaningfully engage with other communist member nations.[58] If such treatment was meant to modify North Korean behavior and bring it back into the Soviet fold, it failed to achieve this end; it only underscored for the North Koreans the correctness of their course as demonstrated a year later during the Second Asian Economic Seminar held June 16–23, 1964, in Pyongyang with strong Chinese support. This economic summit was attended by thirty-five nations, with the obvious exceptions of the Soviet Union and India. The purpose of the meeting was to propound those national socialist qualities to which both North Korea and China subscribed: national self-reliance; an independent economy; growth through the strength and employment of citizenry and resources; equality among nations; and economic cooperation between and among nations. The North Koreans (and Chinese), however, did not pass up the opportunity to lambaste the Soviets as Nan Han-chen, head of the Chinese delegation to the summit, did:

> ...there are often cases in which they (the Soviets) have no respect for the independence and sovereignty of the Asian and African countries, and flagrantly interfere in the internal affairs of these countries...in order to impose on other people their revisionist line of not opposing imperialism and not waging revolutionary struggles, they have even gone so far as to cancel aid, withdraw experts...as a means of applying pressure.[59]

The most immediate outcome of the Pyongyang economic summit was the reaction it elicited from the Soviets, who responded in kind through Pravda, the Soviet official publication akin to North Korea's Rodong Sinmun.[60] Not surprisingly, this led to editorial retaliation by the Rodong Sinmun, which had a spiraling back and forth effect between the two communist nations.

So the relationships between the three communist countries continued throughout 1964. The prevailing political mood within North Korea with regard to its relationships with the two communist giants can be traced through editorials appearing in the Rodong Sinmun. North Korea's disillusionment with the Soviet Union during the first half of the decade is captured in a 1964 editorial run in the publication.[61]

> In the process of providing assistance in rebuilding our factories, you have sold us facilities... and materials at prices far above those prevailing in the international market, while taking away from us in return many tons of gold, huge quantities of precious metals, and other raw materials at prices substantially below those prevailing in the international market.[62]

Soviet-North Korean bilateral relations, however, took a decided turn for the better in 1965 with Khrushchev's ouster from power in October of the preceding year.[63] The Brezhnev-Kosygin team succeeded Khrushchev and one of its first orders of business was to undertake some measure of reconciliation with both Pyongyang and Beijing; Brezhnev and Kosygin embraced a broader vision for repairing socialist solidarity and conditions within North Korea provided fertile ground for Soviet overtures. One major reason is that North's Korea's adherence to China's blueprint for socialism simply was not working for either North Korea or China. By 1965, North Korea had begun implementation of its Seven-Year plan and was falling short of its goals as outlined under the plan.[64] And as disappointing as North Korea's results were, China found itself in even more dire economic straits, which caused Kim to question the veracity of the Chinese plan. This disillusionment was further fuelled by the need for North Korea to append a three-year extension to the original Seven-Year plan because North Korean leadership ultimately found economic growth and expanded defense capabilities to be mutually exclusive ends. Another reason North Korea was susceptible to Soviet overtures was Kim's continued concern over the threat the U.S. and South Korea bilateral alignment presented on the Korean peninsula. Given China's own economic problems, it was increasingly unable to offer the necessary military assistance needed to make North Korea feel secure. Finally, just as the Cuban Missile Crisis had become a stain on Soviet honor by virtue of its apparent unwillingness to stand up to imperial aggression, Soviet support of the Vietnam War provided the opportunity for redemption. Consequently, North Korea may have begun to see the Soviet Union as a more reliable guarantor of socialism. The Soviets, of course, stood to benefit from a more congenial relationship with the North Koreans by wooing back into its camp a major supporter of its ideological socialist rival.

The first official contact under the new Brezhnev-Kosygin doctrine of conciliation took place between Soviet and North Korea leaders during an anniversary celebration of the October Revolution in Moscow at which agreement was reached for an official state visit to North Korea by Kosygin, a visit he made in February 1965. Measured in terms of advancing Soviet-North Korean rapprochement, Kosygin's visit was a success. Both countries stressed the importance of their bilateral treaty of friendship, cooperation and mutual aid and the unity attendant to the agreement.[65] What ultimately emerged from their new bilateral commitment to rapprochement was precisely what North Korea had hoped for: greater economic assistance and military support. It should be recalled that while Khrushchev did not completely sever economic ties with the North, they were diminished and during his last two years in power he did eliminate all military assistance.

Almost immediately following Kosygin's February 1965 visit to North Korea the Soviets resumed the flow of assistance to the regime. For example in early March 1965 a delegation of North Korean technicians visited the Soviet Union to receive assistance in tackling one of its biggest challenges—oil supply. The two countries also signed several scientific and cultural exchange agreements during spring 1965. Broader rapprochement with the Soviet Union had the added benefit of favorably influencing North Korea's economic and cultural relationships with the countries of Eastern Europe.[66]

Important as the resumption of economic ties with Moscow was, for North Korea it was regaining access to Soviet military assistance that was of vital importance in 1965. For example, North Korean angst was triggered by the commencement of the U.S. bombing campaign in North Vietnam and the broader army and air force weapons modernization program the United States had undertaken to bolster South Korean defense capabilities. To counter what it perceived as a growing and dangerous imbalance of military power on the peninsula not in its favor, North Korea sought quick reinfusion of Soviet military assistance, both in weaponry and technical assistance. Thus, on May 31, 1965, the two countries signed an agreement under which the Soviets would assist North Korea in strengthening those areas—air and ground forces—in which disparity existed between it and South Korea as a result of U.S. assistance. Specifically, MIG-21s, tanks, field artillery, antiaircraft weaponry, along with fuel and spare parts were provided.[67, 68]

Progress in Sino-Soviet relations was less positive, although the Soviet's new policy aims for broader rapprochement included China as well. The polemics that characterized Sino-Soviet ideological differences briefly subsided, but in the end, the rift that separated them proved too wide to bridge. While Brezhnev and the Soviets were prepared to extend certain olive branches, much of Soviet policy remained unchanged from Khrushchev's policy pursuits: peaceful coexistence remained the cornerstone of Soviet foreign policy with the West; the proceedings of the Twentieth Congress were reaffirmed; a partial test ban on nuclear weapons was supported; and a united front of socialist nations against the West endorsed.[69] Exclusion of Albania, staunch supporter of the Chinese socialist blueprint, from the guest list for the 47th anniversary of the October Revolution may have served as the impetus necessary to return to polemics as usual. After the celebration, the Chinese returned to the use of editorials appearing in *Hung Chi* to criticize Soviet policy. A November 21, 1964 editorial announced that China would fight "Khrushchevism" bitterly.[70] An editorial appearing nearly one year later attests that Sino-Soviet relations had fully returned to their low point. The editorial made reference to the fact that "capitalism is restored to the Soviet Union" and that Soviet-U.S. collusion was behind the insufficient aid rendered to North Vietnam.[71]

The last half of the decade was one of increased North Korean activity on the peninsula as much for its aim of peninsular reunification as it was for its foreign policy pursuits. The line distinguishing one from the other blurs because North Korean leadership had, by 1966, become quite energized over the Vietnam War, lending what support it could to North Vietnam in its struggle to spread communism. North Korea publicly called on socialist nations to "create diversionary problems that would turn away United States energies from the war effort in Vietnam."[72] To that end, North Korea dramatically increased the number of incidents it undertook across the border with South Korea. For example, the U.S. State Department tracked 50 incidents of "violence, assault, and terror" in 1966. By 1967 such incidents increased to about 600.[73] In January 1968, North Korean naval forces, with support from its air forces, captured the USS Pueblo and held its crew hostage for just under one year.[74] In a nearly simultaneous operation, the North Korean leadership implemented a plan to assassinate President Park Chung Hee by infiltrating a unit of 31 soldiers across the DMZ and into Seoul just outside the presidential Blue House on January 22, 1968.[75]

The North also pursued a more vigorous program of espionage against the South. The case of Lee Soo Keun, former vice president of the Korean Central News Agency (North Korea), serves as a good example of the lengths to which North Korean leadership was prepared to go in order to cause havoc in South Korea and divert U.S. energy and attention away from North Vietnam. Lee had "defected" to South Korea in 1967 amid great press coverage of the event; he was, at that point, one of the highest-placed defectors.[76] It was later learned, upon his capture in Saigon as he tried to make his escape through Cambodia back to North Korea, that he had actually been a spy and circumstances surrounding his defection had been a rouse—he was later hanged.[77]

In summary, North Korea's bilateral relationships with the Soviet Union and China shifted during the second half of the decade—interactions with China became further constrained as a result of Mao's Cultural Revolution and those with the Soviets continued under the rubric of rapprochement. Mao's Cultural Revolution essentially amounted to a political struggle within China, which ultimately led to civil unrest and placed China on the brink of civil war. This level of social domestic discord ran counter to Kim's notion of socialism and the role of the people vis-à-vis the leadership. The situation within China led North Korea to criticize China's Cultural Revolution in particular and its road to socialism generally. The end result was that Sino-North Korean engagement significantly decreased. Engagement with the Soviet Union, on the other hand, continued to flourish to the extent that new trade accords were consummated between the two countries. For example, a new trade agreement was signed in 1967 that provided North Korea assistance in the construction of factories and industrial complexes.[78]

Thus, 1965 was pivotal because it represented a transitional year not only for North Korea's rapprochement with the Soviet Union and some distancing of itself from Chinese socialist ideology, but also because it was from this point that Kim Il Sung began to chart a course of greater political independence from both countries and openly adopt a philosophy of North Korean ideological and economic independence and self-reliance—*Juche*— a topic discussed earlier. Kim had come to realize, as a result of North Korea's experiences with both China and the Soviet Union during the 1950s and 1960s, that although each communist benefactor was in a position to provide important assistance to North Korea, the cost of ideological subservience to either was too high a price to pay.

THE SEVENTIES: MILITANCY, REUNIFICATION, AND THE UNITED STATES

The decade of the seventies was generally characterized by North Korea's continued single-minded pursuit of its primary goal—reunification of the peninsula under the rubric of communism. There remained little distinction between domestic and foreign policy efforts in this regard as both were seen as viable means for achieving reunification. To this end, North Korean leadership focused its energies in five key areas: (1) taking advantage of and fomenting political instability in South Korea; (2) raising its own international stature while minimizing the impact of South Korea's attempts at increasing its own; (3) creating opportunities to engage in direct bilateral negotiations with the United States; (4) using both China and the Soviet Union to build international support for its reunification formula; and (5) building a united international front that would isolate the United States, forcing it to withdraw its forces from the Korean peninsula. It pursued these aims through two seemingly antithetical policy implements: militancy and diplomacy. By militancy I mean the North Korean leadership's willingness to employ violence or subterfuge as a means of policy pursuit. Diplomacy, of course, was those efforts undertaken to build international relationships and support for its policy aims.

One of the major diplomatic events that unfolded early in the decade was the joint North-South communiqué issued on July 4, 1972, in which both sides agreed to establish an atmosphere conducive to peacefully pursuing a path toward reunification of the peninsula. It reads in part:

> ...the two sides, in an effort to remove the misunderstandings and mistrust and mitigate increased tensions that have arisen between the North and the South as a result of long separation, and further to expedite unification of the fatherland, have reached full agreement on the following points... First, reunification shall be achieved through independent Korean efforts without being subject to external imposition or interference... unification shall be achieved through peaceful means... as a homogeneous people, a great national unity shall be sought above all...[79]

Other portions of the communiqué called for each side to refrain from the use of vituperative language against the other; implement various exchanges; and establish a military hotline between Seoul and Pyongyang in order to avoid "incidents" between the two sides. It also provided for the creation of the South-North Coordinating Committee venue in order to advance discussions on unification; the Committee, much like the rest of the communiqué, would wind up being declared all but dead by the end of the decade.

Upon its release, however, the communiqué was hailed as a major breakthrough by all concerned and many finally began to see a light at the end of the tunnel and the prospect for peace on the peninsula. One U.S. government Asian security analyst commented, "When I first took my present job assignment two years ago, I would have wagered my life savings that the two Koreas would not have been unified in my lifetime. Now the question is will they be unified before I am reassigned."[80] Many, who saw this achievement within the broader context of Sino-U.S. rapprochement regarded it as proof of eroding support for North Vietnam in its war; some even began prognosticating the demoralization of North Vietnam and its eventual defeat. Little did they realize that the light they saw in the tunnel was the proverbial oncoming train, not the end of a long journey—what short respite the communiqué provided presaged a very active and violent decade on the peninsula.

The relatively brief glimmer of hope provided by the joint communiqué had all but vanished by 1974 as the North's militant posture began markedly increasing. The year started out with the North Koreans sending a letter, dated March 25, to the U.S. Congress urging that the two sides, to the exclusion of South Korea, conclude a peace treaty to replace the armistice signed in 1953.[81] The letter also demanded removal of UN and U.S. troops from the peninsula. This correspondence, although not particularly worthy of serious consideration on its face, does provide important insight into North Korean thinking, particularly with regard to the specific exclusion of South

Korea from this proposal and any negotiations with the United States generally. Exclusion of the South was important to the North Korean regime because: (1) inclusion of South Korea in any negotiations would be tantamount to recognizing South Korea as a legitimate government and would validate the existence of two separate and equal Koreas—from Pyongyang's viewpoint the only legitimate government on the peninsula was its own; (2) it was an attempt to marginalize South Korea internationally and drive a wedge between the two allies; (3) South Korea was not a signatory to the 1953 Armistice; and (4) South Korea remained the target of North Korea invectives as it continued to characterize the South as a U.S. "lackey" and supporter of imperialism.

North Korea's willingness to employ militancy in pursuit of its policies became readily apparent in three events of 1974. The first was an incident that occurred in the Yellow Sea (Western Sea) on February 15 when the North Korean navy seized one South Korean fishing boat and sank another.[82] In June, the North Koreans sank a South Korean patrol boat which led to near engagement between the two air forces as each side dispatched planes to the scene.[83] The most audacious event of 1974, however, took place on August 15 when an assassination attempt was made on President Park Chung Hee's life; the attempt failed but Park's wife was killed in the attack.[84] Use of violence as a means for achieving North Korean policy goals continued into the decade and was fueled by the fall of South Vietnam in April 1975. On August 18, 1976 the now infamous axe murders of two U.S. Army officers occurred at Panmunjeom within the Joint Security Area.[85]

This series of acts was not violence for the sake of violence, rather the broader and articulated aim the North Koreans pursued was threefold. First, it was a continuation of their policy for creating diversionary problems for the United States as a means of supporting North Vietnam's struggles against the United States and South Vietnam. Second, from the North Korean perspective it kept the United States and South Korea off balance with regard to where and in what forms the next incident might occur. The intent may have been to help convince the United States that concluding a peace accord with North Korea, as proposed in the March 25, 1974, letter to Congress, was more favorable than the existing state of affairs. Finally, North Korean actions were certainly a means of trying to create greater opportunity for reunification on the regime's own terms. This is particularly true in the case of the assassination attempt of South Korean President Park Chung Hee. Park, in addition to building a strong economy for the nation, was also notorious for the authoritarian rule of his administration; he was also avidly anticommunist and had his own vision for reunification of the peninsula under South Korean rule.[86] Under his leadership, numerous laws and agencies were created to control the potential spread of the communist threat and to consolidate his own power. The Central Intelligence Act,

National Protection Law and Political Activities Purification Act are but a few of the laws enacted.[87] He also created the Korean Central Intelligence and Military Intelligence Agencies. Then in 1972 he enacted what came to be known as the Yusin Constitution, which greatly increased his executive powers making him, for all practical purposes, a dictator-president.[88] This, of course, presented an obstacle to Kim Il Sung's own vision for reunifying the peninsula, one he chose to address through assassination of his political rival.

North Korean diplomacy concentrated on establishing ties with third world nations while continuing its policy of maintaining neutrality in its relationships with both China and the Soviet Union. The goals of diplomacy were fairly straightforward: building a coalition of nations sympathetic to North Korea's reunification goals; isolating South Korea in hopes of casting its position as being subservient to that of North Korea; and creating a united group of nations that would bring pressure to bear on the United States, forcing it to remove its troops from the peninsula. Kim focused much of his attention on the smaller Soviet satellite countries of Eastern Europe and African countries. For example, in 1975 he visited Rumania, Yugoslavia, Bulgaria, and Algeria. At the conclusion of each visit a joint communiqué was issued expressing strong support for Pyongyang's reunification formula. In the case of Yugoslavia and Rumania, both countries also called for the removal of all foreign militaries from other countries, a not- so-veiled reference to the U.S. troops stationed in Korea. By August 1975, at the Foreign Ministers' Conference of the Non-Aligned Nations held in Lima, Peru, Kim's efforts at international diplomacy paid dividends as North Korea was voted in as a member nation; South Korea's application for admission, however, was declined.[89] The Conference also issued a statement demanding that all foreign troops in Korea under the control of the United Nations be removed and that a peace accord be concluded.[90]

In 1976, despite some diplomatic setbacks in Scandinavian countries, North Korea expanded the number of countries with which it had diplomatic relations, adding Angola, Nigeria, Papua New Guinea, and the Seychelles.[91] By the end of the year, Pyongyang boasted diplomatic relations with 138 nations; South Korea claimed such relationships with 142.[92] This pattern was generally followed throughout the remainder of the decade. For example, during the first half of 1979 alone, Pyongyang hosted 200 delegations from 80 countries and dispatched 130 delegations to 60 countries.[93] By the time of the Havana Round of the Foreign Ministers' Conference of the Non-Aligned Nations in 1979, conferees had officially adopted North Korea's position on reunification of the peninsula.

North Korea's relations throughout the decade with both the Soviet Union and China maintained the earlier status quo with Pyongyang carefully walking a razor-thin line between the two so as to avoid offending either. North Korea, however, remained uneasy with the growing détente in

Sino-U.S. relations.[94] Despite this turn of events, alienating Beijing was not an option particularly given Pyongyang's increased militant posture against the United States and South Korea. Illustrative of North Korea's broader engagement pattern with China was the manner in which it handled quite similar events involving China and Vietnam. While denouncing Vietnam's invasion of Cambodia in January 1979, North Korea refrained from similar criticism of China in its invasion of Vietnam the following month. This type of careful support netted, from Pyongyang's estimation, important political dividends such as Beijing's public support for its claim to be the sole legitimate government on the peninsula and its reunification policy.

Soviet interest in maintaining stable relations with North Korea during the period increased as a result of China's improving relations with the United States. The Soviets were also concerned with permitting even closer ties to develop between Pyongyang and Beijing. Thus, North Korea took on greater importance in Moscow's regional calculations. Not only did the Soviet Union offer public support of the North Korean position on reunification and its claim as the sole government for Korea, the two countries also entered into a new agreement on trade and economic cooperation in January 1976 and permitted automatic extension of the 1961 Soviet-Korean Treaty of Friendship, Cooperation and Mutual Assistance.[95]

Domestically, the situation in North Korea was mixed. There was progress for Kim Il Sung in further consolidating his own political position but the economic formula Pyongyang had long touted as having been so integral to North Korea's success began showing signs of strain midway through the decade.

The concept of *Juche* and its tenets underwent final evolution from state philosophy into near-religious dogma during the seventies. Its tenets were inculcated into the public so that it became more than a mere political doctrine, but rather a way of life, transitioning into what came to be known as "Kim Il Sungism."[96, 97] Illustrative of this point is the increased deification of Kim throughout the decade as well as the glorification of his family's lineage—his own life, his father and mother, brother, and his former wife were all extolled. In 1977 a film was produced about the lives and deeds of Kim and his family, furthering the nationwide cult-like adoration of him; it was in fact the fist time his image had appeared on screen.[98] It was also during this period that public reference to Kim Jong Il began to occur. According to Young C. Kim, until 1974 no newspaper articles had ever carried coverage of Kim Jong Il, but articles run in the Japanese newspaper, the *Yomiuri Shimbun*, after reporters returned from a trip to North Korea indicated the younger Kim was well placed within the KWP and had been designated as the elder Kim's successor.[99] By 1977 there was widespread speculation that the KWP Central Committee had finally endorsed Kim Jong Il as Kim Il Sung's successor.[100] By 1979 North Korean media began carrying references to "Tang Chungang" or the "party center" and used the term in such a manner that it more likely referred to an individual rather than any institution.[101]

Signs of what would become North Korea's perennial economic woes began to reveal themselves about the middle of the decade. Contrary to the somewhat rosy picture painted of the economy in 1973 when predictions of meeting the goals of the Six Year Plan ahead of schedule abounded, followed in 1975 by pronouncements of having achieved those milestones sixteen months ahead of schedule, by 1976 it was evident that the policies had gone awry. The first indication was Kim's constant demands to "normalize the economy, economize on supplies, and improve the quality of goods."[102] If the rhetoric did not serve notice of impending problems then North Korea's inability to repay its debts did. The Japan External Trade Organization (JETRO) calculated North Korea's trade deficit for the period 1973–1975 to have totaled approximately $1.4 billion (U.S.).[103] In September 1976, Pyongyang requested a reprieve from repaying $293 million (U.S.) in debts to Japanese firms.[104] By 1977 a fuller picture of the stresses on the economy began to emerge particularly in the areas of enterprise management, logistics, mining, agriculture, and electricity production. The biggest problem confronting North Korean industry, however, was its inability to develop and maintain the necessary distribution systems to get needed materials to factories, consequently leaving a good deal of production capacity idle.[105] Drought also impacted agriculture and electrical production capacity; what limited farmland was available was decimated by the effects of a continuing drought. Further compounding this problem was the fact that nearly two-thirds of the country's electricity was produced by hydroelectric power plants—with a shortage of water there was a commensurate shortage of electricity.[106] That little headway was made on these issues during the remainder of the decade is evidenced by the fact that in 1979 the lack of an adequate logistics system remained a focal point for the KWP's Central Committee plenary session convened in June 1979.[107]

Engagement with the United States was generally characterized by North Korea's continued overtures to initiate direct negotiations in order to conclude a peace accord and push for removal of U.S. military units from the peninsula. The rationale was fairly straightforward: with U.S. military units removed from the peninsula, a weakened and internationally isolated South Korea could more easily be subsumed under North Korean control. Overtures for negotiations with the United States were interspersed with episodic swings toward belligerence and militancy: the axe murders in the Joint Security Area at Panmunjeom and North Korea's move toward a war footing in its immediate aftermath serve as a case in point. Despite its record of militancy and belligerence, however, there were also examples of moderation demonstrated toward the United States, a good example of which was elicited in the wake of Jimmy Carter's presidential election victory (1977–1981). The reason for such moderate behavior lay in Kim's belief that Carter, because of his campaign pledges, was committed to a policy of U.S. troop withdrawal from the peninsula.[108] Consequently, Kim sought to avoid jeopardizing the goal he had pursued for so long. An example of the regime's moderate approach can be seen in how North Korea handled the downing of a U.S. CH-47 helicopter (Chinook) that accidentally strayed into North Korean territory in July 1977.[109] In contrast to its usual histrionics, the North Koreans assumed a rational approach, negotiated in good faith and reached agreement on the issue within three days, returning the remains of three U.S. Army soldiers and one injured soldier.[110] Unfortunately for North Korea, Kim miscalculated the Carter administration's policy direction on the peninsula: U.S. aid to South Korea actually increased and Team Spirit, a joint U.S.-ROK military exercise, continued not only through the remainder of the Carter administration but well into the 1990s.[111]

THE EIGHTIES: ECONOMIC SETBACKS AND THE CARROT-AND-STICK APPROACH—PYONGYANG STYLE

Several important events and trends came to define the decade of the eighties that in retrospect can be considered building blocks for the present situation on the Korean peninsula. Among these are included: North Korea's loss of international prestige vis-à-vis South Korea; an increasing number of economic setbacks that forced the North to redefine its priorities; official acknowledgement of plans to create a diarchy between Kim Il Sung and son Kim Jong Il as a means of assuring a peaceful transfer of power after Kim's death; creation of the foundation for South Korea's present-day "Sunshine Policy" of engagement with the North; and the North Korean regime's increasing sense of geopolitical isolation, insecurity, and the manifest behaviors attendant to such perceptions.

North Korea's loss of international stature resulted primarily from two causes. First, Pyongyang's penchant for committing heinous acts as a means for disrupting and destabilizing the political atmosphere in the South became even more desperate during the 1980s, alienating some of its supporters. Second was the trend toward rapprochement between South Korea and several socialist nations, to include China and the Soviet Union, the result of its comparative economic miracle. The prevailing economic situation within the socialist bloc of nations indeed forced some to reevaluate the effectiveness of the command economy (centrally planned economy) model and their respective relationships with nonsocialist nations.

Examination of North Korea's behavior during the decade reveals an important shift in its method of engagement with South Korea, and by extension the United States; it assumed a curious carrot-and-stick approach, which in the end, cost it a good deal more than it garnered. This period can be considered the advent of the North's present-day "now on, now off" method of engagement with South Korea and other nations through the Six

Party Talks. Consider, for example, the bombing the North undertook in Rangoon, Burma on October 9, 1983, that killed seventeen South Koreans of a visiting delegation, four of whom were cabinet members in the Chun Doo Hwan administration.[112] The North had in fact only one day earlier approached the United States through the Chinese in Beijing about initiating tripartite discussions between the United States, South Korea and itself over the future of the Korean peninsula and publicly announced its willingness to do so again in January 1984. As the blast occurred only minutes before the arrival of President Chun, one can surmise that the goal was to destabilize the South Korean administration through yet another assassination, but what it netted for North Korea was a loss of diplomatic ties with Burma, Costa Rica, and Western Samoa as each severed official relations with the regime.[113] In the same year, the North Koreans seized two South Korean fishing vessels. Yet in the wake of the floods that occurred in South Korea in September 1984, North Korea offered to provide assistance in the form of 50,000 sacks of rice, 550,000 yards of cloth along with medicine and cement.[114] The South Korean government was rightly suspicious of the gesture, but agreed to accept the offer of assistance to deny the North a propaganda opportunity.

In 1985 North Korea agreed to and participated in cross-border family reunions, which permitted 151 separated family members in both halves of the peninsula to reunite through visits.[115] This was the first program of its kind on the peninsula since the establishment of the two Koreas. But by November 1987 the pendulum had reversed course again and North Korea detonated a bomb on a Korean Airlines (South Korea) civilian airliner killing all 115 passengers and crew as a means of disrupting Seoul's hosting of the 1988 Olympic Games.[116] However, this act had been preceded by North Korean overtures for reconciliation between the two Koreas. As late as July 1987, Kim had called for the two sides to reduce their respective military strengths, turn the DMZ into a peace zone, and eliminate large-scale military exercises.[117] Such errant and unpredictable behavior has been described in various ways, but the root cause is reasonably identifiable: North Korea's single-minded pursuit of reunification on its terms through employment of short-term, maximum effect means. This led to convulsive, erratic, and seemingly unconnected policy pursuits throughout the decade.

The decade also witnessed a sharp increase in South Korea's international stature, which in the zero sum game of international diplomacy, translated into a commensurate decline in North Korea's own international stature. As noted earlier, its foreign policy hinged on building a coalition of nations comprised of communist bloc and nonaligned nations in order to bring pressure to bear on the United States and South Korea for U.S. troop withdrawal and reunification of the peninsula. Consequently, as more socialist nations began formally recognizing South Korea, it threatened Pyongyang's vision for reunification, a trend that became more pronounced during the latter half of the decade when the Soviet Union and China undertook rapprochement with the South as well. Symbolic of this trend was China's participation in the 10th Asian Games hosted by Seoul, something that unnerved the North not only because it signaled increasing improvements in the Sino-South Korea relationship, but also because it was open recognition of the existence of "two Koreas." This trend continued throughout the remainder of the decade and early 1990s until full diplomatic relations were established between China and South Korea in August 1992, despite Pyongyang's vehement protestations.

In the Chinese calculation, recognizing South Korea made good foreign policy sense; China was pursuing modernization and expanded influence in the Asia region and could ill afford to isolate itself behind a wall of socialist ideology. If its goals were to be achieved broader regional engagement policies were the key. Additionally, China's greatest ideological competitor had taken itself out of the game. The Soviet Union, under Gorbachev's new foreign policy initiatives termed "New Thinking," was no longer interested in continuing the ideological and geopolitical feud with China, which included their long-standing competition over North Korea. In fact, the Soviets established formal diplomatic relations with South Korea in September 1990 after a period of heightened economic intercourse and commercial exchange. Thus, China understood that North Korea had no alternative other than to stick with China. But Chinese leadership was also mindful not to alienate the North in order to minimize the possibility of North Korea taking provocative acts and destabilizing the region, which it saw as beneficial to no one. Thus, by decade's end Sino-North Korea exchanges were for the most part limited to cultural ones.

Mikhail Gorbachev's ascension to power in the Soviet Union introduced policies that offered diminished Soviet support of North Korea. The result of deteriorating economic conditions, Gorbachev embarked on a course he felt would cure the ills of the Soviet Union, a course with three separate components: (1) *perestroika*, which were economic reforms and restructuring; (2) *glasnost*, or openness; and (3) *novoe myshlenie* or "New Thinking" with regard to Soviet foreign policy pursuits. These concepts coalesced particularly with regard to policy pursuits on the Korean peninsula. The Soviets were impressed by South Korea's economic miracle and sought opportunities for expanded economic contacts in hopes that they would find a way of reviving their moribund socialist economy, particularly in the Soviet Far East. Simultaneously, the Soviets began to see greater cost and less strategic advantage in continuing to prop up the North Korean economy and providing it with a steady stream of technical assistance and military hardware. Soviet participation in the 1988 Olympics hosted by Seoul served as an appropriate segue for broader rapprochement with South Korea. In the wake of the Olympics, Moscow pursued an aggressive program of improved commercial and economic ties.[118, 119] For example, South Korean conglomerates

Lucky-Goldstar, Daewoo and Samsung participated in an electronics fair in Leningrad in 1988.[120] Total trade between the two countries increased twelve-fold, from $48 million in 1983 to $599 million in 1989.[121] Joint ventures between Soviet and South Korean firms were also established.

Rapprochement with South Korea was not limited to China and the Soviet Union. Hungary and Poland actually outpaced Soviet rapprochement efforts as both had established diplomatic relations with South Korea by the end of 1989. Thus, in the zero-sum game of international politics, economic necessity won out over political ideology. This offers an important lesson for current efforts to convince North Korea to ameliorate its behavior. The command economy has been, and remains, the inherent weakness of the socialist nation. If confronted ideologically, the response tends toward recalcitrance. It is, however, economically vulnerable as South Korean president Roh Tae Woo (1988–1993) proved.

Roh embarked upon a broader engagement program with communist nations and markedly expanded dialogue with North Korea, which represented a significant policy departure from those of his predecessors, if not in content then certainly in degree. It also laid the foundation for South Korea's present engagement policy with the North Korean regime. What Roh sought was full détente with communist bloc nations, to include Pyongyang, via his policy of *Nordpolitik*. Recall that South Korea established diplomatic relations with China, the Soviet Union, Hungary, Poland, and other socialist nations during his tenure. The rationale upon which the policy was based was that South Korea could use rapprochement as a catalyst for improving relations with Pyongyang; in effect, pressure Pyongyang into broader engagement.

While this program did not contain many of the economic inducements associated with Kim Dae Jung's Sunshine Policy, it did provide the necessary precursors to establish a more conciliatory tone and framework. Roh's policy called for cessation of diplomatic competition and cross-border vituperation; assisting North Korea in improving its relations with both the United States and Japan; permitting South Koreans who resided overseas to visit the North; undertaking exchanges in all fields; and for Roh to visit Pyongyang to negotiate differences directly with Kim Il Sung.[122] That this constituted a substantive policy shift in favor of détente and not a tactic to gain the short-term advantage over Pyongyang is underscored by the fact that Roh instituted his policy of *Nordpolitik* after the January 1988 revelation that North Korea had dispatched its agents to plant the bomb that brought down the South Korean airliner in November 1987.[123] Roh soon learned gaining accommodation from Pyongyang as a result of Seoul's new olive branch was easier to conceptualize than execute. North Korea refused to take the course of rapprochement followed by other socialist bloc nations, underscoring the continued difficulty of working with a North Korean regime ensconced in *Juche* doctrine.

From an economic standpoint, the 1980s continued trends that had begun to emerge a decade earlier, forcing North Korean leadership to reprioritize national economic policy goals. How the leadership reprioritized these goals can best be seen in what the domestic media focused on. During 1981, for example, the lion's share of coverage was devoted to economic issues (54 percent), with other issues falling a distant second: politics (20 percent); reunification (19 percent); and foreign affairs (4 percent).[124] Exacerbating its economic problems was North Korea's changing relationship with China. For example, despite past trade links to Beijing, by 1986, trade with China had dropped to 19 percent of its total trade volume, exactly half that of the country's trade volume with the Soviet Union.[125] The root cause of the changing relationship between China and North Korea was China's broader rapprochement efforts in the region and with the United States, which necessitated that China bury the hatchet in its ideological war with and vituperations of both the United States and South Korea.

In contrast, the Soviet Union, at least until the seeds of Gorbachev's reforms began bearing fruit in the latter half of the decade, remained North Korea's primary benefactor providing technical, economic, and military assistance. By 1983, North Korean dependence on Soviet assistance had become extensive, relying on the Soviets to provide 63 percent of its electricity; 50 percent of its oil derivatives; and 42 percent of its steel products.[126] In 1987 it was reported that the Soviet Union was assisting in 14 projects, to include construction of a nuclear power facility and that overall 64 major industrial projects had been completed.[127] While the rationale for North Korea wanting to continue the relationship with the Soviet Union is obvious, what benefit was there for the Soviets to continue such a massive infusion of assistance? From a geopolitical and strategic standpoint, the Soviets were concerned with the growing rapprochement between China and South Korea and a fear they would be isolated from the region—a continued relationship with North Korea provided for a presence in East Asia. Second, the ideological feud between the Soviet Union and China remained intact and thus a strong relationship with North Korea provided leverage against the Chinese. Third, North Korean ports provided the Soviet navy with deep water ice-free ports in the region.

One of the more important tasks Kim Il Sung personally undertook was ensuring establishment of a proper framework for transferring power to his son, Kim Jong Il, through a diarchic arrangement, the first in socialist history. The younger Kim's succession was officially declared in 1980 during the Sixth WPK Congress, confirming that past references to the "Party Center" during the seventies were indications of succession preparation.[128] With this revelation, Kim Jong Il took charge of the Party's day-to-day operations and efforts were made to raise his stature domestically, for example displaying his portrait in all public buildings. He remained, however, in a position of understudy to the elder Kim.[129]

The process of solidifying the younger Kim's position continued throughout the decade with Kim Jong Il assuming a greater role in the daily affairs of the party and taking on more of his father's duties. By 1987 two historical sites had been dedicated to recognize his accomplishments[130]; and in 1989 Mt. Paektu was redesignated Jong Il peak.[131] In the same year a flower, Kimjongilia, was also named after him and displayed in greenhouses in each provincial capital.[132]

Finally, one of the more curious trends during the period was North Korea's own willingness to at least minimally employ certain tools of capitalism as it sought to resuscitate its economy. In this regard, 1984 represents a transitional year as this was when the regime began attempts to establish joint commercial ventures with both socialist and nonsocialist nations. Following in the footsteps of China's broader embrace of capitalistic opportunities, in September 1984, North Korea enacted its joint venture law to induce foreign investment in the country; the 26-article document closely resembled the Chinese joint venture law.[133] Two years later in August 1986, it created the North Korea International Joint Venture General Company in collaboration with *Choch'ongnyon*, an association of pro-Pyongyang Korean residents in Japan, the purpose of which was to attract investment capital from Japan using the group as an intermediary.[134] Then, in 1988 the regime also created the Ministry of Joint Venture Industry in attempts to better identify and consummate joint commercial venture opportunities worldwide.[135] That these efforts garnered little interest and had negligible long-term impact can be deduced by the relatively quick succession of remedial steps taken by the regime during 1984–1988. And of the 135 joint projects initiated, 77 were undertaken jointly with pro-North Korean firms in Japan, and none of the projects amounted to much financially.[136] The lack of any substantive response from the world community led the regime to enact several modifications in 1992 to the existing joint venture law in hopes of attracting foreign investors, measures which also failed to garner any real support.[137] Nor should this come as a surprise as the country continued its history of defaulting on loans received from other countries. For example, North Korea was the first country ever to officially be declared in default on international loans, to the tune of $770 million (U.S.) to Western European concerns and 30 billion yen to Japanese firms.[138]

Another measure considered for a time to raise venture capital was the issuance of treasury bonds, although this never evolved into anything concrete. While none of these measures ever amounted to much in terms of economic improvements, they may in fact hold the key for how best to cajole the regime back into the international community of nations and away from its present addiction to nuclear weapons. Despite its ideologically driven vitriol and mercurial behavior, such examples of a willingness to consider capitalist measures as a means of achieving economic stability give some indication that North Korea is both pragmatic and, to a degree, flexible. The challenge will be how to craft a viable long-term policy that molds its behavior to a level of reasonableness that comports more with international norms.

5

From Belligerent Reunification to Belligerent Survival

The Communists presented many arguments in support of the 38th parallel...
none of which were any good... Some were downright ridiculous... When
their arguments failed them they took refuge in vituperation, insults, and rage.
You could always tell their estimate of the progress they were making from the
amount of obnoxious propaganda that blared forth on the Communist radio
and in their press. When they were not doing so well it intensified. I presume
this was their idea of putting pressure on their opponents.
>   —Admiral C. Turner Joy, *Negotiating While Fighting: The Diary*
>   *of Admiral C. Turner, Joy at the Korean Armistice Conference*

THE NINETIES

The decade of the nineties is characterized by several significant events,
for example the 1993–1994 nuclear standoff and the associated Agreed
Framework that at least helped table the crisis; the death of Kim Il Sung;
and the advent of South Korea's Sunshine Policy toward the North. The
period 1988–1995 also witnessed what I believe to be the most profound
change in the situation on the Korean peninsula since 1948, one which has
had continued ramifications for the world ever since. It was during this
period that several events coalesced, forcing the North Korean regime to
abandon its theretofore policy pursuit of reunifying the peninsula under
communist leadership to one of ensuring its own survival, which resulted in
a change in the nature of the demands for which North Korea negotiated.

In short, the regime came to recognize the need to move from the politics of socialist reunification to the politics of survival. It was also during this period that North Korea introduced its new geopolitical "trump card"— a nuclear weapons program—which expanded the profile of the threat it posed, growing from a peninsular threat to a regional one.

The events most responsible for bringing about this shift were: (1) South Korean rapprochement with former Soviet bloc nations and China, which included the loss of North Korea's communist security guarantors; (2) the growing economic disparity between North and South Korea and the associated ability of each to underwrite the cost of its respective security needs; (3) the death of Kim Il Sung; and (4) natural disasters that exacerbated North Korea's economic decline. As mentioned in the preceding section, South Korea's *Nordpolitik* approach to relations with socialist bloc nations proved most successful at undermining an increasingly fractured and economically weak socialist coalition: by the end of 1989 South Korea had normalized relations with Hungary, Poland, and Yugoslavia; by the end of 1990 added to this number were Bulgaria, Algeria, Mongolia, Romania, Czechoslovakia, and, of course, the Soviet Union. The year 1990 also saw German reunification; and by 1992 South Korea had achieved rapprochement with China. Thus, by the end of 1992, North Korea had become diplomatically, if not ideologically, isolated. When these events are considered alongside the death of Kim Il Sung in 1994, which occurred in the midst of negotiating the Agreed Framework, the period can only be described, from the North Korean perspective, as a tumultuous one.

North Korea's growing isolation during 1988–1995 had two immediate impacts. First, it forced the regime to begin seeking a more realistic approach to its foreign policy pursuits. In effect, it sought improved relations with Seoul, Washington, and Tokyo as ballast to stabilize what it saw as an increasingly hostile international situation vis-à-vis its interests. Consequently, as early as 1990, it began extending to Japan offers for bilateral dialogue in hopes of establishing diplomatic normalization; this was followed up by numerous meetings with Japanese delegations. North Korea, of course, had ulterior motives for seeking diplomatic normalization with Japan, namely a piece of the Japanese economic miracle. The regime sought compensation for suffering endured during the colonial period as well as post-colonial economic losses.

These discussions were unilaterally ended in 1992 by the North Koreans when the Japanese raised the issue of their citizens who had been allegedly abducted by North Korea during the 1970s and 1980s, but the fact that the regime even pursued such an avenue with a nation it had in the past regularly vilified was telling.[1] Similarly, overtures were made to the United States to upgrade relations to full diplomatic status, a proposal rebuffed by the United States. The U.S. position was that until Pyongyang agreed to abandon plans for a nuclear weapons program no improvement in relations could be undertaken. Undaunted, Pyongyang also welcomed the Reverend Billy Graham to North Korea, hosted a delegation, the American Freedom Coalition, and began returning remains of U.S. military personnel killed during the Korean War.[2] The regime's overtures toward Seoul were even more substantive. Pyongyang's stance on reunification was modified to recognize the existence of two Koreas, thus adopting a "one nation, two systems" policy; it reversed its position on dual membership in the United Nations for the two Koreas, both of which gained admittance into the world body in September 1991; and North and South Korea signed the Agreement on Reconciliation, Non-Aggression, and Exchanges and Cooperation.

The second impact of North Korea's growing isolation was its increased efforts to pursue a nuclear weapons program as a cost-effective means of equalizing what it saw as an unequal playing field. South Korean rapprochement with socialist bloc nations had accomplished more than just ideologically and diplomatically cutting off the regime—it also had economic ramifications. Moscow, which had functioned as Pyongyang's primary benefactor, particularly of military support and trade, began significantly reducing its support after 1990. For example, the Soviet Union provided the regime 440,000 tons of oil in 1990, which constituted 18 percent of its total oil imports; in 1991 this level dropped to fewer than 50 tons.[3] The former Soviet Union also represented for Pyongyang a significant partner in trade, the levels of which until 1990 represented 50 percent of North Korea's total trade volume. In absolute terms, North Korea's 1990 trade volume with the former Soviet Union reached $2.35 billion of its total $4.66 billion in trade.[4] By 1991, however, because of the former Soviet Union's policy shifts under Gorbachev's leadership and Pyongyang's inability to pay for goods in hard currency, trade dropped precipitously to an estimated mere 3 percent of earlier levels.[5] Although initially increasing military aid to the regime when first assuming power in the former Soviet Union, Gorbachev's reform programs ultimately reduced such aid to nothing by the end of his term. And under Boris Yeltsin the two countries' mutual security agreement was allowed to lapse. (While Moscow and Pyongyang would later enter into another agreement, mutual security would not be a part of it.)

Reduced support further exacerbated an already dire economic situation. North Korea's 1990 and 1991 gross national product (GNP) figures indicated significant declines of -3.7 percent and -5.2 percent, respectively.[6] These figures pointed to a marked decrease from the falling but still positive 1989 GNP levels of 2.4 percent. Agricultural production also suffered; by 1992 there was a two-million-ton shortfall in grain production. Decreased access to energy also contributed to North Korea's problems—flooded coal mines caused an associated reduction in its production, leading to electricity shortages—along with decreased oil imports from China, the Soviet Union and Iran.[7] By 1995, the regime confronted massive flooding, which continued into 1996 followed by drought in 1997, impacting its ability to grow enough food to sustain its own citizenry. In short, by 1991 the regime had fully entered a cycle of dire economic conditions from which there was no extrication without outside economic assistance. Its decreased economic capacity had inescapable security repercussions. During 1990–1993, for example, North Korea's defense budget decreased by 58 percent, from $5.23 billion to $2.19 billion.[8] This downward trend is juxtaposed against South Korea's increasing defense budget during the same period, which grew by 13.6 percent, from $10.62 billion to $12.06 billion; a defense budget nearly six times greater than North Korea's.[9] In short, North Korea had reached a point where it could no longer effectively compete with South Korea's defense program nor the traditional U.S.-South Korea bilateral security alliance, particularly given that it could no longer rely on the protection afforded from the former Soviet Union's security umbrella. The road it chose to offset its growing security deficit, which also came to serve as a means for trying to improve its economic problems, was development of a credible nuclear weapons program—a cost-effective geopolitical equalizer that offered the dual benefit of being an effective bargaining chip.

North Korea's New Geopolitical Card—The Nuclear Option

While North Korea outwardly began courting use of nuclear weapons during the 1990s, the contributing reasons for which are outlined above, the seeds for this troubling trend may have been sown as early as the Korean War. Ironically, North Korea's use of nuclear weapons as an implement of statecraft may actually be a lesson learned from U.S. use of its own nuclear arsenal during the Truman and Eisenhower administrations.[10] The threatened use of nuclear weapons under these administrations was never overtly communicated nor realistically considered as a tactical option, rather indirect means were employed to communicate their potential use, leaving to inference the degree of probability as to their employment—movement of bombers with a capability of carrying nuclear weapons into strategically important locations; deployment of incomplete nuclear weapons; and well-timed, controlled disclosure as to their movement.[11] The goal of these activities was to indirectly communicate to the Soviets and Chinese, diplomatically, that should negotiations to conclude an armistice fail, the United States could well expand the level of hostilities beyond conventional means. The lesson learned perhaps by North Korean leadership was that while might may not necessarily always be right, it is at least effective as an attention-getter.

Fast forward to the mid-1980s, a period that provides the practical elements of North Korea's nuclear program. By 1984, U.S. satellites had detected construction of a large Soviet nuclear reactor, reportedly of the type capable of producing the plutonium needed for construction of nuclear weapons.[12] Recall that this accords with the final period of enhanced relations between the former Soviet Union and North Korea prior to implementation of Gorbachev's policy of "New Thinking." By the late 1980s, North Korea had begun its full-court press toward nuclearization with construction of a plutonium reprocessing plant as well as a third nuclear reactor located at Yongbyon.[13] Mindful of the imminent danger a nuclearized North Korea presented, the first Bush administration, in 1990, extended a series of carrots to the regime as a means of cajoling the North Koreans to sign the International Atomic Energy Agency (IAEA) nuclear safeguards agreement, which included an inspection regime to which its declared nuclear facilities would be subject. North Korea signed the agreement in February 1992, thus assenting to IAEA inspections of those declared nuclear facilities. Another lesson learned by the North Koreans: even the world's only remaining superpower negotiates when in the shadow of a growing nuclear threat. To be sure, the first Bush administration had enough geopolitical savvy to understand both that the North presented a growing threat to peninsular and regional security and that the way to address the threat was through engagement. The irony is that it may have been the administration's moderate response that served as impetus for the regime's future nuclear brinksmanship-style diplomacy.

The process proceeded without incident until IAEA inspectors discovered inconsistencies in the amount of plutonium the regime claimed to have produced and the amount actually produced, leading the IAEA one year later, in February 1993, to demand the right to inspect facilities not listed in the original 1992 agreement. In retaliation, North Korea threatened withdrawal from the Nuclear Non-Proliferation Treaty (NPT), leading to a heated cycle of back and forth demands and counter demands. The period 1993–1994 proved to be the most ominous on the peninsula since the Korean War with regard to possible recommencement of hostilities. Growing tensions were diffused when in June 1994 former President Jimmy Carter traveled to North Korea and met with Kim Il Sung, during which Kim appeared amenable to freezing North Korea's nuclear program in return for appropriate economic inducements. This, in turn, led to a series of talks convened in Geneva, the objective of which was to hammer out a formal agreement based on an exchange of economic benefits for a freeze in North Korea's nuclear program. The negotiations, originally planned to begin July 8, 1994, got off to a rocky start as Kim Il Sung, the only leader the reclusive nation had known to that point, died. Concerns that Kim's death would derail any progress achieved to that point, however, proved unfounded. Intermediate agreement on objectives was achieved on August 12, 1994 when both sides consented to terms for a freeze in the North's nuclear program laid out in the Agreed Statement, which was later formalized in October 1994 into what has come to be known as the Agreed Framework, thus diffusing the crisis.

Neither the agreement nor the process is without its detractors. The Framework has come to represent at once the quintessence of negotiated efforts to persuade North Korea to denuclearize and the folly of negotiating with the regime. Supporters of the Framework contend that while not perfect, it did help freeze the regime's nuclear program for a time, in stark contrast to the results achieved under the Bush doctrine of CVID.[14] Detractors claim that because the agreement covered only North Korea's plutonium-based nuclear weapons program the regime was essentially handed a means for circumventing the Framework through development of uranium-based weapons. They contend it was a policy of "appeasement."[15]

The Framework contained a number of provisions important to each side. North Korea was required to freeze its graphite-moderated nuclear reactors and related facilities and eventually dismantle them; and had to submit to IAEA monitoring to ensure compliance.[16] Additionally, all spent fuel, which could be used in the production of nuclear weapons-grade material, would be stored and ultimately disposed of. In return, North Korea would receive proliferation-resistant light water nuclear reactors (LWRs) incapable of producing plutonium; heavy fuel oil in place of energy forgone as a result of shutting down its reactors, an amount that would reach 500,000 tons annually at some point in the future; full normalization of diplomatic and economic relations with the United States, to include removal of sanctions; and a security guarantee that the United States would not use nuclear weapons against it.[17] (See appendix for the complete text of the Agreed Framework.) With finalization of the Framework, it appeared the world had not only averted a nuclear crisis on the Korean peninsula, but had denuclearized a potentially dangerous adversary. The hiatus that followed in the wake of the agreement was relatively short-lived, however, as by 1998 the regime had introduced to the world yet another component of its nuclear weapons program—ballistic missiles. On August 31, 1998, North Korea launched a multi-staged rocket in an attempt to put a small satellite into orbit, causing a good deal of concern and consternation within the international community. (This topic is covered in greater detail in the following chapter.)

If the period preceding the 1994 Agreed Framework can be seen as the introduction of North Korea's new brinksmanship-for-economic-benefits style diplomacy, then the 1998 incident should be viewed as a significant honing of that art. Given that the Agreed Framework had been in place for nearly four years and that one of Pyongyang's continuing priorities during that time was improved relations with Washington, there appears to have been little military value in launching the missile. There was, however, from Pyongyang's perspective something to be gained diplomatically and economically by having done so. As early as late 1997, North Korea had begun to complain of the slow progress on the international community's fulfillment of commitments made to it under the Framework: there were delays in the construction of the LWRs; heavy fuel oil deliveries had become similarly delayed; and economic sanctions remained in place against it. Further, in proceedings under the Four Party Talks venue convened in Berlin during March 1998, the regime learned that the Clinton administration had linked the lifting of economic sanctions to progress under the Talks in improving the security situation on the Korean peninsula.[18] As a result of what it saw as unacceptable delay under the Framework and the new focus on the Four Party Talks, Pyongyang essentially stonewalled discussions and threatened to reopen its nuclear facilities and reprocessing plant at Yongbyon.[19]

Following the August missile launch, however, negotiations between the United States and North Korea produced a new commitment under which North Korea would discuss permitting inspection of its newly discovered underground facility and reaffirmation of previous commitments: storage and monitoring of its on-hand plutonium stock in exchange for immediate commencement of construction on the LWRs (November 1998) and delivery of promised heavy fuel oil. In this regard, the missile launch, whether a primary or secondary objective, might be viewed as the proverbial "shot across the bow" and a warning to Washington that North Korea remained, despite the Agreed Framework, a dangerous adversary and that commitments made to it needed to be fully honored.

Relations with North Korea in the New Millennium

By the opening of the twenty-first century, the international community had cause for some measure of optimism regarding the situation on the Korean peninsula: former President Kim Dae Jung's Sunshine Policy was in full swing; the two Koreas signed the historic North–South Joint Declaration in June 2000; North Korea had begun to shed some of its reclusiveness by establishing diplomatic relations with a growing number of countries; and relations between the United States and North Korea had reached a new level of engagement manifested in two historic high-level state visits—one in Washington and the other in Pyongyang.

The crux of Kim Dae Jung's Sunshine policy, officially known as the Policy of Reconciliation and Cooperation toward North Korea, rested on his belief that cooperation with North Korea could proceed in those areas where mutual agreement was more easily achieved while eschewing the more complicated ones such as security, reunification, and political differences. Three important assumptions upon which the policy was based were that: (1) North Korea would not disintegrate any time in the near future; (2) that its eventual move toward a market economy was inevitable; and (3) that assistance such as that afforded under the Sunshine Policy would speed North Korea toward a market economy.[20] The policy was also guided by three fundamental principles: (1) Armed provocation by North Korea would not be tolerated; (2) South Korea would not follow the German model of reunification, thus eschewing absorption of the North in favor of some other means of reunification; and (3) the South would actively seek to cooperate with the North.[21] Ambassador Yang Sung Chul, former South Korean ambassador to the United States, in a speech delivered on December 4, 2000, offered the following description of the Sunshine Policy: "[The Sunshine Policy] separates not only non-controversial from controversial problems, but civilian from governmental tasks, the short-term from the long-term agenda and the domestic from the international issues." Former President Kim Dae Jung went further in explaining the parameters of the Sunshine policy in a speech which has come to be known as the Berlin Declaration, during which he assured Pyongyang that Seoul: (1) guaranteed its safety from attack; (2) promised assistance in its commercial and infrastructural development in order to help in its economic recovery; and (3) would support the regime in its efforts to reenter the international community of nations.

In practical terms the policy amounted to economic and cultural outreach to North Korea. Economically and commercially, through the first quarter of 2003, for example, the policy produced the following representative results: $1.2 billion (U.S.) in food, fertilizer and other aid to North Korea during the period 1998–2002 and $500 million in payments from Hyundai Asan to win business concessions; construction of the $2.3 billion (U.S.) joint North-South commercial project at Kaesong; and the $540 million (U.S.) Hyundai Asan spent in developing the Mount Kumgang tourist resort located in North Korea.[22] Social outreach refers specifically to those efforts undertaken to reunite family members separated by the permanent division of the peninsula in 1948. As a result of their historic summit in June 2000, both Kim Dae Jung and Kim Jong Il agreed to allow reunion of family members who had been separated for decades, the first of which took place in August 2000 and involved 100 families.[23]

The policy mainstay of the South Korean government since its introduction in 1998, the Sunshine Policy has met with mixed reviews both within South Korean governmental circles and internationally. The primary objections to the policy have been its recognition of a repressive regime; the economic and commercial support it provides; and lack of any demand for demonstrable reciprocity on the part of North Korea. Generally speaking, the Clinton administration's position was supportive of the Sunshine Policy. In fact, the administration itself used a food-for-talks formula to coerce North Korea to participate in the Four Party Talks. Secretary of State Albright's visit to Pyongyang to meet with Kim Jong Il in October 2000, the highest ranking U.S. official ever to do so, can also be construed as support for a broader policy of engagement with Pyongyang. In contrast to the U.S. position, however, Japan, in the wake of the 1998 missile that overflew its home islands, was more guarded in its support of such a policy.

Clearly the high point of the decade came in 2000 with the summit held in Pyongyang between North and South Korean leaders Kim Jong Il and Kim Dae Jung. The summit represented for the two Koreas the culminating point of their relationship since 1948; for the world community the summit provided promise of a reprieve from the inter-Korean strife that had come to represent peninsular relations. If the summit represented a high point in inter-Korean relations, then the signing of the South-North Joint Declaration was clearly the summit's zenith. General in language and tone, what the five-article statement did provide was agreement on: (1) a general course toward reunification; (2) the legitimacy of each side's respective road toward reunification, that is, South Korea's concept of a confederation and the regime's idea of a loose federation; and (3) expansion of economic, cultural, and social engagement to facilitate the broader aim of reunification.

As a result of the summit, and in keeping with the broader aims of the Sunshine Policy, there was notable expansion of inter-Korean interaction during 2000: Seoul provided to North Korea some 300,000 tons of rice and 200,000 tons of corn, repayment of which was required over a 30-year period; liaison offices for both sides were reopened at Panmunjeom; ministerial talks were resumed; and the particulars for a joint commercial project at Kaesong were solidified.[24] In reciprocation, and in keeping with its newly acquired propensity for extracting economic gain for its concessions, Pyongyang was demanding by year's end some 2 million kilowatts of electricity from South Korea. Thus, as one reviews the recent history of negotiations with North Korea, the period 1990–2000 can generally be regarded as the period during which North Korea developed, honed, and extended its nuclear brinksmanship-for-economic-concessions style of diplomacy.

The year 2000 was also notable for the unexpected flurry of diplomatic overtures undertaken by the North Korean regime in an effort to raise its international profile, particularly after the June summit. The year began with the regime establishing formal relations with Italy in January. By May, it had also established formal ties with Australia; the Philippines followed suit in July. North Korea's first foray into multilateral diplomacy came one month after the South-North summit when it made application for membership into the ASEAN Regional Forum (ARF), which was accepted.[25] By the year's end it had also established formal relations with the United Kingdom. Interspersed with its notable diplomatic outreach overtures were two landmark events in U.S.-North Korean relations: the exchange of reciprocal high-level visits between the two countries during October 2000. North Korean envoy Jo Myong Rok, first vice chairman of the North Korean Defense Commission (and second highest ranking member of the military just after Kim Jong Il), visited Washington as special envoy to Kim in his capacity as Defense Commission chairman. The regime's objective was to undertake discussions of the security situation on the Korean peninsula ostensibly for the purpose of improving relations with Washington, which was accomplished through a series of strategic talks Jo undertook with administration officials, to include the president, secretary of state, and secretary of defense.

Specific topics of discussion included North Korean missile proliferation and a freeze on its nuclear weapons program; Washington's positive consideration of removing North Korea from its list of terrorist-sponsoring nations; and establishment of liaison offices in each country as a first step toward achieving full bilateral rapprochement, a major point contained within the Agreed Framework but on which little progress had been made. Also a part of the discussion was Pyongyang's willingness to consider halting its Taepodong missile program if the international community provided financial assistance for launching a North Korean satellite from a third country for scientific and peaceful purposes. Finally, Jo delivered to Clinton an invitation from Kim to visit Pyongyang.

Perhaps even greater than the surprise of the visit itself was the unexpected reversal of roles—Pyongyang offered its own carrot to Washington as it promised to take a "very important step" if Washington was prepared to ensure the regime's security and longevity. Precisely what that step would be was unclear, what was definitively decided, however, was that Secretary of State Albright would visit Pyongyang to directly share Clinton's views on Korean security, an event that took place within two weeks of Jo's visit. After Albright's visit, discussions over the regime's missile export program to the Middle East and development of its own long-range missile program became priorities, for which a meeting was convened in Kuala Lumpur, Malaysia, in early November 2000. The lack of progress in discussions failed in the end to produce any agreement and ultimately ended serious consideration of a U.S. presidential visit to Pyongyang, bringing to a close both the year and Clinton's presidency. The year 2000, which began with optimism and perhaps an even slightly giddy air of growing détente in U.S.-North Korean relations, would be left to the incoming Bush administration to carry to successful conclusion.

The change in administrations from Clinton to Bush brought with it a change that moved U.S. policy toward a more hard-line approach, which has over the past six years coalesced into the Bush Doctrine—reliance on CVID as both a goal and strategy—and migration away from engagement based on the principles of the Sunshine Policy. President George W. Bush offered at the outset of his administration what can only be regarded as tepid support for broader engagement with North Korea, which was then followed by a six-month policy review of U.S. policy toward North Korea. Although the official language Bush used to describe the results of the policy review signaled continued support for engagement with North Korea in order to achieve peace and stability on the peninsula, the reality has proved quite different. In his official statement of June 7, 2001, President Bush remarked:

> I have directed my national security team to undertake serious discussions with North Korea on a broad agenda to include: improved implementation of the Agreed Framework relating to North Korea's nuclear activities;

verifiable constraints on North Korea's missile programs and a ban on its missile exports; and a less threatening conventional military posture. We will pursue these discussions in the context of a comprehensive approach to North Korea which will seek to encourage progress toward North-South reconciliation, peace on the Korean peninsula, a constructive relationship with the United States and greater stability in the region.

But as early as the end of 2002, the Agreed Framework and any potential progress anticipated as a result of the 2000 South–North summit had been all but squandered on both sides of the peninsula. While the United States, through the efforts of Ambassador Jack Pritchard, tried to get the Agreed Framework back on track, the sticking point of which was inspection of North Korea's nuclear facilities, the regime assumed a cautious posture citing Bush's "axis of evil" speech as its major point of concern. In the wake of the regime's October 2002 admission to developing a highly enriched uranium program, the United States ceased shipment of heavy fuel oil, while in December 2002 North Korea expelled IAEA inspectors and removed surveillance equipment designed to monitor its nuclear facilities. Relations between Washington and Pyongyang, it appeared, had returned to their normal state of flux and rancor.

Bush on North Korea: Mission Being Accomplished or Rolling Blunder?

It was fairly evident from the outset of the Bush administration that it was prepared to take a different course on North Korea than Clinton had pursued, and substantive differences emerged over time.[26] Development of the Bush Doctrine can be characterized as an evolutionary process that moved toward its hard-line position as a result of three factors: administration infighting between moderates and hawkish neoconservatives, a battle in which the neocons ultimately emerged victorious; external events such as 9/11; and North Korean errant behaviors, some of which might have been in direct response to a hardening U.S. position vis-à-vis itself.

From almost the beginning the new administration was at war with itself over North Korea, primarily the result of strong divisions between the State Department and Pentagon. Former Secretary of State Colin Powell and former Deputy Secretary of State Richard Armitage, also Powell's long-time friend, advocated a tough, pragmatic, yet more moderate approach to North Korea for the administration to follow than the policy recommendations of the neoconservatives who populated the administration. They generally agreed with the Clintonian framework of direct engagement with the regime, but felt that the focus of these efforts should move beyond the singularity of the nuclear issue and be more comprehensive in its reach. They saw as integral to the negotiation process inclusion of such issues as North

Korea's conventional weapons threat. The antithetical hard-line philosophy emerged from within the Defense Department with support from the Office of the Vice President. The approach of former Secretary of Defense Donald Rumsfeld and his then deputy secretary Paul Wolfowitz was premised on the conclusions reached in the Rumsfeld Commission Report (1998), a commission headed by Rumsfeld and on which Wolfowitz served as a participating member. The Commission's mandate was straightforward: "to assess the nature and magnitude of the existing and emerging ballistic missile threat to the United States."[27] In its findings, the Commission contended that not only was North Korea, because of its nuclear aspirations and ballistic missile program, an immediate threat to countries in the region, but to Alaska, Hawaii, and the American Midwest and Southwest as well. The Commission also surmised that as a result of the inability of U.S. intelligence to detect early deployment of North Korea's growing nuclear arsenal, the regime might well be able to deploy a Taepodong-2 missile with "very little warning."[28] In short, the Commission found that North Korea represented a clear and present danger to U.S. allies, its regional interests, and the U.S. mainland.

Indications of which direction U.S. policy would follow quickly revealed themselves. On March 6, 2001, Secretary Powell expressed willingness to use the progress made under the Clinton administration as a means for creating an atmosphere conducive to discussions with the regime over its ballistic missile program when he announced that the Bush administration was prepared to "pick up where President Clinton and his administration left off."[29] Within 24 hours, during a meeting with former South Korean President Kim Dae Jung, President Bush quashed Secretary Powell's statement when he indicated that there would be no resumption of discussions with North Korea over its missile program anytime in the near future.[30] This position came at the expense of President Kim Dae Jung's Sunshine Policy, for which he had come to Washington to enlist the new administration's support. So within a day, President Bush had discarded any notion of near-term dialogue with the North, risking possible loss of momentum in discussions with the regime. He also poured cold water on Seoul's Sunshine Policy, one means through which at least a modicum of engagement with the regime had been successful. What the administration was not going to do was becoming clearer; its actual strategy for successfully resolving issues with North Korea remained unanswered. President Bush's meetings with former President Kim also revealed another interesting clue into the future modus operandi of the administration. President Bush commented during a press conference that: "We're not certain as to whether or not they're (North Korea) keeping all terms of all agreements." There was in fact only one agreement with North Korea—the 1994 Agreed Framework. Administration officials explained "this is the way the President speaks," indicating he was referring to future accords, not the one presently in force. Disregarding the obvious contradiction in the use of grammatical tense, how the administration planned to accomplish any future accords based on its decision not to hold discussions anytime in the near future is somewhat curious. That it had decided on a course of action unburdened by any clear understanding of the current situation seems a more likely explanation.

To begin laying the foundation for its new North Korea policy, the administration undertook a six-month long policy review, which concluded in June 2001. The results affirmed earlier signals that the administration was leaning toward a tougher approach with the regime. Specifically, the review provided for the following: (1) earlier implementation of IAEA inspections of the regime's undeclared nuclear sites; (2) expansion of the topics to be negotiated with the regime, which would now include its conventional weapons posture; and (3) the need for greater verification of North Korean compliance in all aspects of its nuclear weapons program.[31]

The events of 9/11 pushed the administration further down a path toward a tough approach with the regime. 9/11 not only provided the basis for the administration's immediate military action in Afghanistan, it was also instrumental in galvanizing its global war on terror, a major part of which included efforts to more closely control the proliferation of weapons of mass destruction—North Korea has, of course, been identified as a major global proliferator of WMD and its associated technology. In December 2002, the administration issued its National Strategy to Combat Weapons of Mass Destruction in which active interdiction of WMD was cited as a major means for controlling their proliferation. This was followed by the creation of the Proliferation Security Initiative (PSI) in May 2003 and creation of its "Statement of Interdiction Principles" in September 2003. PSI, in which eleven countries originally agreed to participate, is a global initiative that establishes specific steps for interdicting WMD shipments and preventing their further proliferation.[32]

With its growing stridence over WMD and their proliferation in the wake of 9/11, the administration paid special attention to North Korea and its activities. The period 2002–2003 marks a nadir in relations between Washington and Pyongyang under the Bush administration. In October 2001 during an Asian economic summit, Bush admonished the North not to try to use its advantage on the peninsula U.S. involvement in Afghanistan.[33] This was followed, in January 2002, by Bush's characterization of North Korea, Iraq, and Iran as members of the axis of evil. Adding fuel to the fires of mistrust that already burned between Washington and Pyongyang, it was revealed two months later that there existed a U.S. plan that specifically targeted North Korea for nuclear strikes.[34] With North Korea's admission to pursuing a secret uranium-based nuclear program in October 2002, the administration announced it was halting shipment of heavy fuel oil under the Agreed Framework until North Korea abandoned its newly acknowledged program.[35] This effectively signaled the end of any cooperation under the

Agreed Framework. North Korea announced its planned withdrawal from the NPT on January 10, 2003, and by April 2003 North Korea indicated it had begun reprocessing spent plutonium fuel rods to which it had regained access after removing the seals from the nuclear facility where they were stored, the result of expelling IAEA inspectors in December 2002. And in November 2003, the Korean Peninsula Energy Development Organization (KEDO) announced suspension of the project to provide North Korea two tamperproof LWRs, which officially signaled U.S. intent to fully and finally bring an end to the Agreed Framework and its attendant processes. It also signaled the final transition of U.S. policy on North Korea from the Clinton administration's policy of engagement to the Bush team's harder-line approach.

The real issue with regard to the Bush administration's shift toward a tougher North Korea policy is not if or how it differs from the Clinton administration's approach. The real question is just how successful each of these approaches has been in laying the groundwork necessary for achieving an end to the regime's nuclear and ballistic missile programs.

U.S. North Korea Policy: Clinton vs. Bush

Despite progress toward the end of his presidency, Clinton's North Korea policy was not without its critics. Representative of them was Senator Bob Dole who felt that Clinton was "propping up an odious regime that is closer to full collapse than at any time during the past forty years." Dole offered that insight over twelve years ago. Whether such criticism genuinely reflected his ideas or was the result of a contrarian and partisan approach to Clinton's policy, time and recent events have proven it inaccurate. Full collapse of the regime has been predicted for nearly two decades, yet it remains a thorn in the side of the international community.

The passage of time, however, has not rendered any kinder some assessments of Clintonian policy. White House spokesman Tony Snow has characterized Clinton's direct engagement policy with North Korea as attempting to woo Kim Jong Il with "flowers and chocolates" and that the Bush administration had "learned from that mistake."[36] What precisely the Bush administration has learned was left unclear. What is known, however, is that under the aegis of the Bush Doctrine North Korea has, over the past six years, expelled IAEA inspectors; regained access to previously stored spent plutonium fuels rods; restarted its nuclear reactors; conducted a missile test in defiance of U.S. demands while forcing Bush to back away from pre-launch tough talk; and has conducted a nuclear weapons test. All of this transpired while the only venue for negotiation, the Six Party Talks, remained in limbo. In the process, the United States and South Korea, its traditional ally on the peninsula, increasingly pursue divergent paths on North

Korea issues, with South Korea extending economic outreach under continuation of the Sunshine Policy while the United States pursues its harder-line approach. By any reckoning this could be considered a rather precipitous learning curve. It wasn't until the administration undertook some measure of constructive engagement with North Korea beginning in 2007 that it could claim anything akin to progress in negotiations.

Many of the preceding events have, at one time or another, been at least superficially covered in the domestic U.S. news media. Perhaps because of the need to quickly move to the next sound bite or to avoid being overtly critical of administration officials, which helps to maintain "access" to news sources, the media has never covered the real significance of some of these events. In order to get at the real substance, however, one must read the subtext: not only has North Korea stymied U.S. efforts under the current administration to bring about an end to its nuclear and ballistic missile programs, it has also handed the Bush team two surprisingly stunning defeats in the process. The first occurred during winter 2002 to spring 2003 when the regime expelled IAEA inspectors, regained access to spent plutonium fuel rods, and then announced it had begun reprocessing them. The importance of these events can only be understood when considered within the context of the Clinton administration's response to similar circumstances. When confronted with the prospect of North Korea expelling IAEA inspectors and regaining access to spent fuel rods in furtherance of its nuclear weapons program, Clinton drew a line in the sand from which he did not back away. His initial response was to work through the United Nations in order to have sanctions imposed against the regime. When the regime responded with its usual belligerence by indicating that any imposition of sanctions would be considered an act of war, Clinton called its bluff by beginning contingency planning for war that would bring an additional 50,000 ground troops along with military hardware to the peninsula—Bradley Fighting Vehicles, air defense systems, helicopters, planes, and other warfighting equipment.[37] He also dispatched an advance logistical planning team to begin planning the infrastructure that would be necessary to bring additional military units onto the peninsula.[38] The message was clear and unequivocal that maintaining the fuel rods under international monitoring and control was worth going to war over.

When Bush's response during 2002–2003 is juxtaposed against the reaction of the Clinton administration, the difference is remarkable. The U.S. response under Bush focused on three areas in particular: (1) continued demands for North Korean acquiescence; (2) efforts to further paint the issue of North Korea's nuclear and ballistic missile program as a global issue rather than a bilateral (or trilateral if one considers the U.S.-South Korea alliance) one; and (3) attempts to establish both means and venues for dialogue, all of which were undertaken amid a cacophony of heated rhetoric between Washington and Pyongyang. The acrimony between the United States and North Korea was particularly sharp during the first half of 2003. With Bush declaring that "America and the world will not be blackmailed" and White House spokesman Ari Fleischer insisting that the North not "intimidate and blackmail the international community," the administration at once created an atmosphere that was less than conducive to dialogue while simultaneously putting a "global" face on its position. In addition to the normal bellicose retorts of the regime, it also withdrew from the NPT. Amid all of this, there were examples of more substantive discord—North Korea fighter jets shadowing a U.S. reconnaissance aircraft; the North symbolically firing a missile into the Sea of Japan (East Sea) the day before president-elect Roh Moo Hyun was to be sworn in; and the U.S. announcement that stealth aircraft will be redeployed to the peninsula.

It is within this tit-for-tat atmosphere that the administration sought to create a venue for dialogue. One of the first actions taken by the administration was to dispatch U.S. Assistant Secretary of State for East Asian Affairs James Kelly to Beijing in April 2003 for discussions with the regime. Although these talks produced no meaningful resolution to the immediate problems of North Korea's nuclear program, they did lay the necessary groundwork for the creation of the Six Party Talks. The regime finally agreed to participate in the Talks on August 1, with the first round of discussions taking place in Beijing on August 27–29. So ironically, talks became the order of the day for an administration that touted a tougher line.

As important as the dialogue process is, in order for it to be effective it must be undertaken within a comprehensive framework of constructive engagement and not as a direct response to actions taken by the North Korean regime. In this case, instead of dialogue serving as a means for moving negotiations forward, U.S. efforts likely came across as weak, something the regime has sought to exploit at every opportunity. That there was such a notable difference in the responses of the Clinton and Bush administrations to very similar circumstances is likely not to have escaped the notice of our North Korean adversaries, a fact that I believe has colored the regime's perception of how to deal with the current administration. This might well have contributed to its calculations leading up to its second surprise victory over the Bush administration—the July 2006 missile launch followed by the October nuclear detonation.

What is notable when considering the circumstances surrounding both events is North Korea's open disregard of U.S. assertions that the regime was acting counter to the world's expectations of transparency in its behavior and the promise of consequences for its actions. The questions that bear some consideration are what North Korea felt it had to gain by conducting the tests and why it felt it could do so in the face of strong U.S. opposition. One plausible consideration is to take the regime's argument at face value— it was pursuing what it sees as its sovereign right to develop a nuclear weapons program. While this may or may not be true, it fails to adequately address the issue. The regime has maintained its right to develop such a program all along so it wasn't trying to assert a newly proclaimed right. Another possibility is that the regime, confronting a continuing stalemate through the Six Party Talks venue, sought to "shake things loose" and pressure the United States to return to the negotiating table with terms more favorable to its position. Adding to this theory's plausibility is the fact that there existed at the time an agreement that the regime had signed to scrap its nuclear weapons program; not surprisingly, it added major caveats to the agreement within twenty-four hours and allowed it to languish, with little demonstrable progress through the Talks venue from November 2005 through December 2006. In the face of a growing lame-duck presidency, perhaps the regime calculated that the Bush administration might be more flexible in its position if its hand was forced. In any case, what did not seem to enter into its considerations was any genuine concern over U.S. response to its actions.

How then does one measure the success of the very different approaches under the Bush and Clinton administrations? Quite simply, through their results. Neither, of course, achieved the ultimate aim of denuclearizing the regime. Under Bush's approach, however, to his credit, he has enlisted the assistance of China to a greater extent in order to facilitate negotiations with North Korea. (Clinton also enlisted the assistance of the Chinese, but the difference is a matter of degree.) China can be of assistance in the process, but as mentioned earlier, it has its own agenda both regionally and in its bilateral relationship with North Korea, which ultimately mitigates the benefit of Chinese involvement. Under Bush, the Six Party Talks venue was also created and remains the only existing multilateral forum through which to engage the regime, although there has been little meaningful U.S. strategy associated with its proceedings and even fewer substantive results. This notwithstanding, I believe the Talks hold potential for ultimately facilitating resolution of the North's nuclear programs. It will, however, require developing a substantive and creative strategy for moving forward.

In contrasting style, Clinton's approach of engagement, whether one sees it as a "flowers and chocolates" approach or as a necessary antecedent to resolving North Korean issues, also had its strong points. His efforts during 1993–1994 produced the Agreed Framework, although the agreement was certainly not without its flaws—it left major elements of the potential North Korean nuclear threat either unaddressed altogether, such as its highly enriched uranium program, or unattended until late in the Agreed Framework process, such as the requirement for North Korea to come into compliance with IAEA safeguards only after key components of the LWR were delivered. And it wasn't until very late into his first term and early second term that Clinton actually began crafting a policy on North Korea with any coherence, the turning point for which was the U.S.-South Korean 1996 proposal for creation of a Four Party Talks venue. The Four Party Talks were designed to address Korean security issues and involved the United States, China and the two Koreas. Clinton's approach also helped contribute to the North's expanded efforts at diplomatic outreach during 2000. Despite the obvious flaws, the Clinton administration's approach did include one important element: it left open, by means of its willingness to engage in broader dialogue with the regime, a road toward possible resolution of the North Korean nuclear and ballistic missile issues, a road that the regime nearly took during 2000. In the end, perhaps a good portion of Pyongyang's efforts during 2000 can be attributed to its desire to gain as much ground as possible before the change of U.S. presidential administrations, but the fact remains that at least the road to greater engagement hadn't been cut off.

Another area in which Bush and Clinton policies have differed is how each perceived the negotiation process with the regime best moving forward. Clinton, recognizing the need for multilateral buy-in, tried to garner South Korean, Japanese, and later Chinese support, but also pursued more direct dialogue with the regime during his second administration. The Bush administration, on the other hand, has elevated the dialogue to a nearly exclusive multilateral track through the Six Party Talks, again with a sudden reversal of course coming in 2007. The two administrations also differ in what role they see China playing in advancing the process of negotiation with North Korea. Until his second term, Clinton largely ignored China's emerging role on the peninsula. By 1996, however, the administration's thinking had evolved at least enough to recognize that China could be instrumental in broader negotiations with the North, hence its inclusion in the Four Party Talks. The Bush administration, along with elevating the dialogue to a multilateral level, has placed a priority on China taking the lead in negotiations with the regime based on the premise that China has at least as much at stake in seeing North Korea denuclearized as does the United States. So much so in fact that Ambassador Robert Gallucci contends the administration has "subcontracted" its North Korea policy to Beijing.[39] That China, for reasons of maintaining regional stability, doesn't want a nuclearized North Korea is an accurate assessment, but it also does not want to see North Korea destabilized either, something the Bush administration doesn't take into account in its assessments. Consequently, the Chinese prefer taking a softer and more patient approach with the regime, which includes providing food and energy assistance. In fact, the Bush administration would likely welcome regime change in North Korea, a position that puts Washington and Beijing at odds with each other. The administration focuses on North Korea as an element of its global war on terror; China sees it as a potential factor of regional destabilization that must be supported so as not to invite a North Korean catastrophe that adversely impacts China and the region.

In the end, each approach has had its measure of success, but each has had its weaknesses as well. What has fundamentally lacked in both cases, however, is a well-planned strategy for broader engagement of North Korea that systemically weans the regime off its reliance on nuclear weapons as its single geopolitical playing card and forces it to act as a normal nation.

Part II

The Practicalities of Engagement

6

North Korea: Engagement Alternatives

No one starts a war—or rather, no one in his senses ought to do so—without first being clear in his mind what he intends to achieve by that war and how he intends to conduct it.

—Carl von Clausewitz, "On War"

For decades experts have predicted North Korea's imminent collapse and have pointed to various indicators portending such: dissolution of the Soviet Union in 1991; drought and flood conditions that decimated agriculture resulting in famine and the death of millions during the mid-1990s; the death of Kim Il Sung in 1994, the only leader North Koreans had known to that point since the country's creation in 1948; and dire economic straits brought on and further exacerbated by less than stellar economic policy choices. Yet an economically fragile North Korea survives. One that has depended on international aid for survival since the mid-1990s, and ironically, presents its greatest threat to East Asia and potentially the world since the Korean War, the result of its dangerous and expanding nuclear weapons and ballistic missile programs. For example, in August 1998, North Korea test-launched a Taepodong-1 rocket in a space launch configuration, attempting to put a small satellite into orbit using a three-stage Taepodong rocket, the second stage of which overflew Japan, offering the first indication that North Korea had begun to develop the technology for advancing its ballistic missile program to the level of intercontinental capability. This was followed by a troublingly rapid succession of events ushered in after the turn of the century beginning with its admission in October 2002 to a secret program to produce highly enriched uranium; the December 2002 expulsion of International Atomic Energy Agency (IAEA) inspectors and the removal of monitoring devices from and reopening of the Yongbyon nuclear power facility; its withdrawal in January 2003 from the NPT and ultimate removal of 8,000 spent plutonium fuel rods from storage; its February 2003 announcement that it had restarted its nuclear facilities at Yongbyon; and by April 2004 the apparent shutdown of the reactor, ostensibly for the purpose of reprocessing spent fuel rods into weapons-grade material. Interspersed with all of this activity was the now familiar vitriol directed at South Korea, for example, threats to turn Seoul into "a sea of fire"; maintaining that economic sanctions would be considered an "act of war"; and of course, outright refusal to participate in negotiations with other nations over its nuclear weapons programs at critical junctures. Yet the international community has continued to provide humanitarian, economic, and energy assistance in various forms to what can only be described as a mercurial North Korea: emergency relief for North Korean citizens through such organizations as the United Nations' World Food Program; South Korea continues to provide such necessities as food and fertilizer; and China remains a major provider of energy assistance.[1]

What then is the basis for the world's continued economic and diplomatic engagement with what has been termed a "rogue regime" that refuses to adhere to the demands of the world community to abandon its nuclear weapons program? How effective have past policies been in securing North Korean cooperation and what are the prospects for success into the future? And what alternatives might exist to offer a more effective and lasting solution to the problem? In short, what is the best way of handling the North Korea issue?[2]

THE NORTH KOREAN THREAT

To ascertain the most effective method of engaging the North Korean regime, one must first frame the problem in its entirety, which in this case requires developing a clear picture of the threat North Korea actually poses. The threat, which at one time was non-nuclear and confined to the peninsula, has evolved into a regional nuclear threat; and there is growing concern that as its ballistic missile capability advances, thus extending the reach of its nuclear weapons, the threat will become more global in nature.

The true basis of the regime's threat posture, however, is threefold. Not only is there concern over the development and possession of nuclear weapons because of its historically unpredictable behavior pattern, but there is also added concern over its propensity to proliferate such weapons through the sale of associated technology. Additionally, and recently overlooked because of the Six Party Talks' singular focus on the North Korean nuclear weapons program, is also the conventional threat still posed by the regime. While essentially limited to the Korean peninsula, it is still credible and dangerous, the employment of which would have far-reaching implications regionally, and to a lesser extent, globally. It would, of course, directly involve South Korea and the United States in immediate fighting on the peninsula; Japan would also become involved to the extent U.S. personnel and equipment flowed through U.S. military facilities within its territorial boundaries and it provided logistical support to U.S. forces under the U.S.-Japan Defense Guidelines; given the security relationship existing between North Korea and China, China's potential involvement couldn't be ruled out; and finally, to the extent a multilateral coalition of forces might be formed to assist in a war scenario on the Korean peninsula, particularly if U.S. forces remain actively engaged in military operations in other parts of the world, global involvement would be unavoidable.

As with many military forces around the world, North Korea maintains both a conventional force structure (army, air force, navy) and an unconventional or asymmetric one, the most immediate threat from which is its WMD program.[3] The product of its *songun* (military first) ideology under which the North Korean military receives the preponderance of resources to the detriment of its citizenry and other parts of the economy, North Korea spends 25 percent of its GNP on military-related expenditures; this figure represents the greatest percentage of GNP expended on military forces among nations of the world.[4] (This is also the highest percentage of GDP North Korea has spent on military expenditures since the period 1967–1971 when expenditures ranged from 30 to 32 percent.)[5] This investment garners for the North the world's fifth largest military and its third largest ground force. Its conventional force structure is comprised of a 1.1 million man army and a nearly 7.5 million strong reserve force which includes paramilitary training, worker-peasant Red Guard and Red Youth Guard units. This is in addition to the tanks, armored vehicles, field artillery tubes, multiple rocket launchers (MRLs), aircraft, and ships possessed by the North Korean military.[6] These numbers illustrate the level of regime commitment to *songun* and strengthening its military capability. Ever prepared to communicate such policy commitments to its citizens and the world, the regime used its 2006 New Year's message as a means of communicating its continued prioritization of the military: "We should confidently build an economic power in the 21st century through a high-pitched drive for affecting a great *songun* revolutionary surge."[7] And despite concluding the DAP in February 2007, the North Korean New Year's message offered only a month earlier called on its military to "mercilessly defeat any invasion of the U.S. imperialists" while characterizing the October nuclear detonation as an "auspicious event in national history."[8]

Having the military and armaments of war is one thing, however, maintaining them is quite another matter and maintaining the effectiveness of its conventional military forces has proved problematic over the past two decades for two important reasons: an inability to undertake force modernization because of a lack of research and development resources and the absence of foreign exchange to maintain its existing force structure and weapons systems. Consequently, while North Korea enjoys numerical force superiority vis-à-vis the U.S.-South Korea bilateral security alliance in terms of military end strength and numbers of weapons systems on the peninsula, this advantage is mitigated by the technological superiority and high state of unit readiness of U.S. and ROK units.

Central to this disparity in technology and unit readiness is North Korea's economic crisis, which has taken its toll on all sectors of the economy, but presently forces the military sector to operate at about 64 percent of its pre-1992 levels.[9] An immediate impact of a shrinking military budget has been the effect on the research and development dollars necessary to upgrade conventional armaments in order to maintain the readiness of North Korean conventional forces. This, coupled with the difficulty of ensuring regular maintenance and availability of repair parts for its large inventory of existing weapons systems, has led North Korea to seek more cost-effective means for creating and maintaining a credible threat against the U.S.-ROK alliance—a WMD program.

The North Korean WMD threat can itself be divided into two categories: conventional and asymmetric weapons. A conventional WMD capability can be described as one that employs the use of conventional weapons systems against high value, high concentration targets, such as cities, in such mass that their potential lethality generally approximates the effect of unconventional WMD. For example, the North Korean Army has forward deployed in the vicinity of the DMZ, which is located roughly 50 km from Seoul, the capital of South Korea, approximately 12,000 field artillery tubes capable of producing a sustained rate of fire of up to 500,000 rounds per hour for several hours.[10] When one considers such a potential barrage on a concentrated area like Seoul, with its population of 10.4 million, the aggregate effect would be much like that of an unconventional WMD. Another important point to bear in mind, of course, is that conventional artillery shells could potentially be replaced with tactical nuclear artillery shells, thereby increasing their lethality.

It is North Korea's asymmetric WMD program, however, that is of more pressing concern to the peninsula, region, and larger global community of nations. North Korea possesses the full complement of nuclear, biological, and chemical (NBC) weapons, along with its ballistic missile program, which serves as the carriage for its WMD threat.

While its biological weapons program has been in existence for nearly a half-century, it remains comparatively immature, though not un-nurtured. Under a mandate from Kim Il Sung in 1980, North Korea undertook an expanded program to develop biological toxins and weapons. Through its National Defense Research Institute and Medical Academy, North Korea has pursued the research of such pathogens as yellow fever, small pox, cholera, anthrax, and the bubonic plague.[11] Their existence may, however, be more ominous than any threat of actual use as the likelihood of their employment on the battlefield is very slim for two important reasons. First, weaponization of such pathogens requires a level of technological advancement not yet achieved by North Korea.[12] Second is the issue of controlling the pathogens once they are released, something that would require a great deal more luck than skill. In short, these pathogens would be virtually impossible to control after their deployment, leaving North Korean forces as susceptible to their effects as any force against which they might be employed. This is not to say, however, that there is no probability of their use. Although North Korea has acceded to the Biological Weapons Convention (1987), there is a scenario under which one might envision deployment of such biological toxins—in a military conflict under which the regime fears its own annihilation—in effect, if it has nothing to lose as a result of employing such weaponry.[13]

Unlike its biological weapons capability, North Korea's chemical weapons program is fully matured with its stockpiles of such weapons estimated at somewhere between 250–5,000 tons and include choking, blood, blister, and nerve agents.[14] Since 1989, the regime has had the capability to indigenously produce such chemical weapons and unlike the constraints associated with biological pathogens, North Korea's chemical weapons agents can be delivered via a vast number of its weapons systems—artillery, multiple rocket launchers, mortars, and missiles—making this capability a potentially devastating tactical offensive weapon against military units and civilian populations. Use of chemical agents also affords greater flexibility and control than do biological pathogens, as persistent biological agents would most likely be employed against hard targets in the enemy's rear, denying use of buildings and facilities for extended periods of time. Conversely, nonpersistent chemical agents might be employed in the area of operations, limiting the potentially adverse impact on North Korean forces while disrupting operations of its adversaries.[15] As North Korea is not a signatory to the Chemical Weapons Convention (1997), the regime would likely not feel bound by the Convention's terms of nonuse of chemical agents in a conflict scenario, as recent evidence may suggest. The South Korean government, through its Ministry of Commerce, Industry and Energy, confirmed in September 2004 that unauthorized shipments by South Korean firms of 122 tons of sodium cyanide, used in the manufacture of sarin nerve gas, was transshipped to North Korea via China and Malaysia.[16]

The greatest threat, however, because of the potential lethality and widespread devastation, is the regime's nuclear weapons program, as much for what is known of it as what is not. The North Korean nuclear weapons program is suspected to be both plutonium and uranium-based, with the former supplied through spent fuel rods obtained from its nuclear reactor facilities and the latter through its vast stores of uranium deposits that can then be processed through its emerging highly enriched uranium (HEU) program. U.S. intelligence estimates indicate North Korea already possesses approximately eight plutonium nuclear weapons and a recent article appearing in the *Korea Times* argues that North Korea may yet be reprocessing spent plutonium fuel rods removed from storage in early 2003, while simultaneously negotiating the modalities of dismantling its nuclear weapons program through the Six Party Talks.[17] Its uranium-based program is harder yet to assess. In contrast to the distinctive aboveground plutonium production reactors, elements of a uranium enrichment program could be hidden underground, escaping detection. Further, there is some disagreement as to when North Korea's HEU program was actually initiated; estimates range from as recently as the late 1990s to as early as the late 1970s.[18] What is known about the uranium enrichment program, however, is disturbing. With its ability to mine thousands of tons of uranium, there is no lack of raw materials.[19] Coupled with this are its past connections to Pakistan through the A.Q. Khan network, through which North Korea may have acquired the required gas centrifuges used in producing weapons-grade uranium, by entering into a "nuclear weapons components for ballistic missile technology" swap.[20] U.S. intelligence estimates that Pyongyang's uranium program could have advanced to the point where it is now able to convert enough of the material to produce at least two uranium-based nuclear weapons annually.[21] It should be stressed that these are estimates, but the available circumstantial evidence would not render such a conclusion unreasonable. Herein, however, lies the advantage North Korea enjoys with regard to its nuclear activities: while intelligence sources are reasonably certain that it has a credible nuclear weapons program, no one knows how advanced it might be. From North Korea's perspective, world conjecture over the level of its nuclearization is just as effective as actually possessing the weapons themselves.

The final component of North Korea's nuclear program, and one central to its success, is its ballistic missiles, the means for delivering any nuclear payload it has or is presently developing. Three factors go into measuring the effectiveness and lethality of a ballistic missile: payload, range, and accuracy. If a missile cannot carry enough of a payload, the damage ultimately inflicted on any potential enemy targets will be less than optimal; the whole point of investing in nuclear weapons technology is to inflict maximum damage and casualties on the enemy. Similarly, limited range means limited deployability. If one cannot reach enemy targets, nuclear weapons cannot be used to their maximum effectiveness. Finally, if one cannot hit important strategic or operational targets at the determined time and place, both effectiveness and lethality are impacted.

North Korea continues incremental improvement of its ballistic missiles in all areas, although there are limitations to its relatively fledgling program. The most notable limitation is its comparatively limited range capability that, at least for the present, limits its destructive capacity to the East Asia region— it does not yet possess an intercontinental capability for delivering its nuclear weapons. A point also worth noting is that range and payload capacities have an inverse relationship: the larger the payload, the less the missile's range. Similarly, the three-stage Taepodong-1 missile launch over Japan in August 1998 revealed a good deal about how the North's missile program had advanced to that point, particularly with regard to stage separation, which is the key for developing intercontinental ballistic missiles. North Korea has yet to overcome another hurdle in its bid to become an intercontinental threat, namely, the capacity to produce a missile with reentry capability. Without such capability, the likelihood of delivering a weapon with any reasonable accuracy is greatly diminished.[22] Additionally, the July 2006 missile launch provides important insight into just how far North Korea's missile program has progressed. Contrary to the message the regime was trying to send to the world, but particularly to the United States, of its growing nuclear capability, the missile malfunctioned in the initial stage and tumbled back to earth within the first minute of flight. Despite all this, its intentions, brazen behavior, and incremental progress in developing a greater missile capability bear close watching.

Under the aegis of the Second Natural Science Academy, formerly known as the Academy of Defense Sciences, the Taepodong-2 missile has been under development to improve its lethality.[23] U.S. intelligence estimates that a three-stage version of the missile could conceivably reach the west coast of the United States, although not with a great deal of accuracy, in what the Bush administration terms a "theoretical capability."[24] But without first surmounting issues of increased range and developing a reentry capability, this is still a "paper capability." The Rumsfeld Report offered a pessimistic estimate of the Taepodong-2 missile as well: "Light-weight variations of the TD-2 (Taepodong-2) could fly as far as 10,000 km, placing at risk western U.S. territory in an arc extending northwest from Phoenix, Arizona, to Madison, Wisconsin. These variants of the TD-2 would require additional time to develop and would likely require an additional flight test." While assessments of this type can, I believe, be safely regarded as unconstrained conjecture at present, one underlying point of the report's findings is accurate: the threat grows with the passage of time, it is not diminished.

So despite its current lack of intercontinental power projection, the potential threat to the Korean peninsula and the region remains a present danger. With its existing arsenal of ballistic missiles North Korea has become a greater potential threat to South Korea, Japan, and the region as a whole, as indicated in the following map.

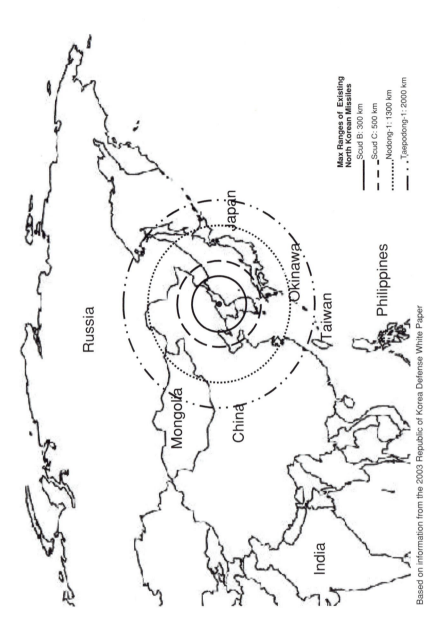

Max Ranges of Existing North Korean Missiles

Scud B: 300 km
Scud C: 500 km
Nodong-1: 1300 km
Taepodong-1: 2000 km

Russia

Mongolia

China

India

Japan

Okinawa

Taiwan

Philippines

Based on information from the 2003 Republic of Korea Defense White Paper

Maximum Ranges of Existing North Korean Missiles.

While its ballistic missile program might be accurately described as being in the developmental stage, its associated technology represents an immediate global threat. For example, a disturbing point about North Korea's ballistic missile technology is its suitability for reciprocal proliferation. By this I mean the suitability for the technology to be further developed by other countries after purchase, which can then be reintroduced into North Korea's missile program at a later date. This has apparently been the case with Iran as technology for Tehran's Shehab-4 satellite launch vehicle may have been derived from the Taepodong-1 and the Shehab-5; and Shehab-6/Kosar satellite launch vehicles may be based on Taepodong-2 technology, technology adaptable to ballistic missiles.[25] Imagine the advantage the regime gains by allowing other countries to bear the cost of and logistics for new missile engine test firings. Tehran is also suspected of assisting Pyongyang with technical teams in order to resolve launch and propulsion issues related to its ballistic missile program.[26]

At this point it might be useful to examine the underlying rationale for such vast conventional and asymmetric military expenditures, since so much of it is undertaken at the expense of other parts of the economy. First, as conceptualized by the North Korean regime, military power provides the basis for the country's autonomy—independence in domestic politics and its foreign relations (*chaju*) as well as economic autonomy (*charip*) can only be achieved through a strong military (*chawi*). Second, as noted above, at least as far as proliferation of ballistic missiles and their associated technology is concerned, it provides a source of foreign exchange; sale of the technology provides the added potential benefit of reciprocal proliferation. Third, from the regime's perspective, its asymmetric weapons provide a measure of security against its adversaries, namely the United States. Having been included in the infamous axis of evil along with Iran and Iraq as first described in President Bush's (43) January 2002 state of the union address, and having seen the outcome of Iraq's inclusion in the axis, the regime sees little reason to be placated by U.S. guarantees of its security. When one considers such a mindset against the backdrop of the North Korean "shrimp amongst whales" worldview, there is little benefit, from the regime's perspective, to giving up its push for nuclear weapons. Fourth, an asymmetric weapons capability provides a means through which to negotiate with larger powers. In short, its nuclear weapons program serves as both an attention-getter while also leveling the playing field. That so much time and effort have already been expended through the venue of the Six Party Talks to persuade North Korea to abandon its nuclear program underscores this point. Irrespective of how vexed it may purport to be or what veneer of bellicosity it may wear at any given time, in the end sitting at the negotiating table with the United States has been and remains a primary objective of the North Korean government. Why? There are two simple but important reasons. The first goes back to *Juche's* determinant of equality. Although its major adversary, undertaking negotiations with the United States translates into a certain legitimacy for North Korea as it perceives parity between itself and the United States through such negotiations. Second, direct U.S.-North Korea negotiations isolate South Korea and undermine the decades-long U.S.-ROK security alliance, which is, of course, a major North Korean goal and something successive U.S. administrations have assiduously avoided.

Its nuclear weapons capability has come to serve as an important underlying construct of its present means for engaging the world, which is a confluence of two factors, namely, an understanding of the global community's sensitivity to nuclear weapons proliferation and a dearth of other statecraft implements at its disposal: a ravaged economy; its military, while still formidable, is a capability limited to the peninsula; and any technological advantage it might enjoy is limited and rests in nuclear and ballistic missile technology, the result of infusing a preponderance of investment into this sector of the economy. Hence through an artful mix of its fundamental statecraft implements, *audacity*, threats to develop, proliferate, and potentially employ nuclear weapons, North Korea's engagement policy with the rest of the world has become one of missile diplomacy with a foundation of brinksmanship.

NORTH KOREAN ENDGAME: IS IT REALLY ZERO SUM?

Given the preceding, what then is the North Korean endgame? Is it to build a nuclear arsenal with the objective of militarily engaging the U.S.-Republic of Korea bilateral security alliance in a peninsular conflict? Is it perhaps to broaden a potential conflict by engaging the United States and its regional allies in a regional war? Or, ultimately to develop its nuclear capability to a level where it is able to threaten U.S. sovereign territory? Against what perceived threat does it pursue its nuclear endgame? Equally important to understand is what it hopes to gain from brinksmanship missile diplomacy.

While the threat North Korea presents to the peninsula, region, and potentially the broader global community of nations has been successfully defined, there has been less success in understanding the longer-term intent—*the endgame*—behind North Korea's nuclear weapons program and even less in creating workable solutions for compelling it to abandon these programs. With little understanding of the dimensions of the problem, however, solutions remain elusive. In this case, the endgame can be summed up in two words: *regime survival*, although the simplicity of the definition belies the concept's complexities. The policy of regime survival is comprised of several components: to develop and maintain a viable nuclear weapons program to offset costs of maintaining a strong conventional military capability; keep the United States and its allies off balance to maintain its independence; and to negotiate while extracting economic and energy concessions necessary to keep the North Korean society from collapsing. Essential to understanding the North Korean endgame is realizing how closely linked nuclear weapons and economic welfare are to regime survival—the latter ever more dependent on external economic assistance. Consequently, trying to use one to gain advantage over the other, something that has characterized the U.S. policy toward North Korea, has and will likely remain an unsuccessful strategy.

The economic carrot-and-stick approach has, however, come to dominate negotiations with North Korea, most readily in the form of humanitarian and energy assistance; not an unreasonable approach given the poor economic conditions existing in the country or the North's past incessant demands for ever greater humanitarian and energy assistance. Because its poor economic circumstances have become North Korea's Achilles' heel, this is where both the Clinton and Bush administrations have focused their energies, for very different reasons, but with similarly disappointing results. Clinton saw economic inducements as a way to move security discussions ahead, hence linking the two. This was precisely the case when the Clinton administration undertook its "food for talks" strategy to lure North Korea into participating in the Four Party Talks, a task in which it only partially succeeded.[27] The North Koreans did come to the table but failed to ameliorate their behavior. Conversely, the Bush administration has attempted to de-link humanitarian assistance and security, but has sought to more closely align such assistance to improvements in human rights and greater accessibility to the North Korean populace. Attempts to persuade a reclusive regime to open its society to foreign humanitarian observers have met with mixed results at best as the degree of access has been unpredictable at any given time.[28] And a strategy directly linking humanitarian assistance to human rights, through U.S. legislation and appointment of a North Korea human rights czar, has been a doomed policy from the start as the regime's many bellicose outbursts suggest.

Juche's determinants of equality and independence and their inherent aversion to "big power chauvinism" simply will not permit North Korea's autonomy to be held hostage to economic gains; history illustrates that the country holds this ideal so fundamental to its existence that it jealously guarded such prerogatives even with its larger communist benefactors, the former USSR and PRC. To expect it will act to the contrary with an adversary will likely lead to continued frustratingly unfruitful results. Thus, any combination of threats to impose economic sanctions or to extend benefits (this includes humanitarian assistance) directly linked to overtly trying to modify the regime's behavior is unlikely to produce the results intended, because acquiescing to such external pressures runs antithetical to the central belief system of *Juche*.

Given its level of recalcitrance, the regime obviously fears some threat(s) against its ultimate survival. Not surprisingly the U.S.-ROK alliance represents its most immediate concern, but more specifically, the United States itself, which is not an insignificant distinction and underscores the different approaches Washington and Seoul have taken to address the rising nuclear tensions on the peninsula. The Bush administration remains critical of past efforts to negotiate with North Korea, most specifically the 1994 Agreed Framework and the South Korean Sunshine Policy, which have come to symbolize for the administration the folly of trying to negotiate with the Kim regime. What Washington has sought for the past six years until its surprising reversal of course in 2007 was to force North Korean compliance via CVID of its nuclear weapons infrastructure, with no promise of additional rewards until such compliance is forthcoming.

Conversely, since 1998, when former President Kim introduced his "Sunshine Policy" toward North Korea, Seoul's approach has been characterized by expanded economic and cultural outreach while avoiding contentious political and security issues, a policy further broadened by President Roh Moo Hyun. For example, in partnership with the Hyundai Group, North and South Korea have agreed to develop Mt. Paekdu, located at the border of North Korea and China, as a tourist resort for South Koreans and have similarly developed Mt. Kumgang, located along the eastern coast of North Korea; the two governments have also considered opening a South Korean railway line to Mt. Kumgang; and they have created the jointly operated industrial complex in the North Korean city of Kaesong.[29] Although these are just a few examples, these initiatives help to underscore Seoul's broader policies of rapprochement with the North. Seoul has also been instrumental in lobbying other participating nations of the Six Party Talks to take a softer approach with North Korea. Seoul, along with Beijing and Moscow, seeks further engagement through discussion and extension of additional economic perks, or at least no further imposition of economic sanctions. Chinese and Russian aversion to the sanctions option became clear in the aftermath of the July 2006 missile launch as both failed to support sanctions against North Korea. (Although both countries did support sanctions after the October nuclear detonation, it remains to be seen how vigilantly they will be enforced; China has already unfrozen some regime bank accounts in a Macau bank purportedly linked to money laundering.[30] South Korea has also backed away from enforcing measures against North Korea under PSI.)[31] Japan as well at one time advocated taking a softer approach with Pyongyang prior to the most recent missile launch. Prime Minister Koizumi Junichiro, for example, as recently as October 2004, remarked that Japan had reservations about the effectiveness of additional economic sanctions and preferred to "work with patience to get North Korea to respond sincerely."[32]

Several other factors have led to North Korea's anxiety over survival of its regime. First, there are the implications of broader U.S. foreign policy objectives generally characterized by greater unilateralism. For example, the administration's reassertion in the 2006 National Security Strategy of its right to strike preemptively against nations it perceives as potential threats and the U.S.-led war against Iraq have likely sown seeds of distrust.[33] As Russian Deputy Foreign Minister Georgy Mamedov described it, "How should a small country feel when it is told that it is all but part of forces of evil of biblical proportions and should be fought against until total annihilation? There is no use expecting countries included in the 'axis of evil' to remain passive."[34] Second, the impact of present disagreements with Iran over its nuclear program, the third leg of the tripod comprising the axis of evil, should not be discounted. Perhaps equally provocative from the North Korean viewpoint are U.S. plans to explore development of a new class of tactical nuclear weapons, the Robust Nuclear Earth Penetrator, designed to destroy hardened and underground targets: much of North Korea's artillery is located in hardened positions within mountainsides in the vicinity of the DMZ.[35] Finally, North Korea likely saw U.S.-led actions through the Korean Peninsula Energy Development Organization (KEDO) as antagonistic, particularly U.S. decisions to halt shipments of heavy fuel oil to the North in November 2002 and suspension of construction of two light water nuclear reactors in November 2003, both of which were elements integral to the 1994 Agreed Framework.

Defining the endgame and its important contributing factors helps to frame the North's thinking within the context of its engagement policies with the United States and its regional allies, it does not, however, address the question of what North Korea feels it has to gain through its brinksmanship approach with the countries of East Asia and the United States. The principal reasons are pragmatic—North Korean unpredictability should not be dismissed as "lunacy." One cannot disregard the value as a bargaining tool the anxiety a nuclearized North Korea engenders. Consider the extent to which the North Korean government has gone to present itself as a nuclear menace. In addition to the August 1998 missile that overflew Japan and landed in the Pacific Ocean, in January 2004, in an effort to convince the world it had already reprocessed 8,000 spent plutonium fuel rods necessary to develop nuclear weapons, the regime permitted a group of private citizens, among whom was Ambassador Jack Pritchard, former Special Envoy for Negotiations with North Korea, and Dr. Sig Hecker, former Director of Los Alamos, to inspect its nuclear facilities and confirm that the spent fuel rods had been removed. Added to these events of course have been those of July and October 2006. Development of a nuclear capability, or even the threat of its development, has and continues to serve as a powerful bargaining tool at the negotiating table for the regime.

Under the scenario the Bush administration has created—one in which anything short of CVID is unacceptable—the regime gains through the status quo. Kim understands the benefit of creating the air of a menacing North Korean threat and the sensitivities of the United States and its regional allies to such a threat. The ability to create uncertainty about the state of

North Korea's nuclear weapons program and its willingness to either use them or share technology remains a potent bargaining tool: the greater the uncertainty surrounding the nation's nuclear weapons program, the more attention it garners, thus raising the stakes, and providing North Korea with the ammunition it needs to extract further concessions for prospects of its cooperation. And with continued economic aid coming in from South Korea, energy assistance from China, and humanitarian assistance from the rest of the world, there is little incentive to move forward with any haste discussions of dismantling its nuclear arms program. North Korean leaders are cognizant of the fact that if they don't like the deal they are being offered by the current U.S. administration all they really have to do is wait them out, which is precisely the situation the United States finds itself in presently. The regime can then start discussions afresh with a new U.S. administration, that is, return discussions to square one under a scenario potentially more favorable to its own ends.

There is, however, one key point to remember. Nowhere within its endgame is there room for actual employment of nuclear weapons. Despite its willingness to play the nuclear card as a negotiating tool and to create crises surrounding its nuclear program, actual employment of nuclear weapons would bring about a catastrophic response from the United States and its allies, leading to the destruction of the regime and undermining the fundamental objective: its own survival. *Understanding the endgame is fundamental.* Given the foregoing, what then is the most effective way forward toward achieving resolution of this nearly two-decadelong problem?

THE CASE FOR SOLUTIONS OTHER THAN WAR (SOTW)

How best to engage the regime is an issue that still confounds governments and policymakers involved in trying to resolve the North Korean issue. Fundamentally, there are only five methods of potential engagement with the North: (1) armed conflict; (2) collapse of the regime through means other than armed conflict; (3) fuller accommodation of North Korea's position; (4) imposition of economic sanctions; or (5) some form of negotiated settlement that successfully disarms the regime's nuclear programs while recognizing its sovereignty and forcing its economy to function more normally, the process of *constructive engagement.*

Given the multifaceted threat North Korea poses, can a case be made for intervening militarily and "taking out" its growing nuclear capability? Although a simplistic review of the facts might render an affirmative conclusion, I would argue in the negative. Is North Korea's nuclear weapons program dangerous? Yes. It presents an immediate threat to South Korea and the rest of East Asia and represents a potential future threat to the broader global community of nations. Does North Korea undertake global proliferation of nuclear weapons and its related technology? Absolutely.

The regime has sold missiles to Libya, Yemen, Iraq, Egypt and Syria; it has also purchased and sold missiles and associated technology to Iran and Pakistan.[36] Does it live up to its obligations under agreements into which it enters that are designed to curb its nuclear programs? Experience tells us no. Through some combination of reinterpreting agreements for purposes of convenience and self-interest, being bound by international commitments is not a concept the regime feels compelled to follow. Consider the events surrounding the joint statement reached during the 5th round of the Six Party Talks during which the regime agreed to dismantle its nuclear weapons program, and then subsequently made that agreement conditional to receiving energy perks. Similarly, consider the example of its breach of the 1994 Agreed Framework; while promising to abandon its plutonium-based weapons program it circumvented the Agreement by pursuing a uranium-based nuclear weapons program instead. Given these conditions then, what is the likelihood of successfully concluding a negotiated settlement under which the North abandons its nuclear weapons program? Relatively slim. The regime plainly sees its future linked directly to its nuclear weapons program. Yet the question of whether a military solution is a viable option is not as black-and-white as it may superficially appear to be. A closer examination of the ramifications of militarily engaging the North leads to one inescapable conclusion—that "solutions other than war" or SOTW is the only effective means of achieving successful resolution of the North Korean nuclear issue. Here I define success as not only achieving dismantlement of the North's nuclear weapons programs, but to do so fully and permanently with little or no bloodshed, collateral damage to lives and property, or disruption of systems of government, trade, or economies in the region.

Let's consider the situation on the Korean peninsula under a scenario of conventional warfare. Recall that while North Korea maintains its right to employ nuclear weapons, it is not a policy option of which it is likely to avail itself unless it feels it has nothing to lose by using them. Consequently, the most immediate military threat the regime poses is a conventional one. Roughly 22 percent of South Korea's 48.4 million residents live in the Seoul metropolitan area, which is located approximately 50 km (approximately 31 miles) south of the DMZ. The city is roughly equally divided by the Han River into two sections: *Gangbuk*, the northern section and *Gangnam*, the southern. In the event of a conflict, over 10 million people will attempt to evacuate the environs of Seoul. Roughly half of Seoul's 10.4 million residents would need to cross bridges spanning the Han River, bridges likely high on the target list of North Korean artillery, a point to which we'll return in a moment. While Seoul boasts a modern highway system, it is not designed to handle traffic smoothly under such conditions. I recall my own experiences in Seoul during rush hour; major holiday periods are even worse. During Ch'usok, for example, Korea's Thanksgiving holiday (Harvest Moon Festival), a time when many Seoul residents return to their hometowns, traffic jams of up to 6–8 hours are not unusual. Imagine the gridlock if millions of Seoul's panic-stricken residents took to the streets of the city and highway system nearly simultaneously under a scenario of armed conflict.

Now recall the 12,000 field artillery tubes located in the vicinity of the DMZ with the capacity, for at least a few hours, of delivering up to 500,000 rounds of artillery in and around the city. Against what targets might this artillery most likely be employed? Communications nodes, military head-quarters of Combined Forces Command and U.S. Forces Korea, and of course, highways and bridges would likely be high on the target list. Once bridges are hit they would be useless and strand large numbers of residents; the entire structure doesn't need to be destroyed to render it inoperable. Those caught on highways in traffic jams would, in effect, be stationery tar-gets; hence my earlier characterization of North Korea's artillery capability as conventional WMD—their net effect would approximate that of WMD. Also recall that conventional artillery shells can be replaced with tactical nuclear shells or chemical munitions from the North's vast store of chemical agents. Airports are also likely high-value targets, although the locations of its two largest, Incheon (located on Yeongjong Island in the Yellow Sea) and Gimpo (located in far western Seoul) place them outside the effective range of North Korean field artillery. They are not, however, outside the range of North Korea's short-range ballistic missiles; and airport runways need only one or two hits to render them useless—holes in the runway, shrapnel, and other debris would ground the South Korean civilian aircraft fleet. In short, the situation on the ground would turn into pure bedlam. An additional point to consider is that, the result of a Department of Defense decision to relocate U.S. ground maneuver forces on the peninsula to a location south of Seoul, U.S. forces will be using the same roadways to get to the fight-ing that civilians will use to flee it. The sheer scale of confusion would be staggering.

Under such a scenario, one can anticipate a swift and decisive response from the traditional U.S.-ROK bilateral alliance. Given the technological superiority of U.S.-ROK forces and follow-on U.S. forces onto the peninsula, the ultimate outcome would not be in doubt, which in itself may prove problematic. Consider the situation in Iraq with a considerably less well-armed and organized adversary operating with far fewer numbers. Now consider North Korea with no center, a toppled regime. Regime change in North Korea has been considered by members of the Bush administration in the past, particularly by former Secretary of Defense Donald Rumsfeld in his now less than secret "secret memo." While in the abstract such an outcome can be spun positively, I would argue it hasn't been thought through thoroughly enough; the reality of regime change would be far less desirable than the idea of it. There would potentially be military units under the command and control of no central authority. Recall North Korea's military end strength of 1.1 million active military personnel and 7.5 million reserve and para-military units. They might be armed with nuclear or chemical weapons, or potentially a biological weapons capability—all to be used in defense of the North Korean homeland. In addition, North Korea has a significant special operations capability. U.S. and ROK intelligence estimates that North Korea has over 120,000 soldiers in its Special Operations Forces (SOF) organized into 22 light infantry brigades and 7 independent light infantry battalions.[37] Among the various missions of these military units is to open a second front in the rear areas in South Korea by undertaking such operations as destroying seaport and airport facilities, assassinating leaders, destroying command and control facilities, cutting lines of communications, and harassing military units.[38]

Further compounding this scenario are two important considerations: homogeneity of the population and the potential lack of battlefield linearity. War on the Korean peninsula adds an additional dimension of warfare in that it is war of differing ideologies among an otherwise ethnically and racially homogeneous people; Koreans have shared a common ethnicity, history, and culture for centuries, save the artificial political division of the last fifty-eight years. Homogeneity among a population makes war fighting particularly problematic, as the United States learned in Vietnam and experiences presently in Iraq. Because identity is obscured by common language and ethnicity, differentiating between adversary and friendly forces becomes difficult. So, as in the case of Iraq, unless Saddam loyalists, insurgents, or "death squads" are caught preparing for or actually attacking U.S. forces or the Iraqi people, the only way of ascertaining their presence is through the aftermath of suicide bombings, errant mortar attacks, or detonated improvised explosive devices (IED). In the case of North Korea, these complexities would be compounded significantly.

Another consideration, and one tangentially covered above, is the potential lack of linearity of the battlefield. The traditional battlefield was linear with fairly well-defined areas of operation and rear areas, on which force-on-force operations were undertaken; they were fought at the operational and tactical levels and success was measured by territory gained and controlled and damage inflicted on the adversary's fighting force, both men and equipment. Linearity of the Korean battlefield is an assumption that cannot be made. Force-on-force operations on a traditional battlefield will likely characterize initial phases of a conflict, but conditions will quickly devolve into a quagmire of non-linearity, meaning few, if any, front lines. This will become even more problematic as the United States and South Korea will be fighting an enemy who could appear anywhere armed with some of the world's most potentially devastating and destructive weapons.

This scenario has yet to take into account one of the biggest potential wild cards: China's response to such events. It is hard to conceive of circumstances under which the Chinese would long tolerate U.S. forces conducting military operations against North Korea so close to its own borders. One reason, of course, is that the United States and China remain strategic adversaries, despite the growing economic relationship between them. Second, China and North Korea remain allies, a relationship formally consummated in the 1961 Sino-North Korean Treaty of Friendship, Cooperation, and Mutual Assistance. Third, a scenario under which the United States and ROK ultimately defeat and occupy North Korea, its neighbor, is geostrategically unpalatable. Given the geostrategic relationship that exists between the United States and PRC, China would take a dim view of a U.S. presence so close to its own sovereign territory, particularly if it portends an extended U.S. presence there. Finally, China would not be prepared to accept the projected millions of North Korean refugees who would flee across its borders, a problem with which it grapples presently on a smaller scale.

The military option is messy, uncertain, promises to be protracted, for Koreans would be particularly costly, and could lead to a broader conflict if China felt compelled to somehow engage. In short, the devil that we don't know is likely to be much worse than the devil that we do. Nor is there any political will in South Korea for a Korean peninsula conflict scenario. Consider President Roh Moo Hyun's comments offered during a speech delivered to the Foreign Affairs Council of Los Angeles in November 2004: "Koreans, who haven't gotten over the trauma of the Korean War half a century ago, do not want another war on the peninsula." Public support is similarly lacking. Recall the Korea Gallup Poll conducted in August 2005 cited in an earlier chapter in which 65.9 percent of respondents indicated they would support North Korea in a war involving North Korea and the United States.

Having eliminated the military option as a viable course of action, let's consider the option of forcing regime change through means other than war, essentially speeding the regime's collapse. In the end, while achieved by other means, the end result would largely be the same as engaging North Korea militarily—a North Korea with no center, a situation I maintain is far more dangerous than the status quo. A scenario under which North Korea's central governing apparatus ceases to function as the only viable entity of command and control is a situation of uncertainty that wouldn't be tolerated by Kim Jong Il, the KWP, or the country's military structure, likely leading to imposition of emergency measures, as it might in most countries. In North Korea's case, however, because the regime rules with absolute power, it would likely lead to the National Defense Commission, with Kim Jong Il as its executive head and functioning as a top organ of the state, declaring a state of emergency and mobilizing the military in order to regain control—by whatever means necessary. Outside interference at such a juncture could elicit a desperate response from the North Korean regime; if they feel there is nothing to lose, then all options are on the table— conventional warfare or employment of WMD. Strangely, given the current domestic political conditions in North Korea, the regime of Kim Jong Il offers the greatest relative potential for stability. Change must be initiated and carried out from within.

An important point should be borne in mind when considering regime change under conditions other than war: it would be naïve to assume that once the KWP no longer exercised control over the population that North Koreans would readily flock to the concept of democracy or the purveyors of such a foreign notion, particularly the United States. As North Koreans have lived their lives with near daily propaganda demonizing the United States and all it stands for, it is unlikely they would embrace the United States with open arms; rest assured, U.S. forces will not be greeted as liberators.

It is difficult to envision how the international community might achieve greater accommodation of the North Korean position short of total capitulation to North Korean demands. Despite its history of broken commitments, refusals to engage in dialogue through the Six Party Talks venue and a continued global, regional, and peninsular threat posture, humanitarian and energy assistance has continued to flow into the country, although assistance through the WFP has stopped as of January 1, 2006, at the regime's own insistence. For example, in 2005, according to WFP statistics, North Korea received nearly 1.08 million tons in food aid and other assistance from the international community.[39] To put this in some perspective, only Ethiopia received more assistance with nearly 1.1 million tons.[40] If considered over the ten-year period 1996–2005, North Korea represented the world's basket case. It received over 10.1 million tons of assistance during the period, the most of any recipient nation in the world, eclipsing even Ethiopia, which received roughly 9.3 million tons.[41]

By far China and South Korea have been the largest donors of this vast infusion of assistance. It portends both a greater shift in South Korean sentiment for rapprochement with North Korea and closer South Korean policy alignment with China since the installation of the Roh administration. South Korea and China, for example, in 2005 provided 392,743 tons and 531,416 tons of cereal (in grain equivalent) in humanitarian assistance to North Korea, respectively, which in the case of South Korea amounted to 99 percent of its total assistance offered worldwide; for China it represented 93 percent.[42] (It should be noted that some of this support was direct in nature, that is, it was not provided through the UN World Food Program.)

These figures become particularly significant when one considers the high degree of fungibility of such assistance. To what extent this has occurred is uncertain, however, anecdotal accounts from North Korean refugees would seem to indicate that at least some amount of the humanitarian assistance extended to North Korea has been transshipped to military units and political elites, the former to help sustain its defense posture and the latter for purposes of profit. Lack of transparency and a viable mechanism for tracking distribution of assistance have thwarted efforts to effectively

mitigate the fungibility potential of such assistance. Fungibility of food occurs in other forms as well, which while not directly involving redistribution
of humanitarian aid, ultimately undermines the efforts of aid agencies to
alleviate chronic food shortage conditions. As John Powell, Asia regional director for the WFP testified to the U.S. Congressional International Relations
Committee (Subcommittee on East Asia and the Pacific) in a May 2, 2002,
hearing: "The Army takes what it wants from the national harvest up front,
in full. And it takes it in the form of food Koreans prefer, Korean rice. The
food that WFP provides is overwhelmingly maize or wheat...commodities
not preferred by those in power."

The energy assistance being provided by China to North Korea tells a
similar story. The 1994 Agreed Framework provided North Korea, in return
for freezing its nuclear program, energy inducements including construction
of two light water nuclear reactors and 500,000 tons of heavy fuel oil
annually until construction of the first reactor was completed; the United
States and EU shared the cost of heavy fuel oil shipments, with the U.S.
obligation amounting to over 75 percent of the total. North Korea's October
2002 admission that it was pursuing a highly enriched uranium program
led to the suspension of heavy fuel oil shipments in November 2002. This
was ostensibly a tactic to bring North Korea back into compliance with
its obligations under the Agreement. If the administration's idea was to
impose de facto sanctions, any impact they might have had were quickly
mitigated by Chinese intervention. Since 2002, China has become North
Korea's primary provider of energy assistance, with coal and oil shipments
nearly doubling to over $200 million by 2004.[43]

The North Korean regime links the country's economic and ideological prosperity to its own political survival, which it, in turn, perceives is
safeguarded through maintaining a strong military and nuclear weapons
arsenal. Consequently, efforts to directly negotiate away what it sees as
a security guarantee will likely remain fruitless. Yet, the regime's proven
vulnerability remains its economic instability and lack of fiscal resources.
Consider the lengths, for example, to which the regime went to engage in
direct negotiations with the United States over its assets frozen in a Macau
bank in November 2005. The United States remained steadfast in its position that no discussions would take place on this issue outside of the Six
Party Talks. Some analysts have directly linked the July missile launch with
North Korea's attempt to up the ante and force the United States to engage
in discussions that would lead to a political solution over its frozen assets.[44]
Russian diplomats took this assessment a step further, noting Kim's "irrita-
tion" at the financial sanctions and citing this as the reason for the regime's
underground nuclear test.[45] The point is that the Bush administration clearly
hit the regime where it hurt—financially—and it is from this point that the
administration should seek to exploit the regime's weakness and gain the

upper hand in negotiations over its nuclear weapons program. Not by directly linking the issues, but rather through long-term strategic economic engagement, although the process will not be quick.

There are two means for undertaking economic engagement in pursuit of nuclear dismantlement: through economic sanctions or by broader active economic engagement. For reasons cited earlier, I believe that instituting a regime of sanctions will not only be ineffective, but counterproductive. I do maintain, however, that the use of asymmetric economic statecraft can begin to lay the foundations for change in North Korea.

Before discussing the efficacies of AES, however, it might be useful to first provide some context for North Korea's lingering economic maladies.

7

North Korean Economic Policy: A Blueprint for Failure

> People living in the cities are always better off than those from the countryside. In the city, they can always manage to beg. In the countryside, there is nothing but the grass for the rabbits.
>
> —North Korean refugee explaining the dire conditions in North Korea

The foundations of North Korea's economic meltdown were laid decades before actual manifestation of its poor policy decisions and can be linked to structural impediments created by the regime as well as diplomatic setbacks: (1) state ownership and intensive control of the means of production, to include agriculture; (2) a less than efficient means for ensuring distribution of goods and food within its command economy; (3) development of an input-intensive agricultural sector; and (4) socialist bloc nations' abandonment of their respective command economic structures in favor of economic models embracing greater capitalization and marketization, which in the end isolated North Korea.

Beginning as early as the 1960s, the regime sought to modernize its agricultural base, which had been collectivized in the wake of the Korean War because of security concerns; providing sufficient domestically produced food for its military became a key security component.[1] Modernization of agriculture focused on, among other measures, extensive use of chemical fertilizers and mechanization. Modernization also sought a shift toward higher yield crops, for example maize, in lieu of traditional farming.[2] The yield of such crops could be increased by extensive use of fertilizers and mechanical inputs. So for a time, the policy worked, but it was instituted without regard for long-term ramifications. Over time, overuse of the soil led to depletion of its nutrients.[3] These circumstances, combined with the buildup of chemical fertilizers in the soil made the land unsuitable for farming and actually led to reduced crop yields. This forced farmers to look for new land to cultivate, the solution to which was farming hillsides. In order to do so, of course, farmers were forced to clear the hillsides of natural vegetation and foliage.[4, 5] The unintended result was that this now made the land more susceptible to flooding during conditions of heavy rain, a contributing factor to the extensive damage produced by the floods of 1995 and 1996. For example, the 1995 floods, which occurred in July and August, laid waste nearly 400,000 hectares (988,422 acres) of land, displaced nearly 500,000 people, and resulted in grain loss amounting to nearly two million tons.[6] The floods of July 1996 were less devastating, but occurred in the comparatively agriculturally rich southern region, further amplifying the flood effects of the previous year.[7]

A by-product of denuding hillsides of vegetation is the run-off of soil and rocks that is induced, which can be deposited in nearby rivers, ultimately exacerbating flood and drought effects.[8] As rivers become shallower because of increased soil and rock levels they, of course, are able to hold less water and tend to flood more easily. Conversely, drought conditions are amplified because of reduced water levels, as was the case during the 1997 and 2001 droughts.

The impact of a shrinking agricultural base was exacerbated in the early 1990s by both diplomatic developments and a less than efficient internal distribution system, all of which coalesced into a perfect storm of economic disaster during 1995–1996; 1995 was the first year during which North Korea received external humanitarian assistance. As noted earlier, under its policy of *Nordpolitik*, South Korea made overtures to socialist bloc nations, which ultimately succeeded in bringing about rapprochement. In the zero-sum game of geopolitics, this amounted to a commensurate loss in status and material support for North Korea. None would be so devastating, however, as the loss of Soviet support. Recall that because of its flagging economy, the Soviets, under Gorbachev, sought to reform economic and foreign policies, which included requiring immediate payment from the regime for goods provided. The regime, of course, was in no position to pay for the goods and services it received. Soviet reforms also led to rapprochement with South Korea, essential because of the potential economic assistance South Korea could provide. This shift away from a northern-centered policy to one focused on South Korea led to significant material loss for the regime. For example, Soviet exports to North Korea were worth $1.97 billion (U.S.) in 1990. By 1991, a year after normalization of Soviet-South Korean ties, Soviet exports to North Korea had fallen to $580 million (U.S.).[9] And by 1994, Soviet exports had dropped precipitously to a mere

$140 million (U.S.), which comprised only 6.6 percent of all North Korean trade.[10] Perhaps symptomatic of the impact that the loss of Soviet assistance had domestically was the regime's initiation of the "let's eat only two meals a day" campaign launched in 1991.[11]

Chinese intervention helped to buffer the impact of decreasing Soviet support for a time, but proved to be only a temporary reprieve. In 1993, China provided nearly 77 percent of fuel imports and 68 percent of food imports into North Korea.[12] North Korea's total trade that year with China amounted to approximately $900 million (U.S.).[13]

A combination of the regime's inability to pay for goods in currency and confronting its own reduced crop yields in Northeastern China, however, led the Chinese to reduce their support the following year. By 1994, total trade with China dropped nearly 31 percent to $624 million (U.S.).[14] While China remained North Korea's leading trading partner it proved insufficient at buoying a sinking North Korean economy.

A failing agricultural sector along with significantly decreased assistance from its historic communist benefactors led, in turn, to breakdowns in North Korea's Public Distribution System (PDS), the means through which food, at least theoretically, is distributed to the whole of the North Korean citizenry. In practice, however, the PDS has more resembled a tool for doling out political rewards and ensuring the obedience of the population. The regime pursues a policy of "ideological cleansing" within Pyongyang and other large cities—only those citizens considered to be the strongest ideological supporters of the regime are permitted to reside there; others are forced into the countryside. The PDS favors Pyongyang residents as they are the first to receive food distributions; during times of shortage this means there may be little or nothing distributed to other parts of the country. As a means of controlling the population, food distribution, when it takes place, is typically undertaken in work or other local areas, thus forcing North Koreans to remain in one location. The conditions over the past decade, however, have been anything but ideal causing breakdowns in the PDS. Consider the anecdotal accounts provided in a May 2002 U.S. Congressional report compiled by the Subcommittee on East Asia and the Pacific through accounts of North Korean refugees:

> "Since 1995 I have only received food from PDS once or twice a year for Kim Jong Il's and Kim Il Sung's birthday."

> "We just receive food from PDS for anniversaries in January 1, February 16, and April 15, a ration for 3 days."

> "...And the government announced to citizens that no more food would be provided so they should not expect anything from the government and that everybody had to manage their life by themselves."

Breakdown of the PDS forced North Korean citizens to indeed fend for themselves, leading to increased mobility as they moved around the countryside in search of food; it has also supported the introduction of grain sales in marketplaces. Abandoned for a time, the regime reinvigorated the PDS in late 2005 most likely to reassert its control over the population and to curb growing market sales of grain. How successful it will be in distributing food and supporting the basic needs of North Koreans, however, remains to be seen.

Within this otherwise bleak economic assessment exists a strategic gap through which AES might be applied. Areas holding the greatest promise are light and heavy industries and agriculture. Working in collaboration with other regional powers, the United States is in a position to lead a coalition of nations in developing key North Korean nonmilitary nonnuclear industries in such a way as to increase Pyongyang's dependence on external economic inputs that, in turn, might be used to gain greater leverage over the regime and ameliorate its intransigence regarding its nuclear weapons and ballistic missile programs. Any strategy involving AES, however, must be carefully managed in order to avoid unintentionally increasing the regime's military capabilities through improvement of dual-use technologies—that is those technologies that might also be used for military purposes. This is a particular imperative given the regime's commitment to securing access to foreign science and technology.[15]

8

The Economics of Nuclear Dismantlement

[Sanctions have become] the lazy man's foreign policy, viewed as an instant and painless way of advancing US interests.
—Franklin L. Lavin, "Asphyxiation or Oxygen? The Sanctions Dilemma" (Foreign Policy, No. 104, Autumn 1996)

Since the early 1990s, the United States and its allies have attempted to compel North Korea, through various means, to abandon its nuclear weapons program. To this end, the use of economic statecraft—the threat of sanctions or promise of economic inducement—has figured prominently. That such an approach should form the nexus of U.S. policy efforts makes sense given the precarious state of the North Korean economy. Where the United States has come up short is in developing and executing a strategic policy, specifically in four key ways. First has been the tendency to compartmentalize the problem of the regime's nuclear weapons program, approaching it as a negotiable stand-alone issue. As discussed in earlier chapters, the North Korean philosophy of *Juche* and the regime's world view simply do not allow for such quid pro quo arrangements: developing and maintaining a credible nuclear threat lies at the heart of its very existence and it is unlikely that the regime will obligingly negotiate away what it perceives as its only, and to date rather successful, geopolitical playing card. Issues with the regime's nuclear weapons program should be viewed as part of a larger whole that requires a comprehensive approach in order to achieve resolution.

The second way in which U.S. government policy has come up short is in its demonstrated lack of understanding of the North Korean mindset, which can likely be linked to the moral reprehensibility with which the administration views any dealings with "rogue" regimes. Given the opacity surrounding North Korea's activities and motives, predicting its behavior is a nearly impossible task. In fact, I would argue that the regime regards its "unpredictability" as one of its more potent negotiating tactics. Yet in creating a workable North Korea policy, there is still a good deal of information that can be gleaned from thoughtful analysis of the regime's history and a fuller understanding of the principles it propounds under the *Juche* philosophy. More than a rudimentary understanding of North Korea's history, for example, might have led the administration to reassess the priority it places on China's involvement in negotiations with the North and scale back its expectations of what China can actually deliver. History has demonstrated that neither China nor the former Soviet Union was ever particularly successful in exercising full veto power over North Korean actions.

Another way in which the United States has undercut its own efforts is through past humanitarian assistance to the regime. The basis for providing such assistance was both well-intentioned and humane. Reality, however, requires a blunt assessment of the facts on the ground. With little transparency in how food aid was actually distributed once it arrived in-country, the United States and the world community had no guarantees that such assistance was not being siphoned off to the military or political elites. In fact, anecdotal evidence indicates as much.[1] And as all food aid was transshipped through government controlled facilities, there is good chance that only a small handful of North Koreans, that is, the regime's leadership, ever actually knew from where the food had actually originated, eliminating any chance the United States might garner any residual "good will" with the North Korean population. Consequently, the situation devolved into helping to bankroll a global nuclear threat—feeding the very regime the world seeks to disarm, while the regime was able to use its meager resources to purchase or develop military arms.[2]

Finally, history shows us policies that center on economic sanctions as the primary means for forcing behavior modification in states have largely been unsuccessful. In this regard, North Korea is no exception. Unilateral sanctions imposed by the United States are perhaps symbolically important, but rather meaningless in substance given the level of economic support South Korea and China provide to the regime.

Despite its history of misapplication and often disappointing results, I maintain that the means for moving discussions forward on North Korea's nuclear dismantlement is indeed through some application of economic statecraft. Rather than using economic statecraft as a supporting policy tool within a broader arms control regime or nuclear dismantlement agreement, the focus should be on compelling North Korea to function as a "normal nation" by forcing it to make rational economic decisions about redirecting its few resources away from its nuclear weapons program and into the larger economy. Strengthening economic links to the broader global community of nations, particularly western nations, is one means of achieving this end.

Broader economic engagement on the part of an economically fragile North Korea could in fact spur greater economic dependence. Greater economic dependence on western nations that control the economic means—capital infusion; business links; western manufacturing methodologies—in turn leads to greater exposure to such broader concepts as individual rights, freedoms, and more open societies, at least then laying the beginning foundations for change from within; not revolutionary change, but rather evolutionary progress. The term "asymmetric economic statecraft" best describes this concept: purposefully infusing economic assistance into the North Korean economy with the goal of compelling it to make rational decisions regarding its economy while deliberately increasing regime dependence on western economies and slowly eroding the KWP's absolute commitment to the *Juche* philosophy. Admittedly, this approach does not afford a "quick win" for any single U.S. administration. It is a long-term comprehensive commitment to fundamentally bringing about change in North Korea that reduces its global threat posture. It will require a multilateral effort on the part of the international community, but given the priority North Korea places on improved relations with the United States, it is the United States that would need to galvanize and lead such an effort. This, of course, would demand a good deal of discussion with allies and geostrategic competitors to ensure all are in agreement and compliance. But such an effort would allow the international community to move away from the band-aid approach to the regime's nuclear program while addressing the underlying issues of why North Korea remains a global nuclear threat and to do so within the broader SOTW framework. The present policy of isolating the regime as an international pariah while simultaneously trying to negotiate CVID of its nuclear weapons program has proven, at best, less than fruitful.

Consideration of any such scenario requires calculation of the potential implications of the *Juche* ideology. Application of an AES construct within a *Juche* paradigm is not impossible, but it will be challenging. How the regime is engaged is fundamental to any success. North Korea can be expected to try and stonewall discussions and generally find points of disagreement. Given domestic trends indicating willingness to experiment with alternative economic models and the indications of pragmatism in its position (discussed later in this chapter), however, AES has the potential to work. This approach has the added benefit of comporting, to a greater degree, with Chinese and South Korean engagement policies, which then removes existing fissures in the Six Party Talks framework and potentially brings more pressure to bear on North Korea. (Historically, North Korea has gained greater relative strength by dividing its adversaries and then playing them off each other.)

Again, I would remind critics of a constructive engagement policy approach with the regime of what the CVID "policy" has netted the global community of nations: a good deal of frustration; disappointment; and in the end, the world's newest nuclear power.

THE EFFICACY OF ECONOMIC SANCTIONS

It might be useful to start by providing a simple definition of what is considered an economic sanction. A sanction is action(s) taken by a state or states, either unilaterally or multilaterally, using economic or financial deprivation to impose hardship on a target state or states. Such action is employed to bring about a desired political end or to deny the target nation the resources necessary to carry out its will, for example, by weakening its military posture. Sanctions can be used as either stand-alone implements or as part of a gradual policy of increased response, which could ultimately lead to the use of force should the situation demand it.

Both the term and concept of economic sanctions more fully entered the lexicon of international politics with the end of the Cold War.[3] Consider, for example, that of the 16 nations against which the UN has imposed Chapter VII sanctions, only two—Southern Rhodesia (1966); South Africa (1977)—were the target of sanctions during the Cold War; the other 14 countries have had sanctions imposed on them since 1990.[4,5] One factor that contributed to the growth in popularity of sanctions is that the close of the Cold War brought with it a gradual shift in conceptualizing the traditional security paradigm. Nations began to exhibit greater concern over a wider range of activities they considered to be security threats—undesired and uncontrolled Diaspora; foreign governments providing sanctuary to international terrorists; sale and transfer of arms; the spread of nuclear weapons technology; human rights violations on massive scales; and other events.[6] It would, of course, be both imprudent and impractical to employ the use of force in all of these cases—some events simply do not rise to the level of concern that would demand a forceful response. Trying to do so would deplete a nation's resources and potentially result in domestic economic and political blowback; and public support for the use of force under an expanded paradigm of ensuring security is not without its limits.

Another contributing factor to the popularity of sanctions as a means for achieving political ends is expediency. First, they are relatively inexpensive. Second, the most costly aspect is the creation and maintenance of the necessary infrastructure to monitor compliance. Compare this to the potential cost of sending military forces abroad and maintaining long logistics chains to sustain their activities. For example, current estimates of the monthly cost the United States bears for its operations in Iraq range between $5 billion and $8 billion (U.S.).[7] Third, sanctions are a quick and easy means of demonstrating a government's proactive posture against the actions of the target state with relatively little effort.[8] Additionally, imposing sanctions, particularly in cases where they are meant to address egregious behavior, requires little, if any, new policy development, which greatly reduces the possibility of partisan wrangling in Washington. Finally, as Robert Pape points out in his article, "*Why Economic Sanctions Do Not Work*," sanctions have also come to be seen as a viable alternative to war within the liberal camp; cited as its chief advantage is their ability to successfully coerce target nations while remaining more humane in the process.

Despite such arguments, there is justification for questioning the efficacy of sanctions. Conceptually, a strong case can be made for them; practically speaking there are major drawbacks, most particularly in enforcement. Even in the best case scenario, under UN-backed multilateral sanctions regimes, enforcement presents major challenges. Consider, for example, the difficulty of trying to secure a country's borders on all sides in order to keep out restricted items; key border crossings can be secured, but it is unlikely that any nation's borders can be completely blocked.[9] Another concern is that the target state might well use the imposition of sanctions as a way of rallying nationalistic feelings among its population against the nations imposing sanctions. Short of armed conflict, there is little that lends itself more to the "we-they" paradigm than unwanted and harmful external influence. Consider the domestic effects in Iran of threatened UN sanctions for its pursuit of a nuclear technology capability. Throughout the summer of 2006, the rhetoric remained heated as Iran refused to comply with UN deadlines and undertook massive military exercises to demonstrate its ability to defend itself. Iranian citizens, while divided on Iran's confrontation with the world community, have generally rallied around the government and President Ahmadinejad in what is widely seen as Iran standing up to western intimidation.[10]

Then there is the real possibility of targeted countries finding ways of circumventing sanctions regimes. Consider the oil-for-food program instituted by the UN in Iraq, the largest humanitarian effort ever undertaken by the UN. The UN imposed a comprehensive sanctions regime on Iraq after it invaded Kuwait in 1990. As a result of the sanctions, the Iraqi citizenry suffered serious shortages of food and medicine. In response, the UN created the oil-for-food program in 1995, which was designed to provide relief for Iraq's citizens by allowing the government to sell some of its oil on the world market in exchange for needed humanitarian assistance, namely medicine and food.[11] When the program finally ended in 2003, it did so amid wide allegations of corruption and fraud. What was ultimately discovered, amongst other things, was that Saddam Hussein's regime had obtained over $21 billion (U.S.) in illicit revenues during 1991–2003; the regime had engaged in oil smuggling; and it provided kickbacks to UN officials.[12] Left in place long enough, targeted nations will likely find work-arounds to sanctions.

The 1990 comprehensive sanctions the UN imposed on Iraq point to another shortcoming in such an approach—there is no way to target sanctions in order to control their impact; they tend to produce mass economic casualties because they are shotgun blasts rather than surgical economic implements.[13] In the foregoing example, while the intent was to deprive the Hussein regime of oil profits, it was in fact ordinary Iraqi citizens who suffered the most as a result of the sanctions. North Korea represents another classic case in point; the lifestyle within the upper echelons of the regime hardly compares with the deprivation suffered by the North Korean citizenry. The elite of most societies typically find ways of insulating themselves from the impact of sanctions regimes, while ordinary citizens, lacking similar means to do so, bear the brunt of their impact. Financial sanctions, on the other hand, have a better track record. Imposing freezes on assets, bank accounts, travel restrictions, and similar measures are more surgical in nature.[14] The major drawback is that few nations, with the exception of the United States, have developed the complicated infrastructure to identify and track assets effectively enough to impose meaningful controls on them.

The strength of a targeted nation's foreign relations can also potentially impact the effectiveness of sanctions; the greater number of countries with which a potentially targeted nation maintains friendly relations, the more difficult it becomes to effectively impose and maintain a sanctions regime. Returning to the example of Iraq, the Hussein regime was successful in establishing a circle of 66 UN member nations from which it received kickbacks in return for awarding them contracts to provide humanitarian assistance under the oil-for-food program.[15] North Korea and its 2006 missile testing provides another example. The UN Security Council, without the unanimous support of all five permanent members, was powerless to impose sanctions on North Korea; China and Russia remained the holdouts. And the effects of any sanctions that might be imposed by the United States or Japan as a result of UN failure to do so are mitigated by economic support offered through China and South Korea.

Finally, the relative weight of a country's statecraft implements can also assist in circumventing efforts to impose a successful sanctions regime against it. Consider U.S. efforts to impose sanctions on Iran as a result of its failure to abandon what the United States claims is a growing nuclear weapons program. China has thus far been lukewarm to such action because of its growing appetite for Iranian oil. For example, China signed two agreements with Iran to import massive amounts of oil over the next twenty-five years— 360 million tons.[16] And with China's voracious appetite for petroleum, similar arrangements can be anticipated in the future. It is not in a position to have the flow of its oil supply disrupted. Similarly, nearly 30 percent of the European Union's trade is with Iran, a disruption of which would likely have a significant impact on the EU; hence, France's reluctance as well to pursue a sanctions regime.[17]

This then leads to the question of just how successful, empirically speaking, sanctions have been historically. In a study undertaken by Gary Hufbauer, Jeffrey Schott, and Kimberly Ann Elliot, largely regarded as the bellwether standard for research on the topic of international sanctions, they identified 115 cases where sanctions were imposed during the years 1914–1990. Using this body of cases, they concluded that 34 percent, or forty sanctions regimes had actually been successfully implemented during the period. This equates to success in just one of every three cases.[18] In independent research undertaken by Robert Pape, published in *International Security* in his article entitled, "Why Economic Sanctions Do Not Work," he challenges these findings and offers an even less optimistic assessment. According to his analysis, Pape concluded that in only five of the cases studied by Hufbauer, Schott, and Elliot, a scant 4 percent, could it be concluded that sanctions had actually been successful in bringing about the desired political change. He defined success using three possible criteria: (1) the targeted nation fulfilled the demands of the sanctions-imposing nation; (2) threatened or actual sanctions were applied before the target nation modified its behavior; or (3) no other circumstances explain the modification of behavior in the target state.[19] He eliminated 35 of the previously cited "successful" cases, finding they had actually been resolved through the use of force (18); the demanded political changes never occurred (8); some did not qualify as sanctions (6); or the circumstances were too uncertain to definitively conclude their outcome (3).[20]

This is not to say, however, that sanctions do not have a potential role in the arsenal of tools a nation(s) can use to compel the compliance of other nations. It requires a well-coordinated, long-term commitment and strategy that minimizes target country "work-arounds" and limits the potential political and economic blowback within the target nation.

What case then can be made for the use of economic inducements as a behavior modification tool in international politics? Their effectiveness must be measured under two sets of differing conditions: (1) when employed with nations predisposed to supporting a certain set of policy positions; and (2) when they are used as implements to modify behavior. Using the U.S. experience, an argument can be made that inducements can serve as effective reinforcing implements among nations predisposed to supporting various U.S. policy positions. The United States used such inducements under the Marshall Plan, which was designed to facilitate the reconstruction of Europe after WWII.[21] Also consider the success the United States has had in maintaining support for its global war on terror by directly linking foreign aid to its security priorities since 2002. Aid to Pakistan, for example, a major partner in the global war on terror, jumped considerably during 2001–2004: Pakistan received $275 million (U.S.) in 2004, an increase of over

166 percent over the 2001 figure of $1.7 million.[22] While the percentage increase for Pakistan is illustrative of what inducements can accomplish in the way of maintaining support, U.S. aid figures to Pakistan pale in comparison to its efforts in maintaining a coalition of the willing among other nations. Israel is another major recipient of aid, receiving $3 billion (U.S.) annually which equates to roughly $500 in security for every Israeli citizen.[23] Again, the distinguishing feature of these recipients is their willingness to work cooperatively with the United States and recognition of the intersecting self-interests they share. Can a similar case be made, however, for the success of such measures between nations that have not historically shared friendly relations? Using the examples of South Korea's *Nordpolitik* and Germany's *Ostpolitik*, a reasonable argument can be made for the effectiveness of inducements in bringing about desired political change.

Nordpolitik

The political success of Seoul's *Nordpolitik* policy of engaging socialist nations was detailed in an earlier chapter so will only be summarized here. Seoul successfully ameliorated the antagonistic relationship that had existed between itself and the communist bloc of nations that for decades supported North Korea's vision of a unified Korea under communist leadership. The political success *Nordpolitik* enjoyed, however, was clearly linked to economic circumstances: South Korea's growing economic clout and the flagging economic conditions within the socialist bloc of nations. Consider the case of the former Soviet Union. Gorbachev's new policy initiatives under *perestroika* and *novoe myshlenie* were an open recognition that new ideas about economic development and how such development should be pursued was needed in order to resolve the Soviet economic crisis. This new recognition included a willingness to pursue dialogue and expanded economic relations with past ideological adversaries. South Korea was an ideal partner for the Soviets because the types of economic infusions it sought—direct investment, joint ventures, and trade—Seoul was able to provide and the proximity of the two countries made an economic partnership attractive.

On the promise of expanded economic relations, which included establishing reciprocal trade offices in 1989, movement toward official diplomatic recognition was facilitated; Seoul and Moscow established reciprocal consulates in early 1990. Official rapprochement, in turn, achieved on September 30, 1990, led to expanded economic activity between Seoul and Moscow. For example, the total value of Soviet imports and exports with South Korea amounted to $48 million (U.S.) in 1983 and was indirectly undertaken through third country ports like Hong Kong, Japan, and Singapore.[24] By 1990, the figure had increased to $889 million (U.S.) and trade was being directly undertaken through ports at Vladivostok and Pusan.[25] By 1991, Seoul had agreed to provide Moscow $3 billion (U.S.)

in loans, half of which was designated for the purchase of South Korean manufactured consumer goods.

In return for this much-needed infusion of capital, the Soviets: (1) agreed to support South Korean admission into the UN in opposition to North Korea's position against such action (ultimately both Koreas were admitted simultaneously on September 17, 1991); (2) cast aside their long-standing support for a unified Korean peninsula under communist leadership and became the first major power to recognize the existence of two Koreas; (3) permitted over 36,000 ethnic Koreans who had resided on Sakhalin Island since the 1930s to visit or relocate to South Korea; and (4) issued an apology for the 1983 downing of a Korean Airlines civilian aircraft.[26,27] These were the tangible returns for South Korean economic inducements. The intangibles were perhaps even more significant. Most notable was the shift in Soviet-North Korean relations, a major contributing factor to which was North Korea's historical intransigence over any official recognition of South Korea. Pyongyang's long-standing contention that it represented the only legitimate government on the peninsula created conditions of mutual exclusivity—recognition of one Korea necessarily meant nonrecognition of the other. Thus, Soviet-South Korean rapprochement signaled an end to a long-standing Cold War and ideological relationship and augured a more "normal" relationship between Moscow and Pyongyang.

Despite any successes Seoul might have been able to point to under *Nordpolitik*, the policy was not without its critics. Ironically, the criticisms of this policy approach mirror those of the later Sunshine policy and Seoul's current engagement approach with the North Korean regime—long on give-aways, but short on demands for reciprocity. Critics contended that, if anything, South Korea did not demand enough in return for its $3 billion loan package to the Soviet Union, particularly as it suffered a current account deficit of $2 billion in 1990.[28] High on the list of criticisms was the failure of the Soviets to explicitly renounce Pyongyang's continued posture of hostility toward Seoul. Also criticized was Moscow's continued call for removal of the U.S. military presence from the peninsula, something North Korea had demanded for decades. In the end, however, Seoul's *Nordpolitik* helped to reshape the Cold War landscape by redefining its relationships with socialist bloc nations, further isolating North Korea; achieving rapprochement with both the Soviet Union and China, historically North Korea's main benefactors; and contributing to the reduction of regional tensions among the countries of East Asia.

Ostpolitik

Ostpolitik was to West German foreign policy what *Nordpolitik* was to South Korean external political policies. Ushered in under the chancellorship of Willy Brandt (October 1969–May 1974), *Ostpolitik* provided a new orientation for West Germany—from one that focused nearly exclusively on its relationships with the West to a policy that also sought rapprochement with eastern bloc nations. *Ostpolitik* represented repudiation of the Hallstein Doctrine, which had served as the nexus of West German foreign policy since about 1955. The Doctrine essentially demanded that any nation seeking official recognition by West Germany not recognize East Germany as a separate and sovereign nation.[29]

Although South Korea's *Nordpolitik* was implemented nearly two decades after West Germany's *Ostpolitik*, they shared important similarities. First, both policies relied on extensive use of economic inducements to facilitate political rapprochement with adversaries; both saw economic means as the road toward achieving greater political ends. Second, both policies represented gradual shifts in broader domestic priorities with regard to reunification. Each moved from positions that demanded recognition of their respective government's rights to exercise sovereignty over both halves of their divided nations, which had been a precondition to any further political linkages, to policies that prioritized gradual rapprochement as the road toward reunification. The criticisms of each policy were also similar. Both domestically and internationally, Brandt and Roh were chided for not demanding enough of a quid pro quo for their efforts to establish better relations with socialist nations. Finally, both policies were successful in their expressed goal of achieving rapprochement with the socialist bloc. Although neither achieved them overnight, *Ostpolitik* took longer as it was undertaken during the height of Cold War tensions and *Nordpolitik* during its twilight.

Ostpolitik employed economic inducements in two ways. In some cases they were used to generally promote goodwill with eastern bloc nations; there was no specific quid pro quo that was sought. Conversely, in some instances the economic inducements were linked to specific political actions recipient nations had to fulfill. Brandt launched his new program of engagement with the eastern bloc by signing the NPT (November 1969), an issue that had been controversial in domestic West German politics for years. He then further extended the proverbial olive branch by offering economic inducements to facilitate better relations between West Germany and the eastern bloc nations, a move that played to their Achilles heel. The attitude of eastern bloc nations was aptly summed up by an East German official who pointed out, "... the Federal Republic's economy is booming and ... rolling in money."[30] The conditions that prevailed in West Germany, of course, were a stark contrast to what most of the eastern bloc nations were experiencing under their command economies. Brandt provided, for example, a $550-million (U.S.) credit arrangement to Poland to help underwrite the purchase of West German equipment over a five-year period.[31] *Ostpolitik* also provided for expanded trade ties with East Germany; by 1969, West Germany was East Germany's second largest trading partner behind the

Soviet Union. Trade figures for 1969, for example, were at approximately 1 billion (DM).[32] Commercial ties expanded as well under the West's new policy orientation. The East German government had trucked in from West Berlin rubble left behind from the destruction caused during WWII, which was used in land reclamation projects; the East German government received $0.17 per cubic yard of rubble.[33] East Germany was permitted to export milk and other food items to West Berlin and West Berlin contractors were also used to help rebuild the city center in East Berlin. Thousands of West Berlin workers—contractors, architects, doctors, and nurses—commuted across the border to work in East Berlin.[34]

Nor were the Soviets immune from the attraction of expanded commercial ties with West Germany. On the eve of the historic signing of the Soviet-West German renunciation of force agreement, it was announced that a West German bank consortium had offered $327 million (U.S.) in credits to the Soviets to help finance the purchase of natural gas pipes in order to build a pipeline through Eastern Europe.[35, 36]

The détente achieved under *Ostpolitik* did not end with the Moscow Treaty. Several other important treaties emerged as a result of improved relations between West Germany and the eastern bloc: the Treaty of Warsaw (December 1970), which provided for mutual renunciation of war between Bonn and Warsaw and West German recognition of the Oder-Neisse line as the border between the two countries; the Four Power Agreement on Berlin (September 1971) regularized trade and travel between West Germany and West Berlin; and the Basic Treaty (December 1972), which asserted the sovereignty of East Germany and West Germany and provided for peaceful relations between them. These agreements, while leaving many complicated issues of a divided European continent unresolved, went a long way toward improving security and stability in the region and laid the necessary groundwork for expanded future engagement.

The West German policy of linking economic inducements to improved political relations continued through the country's ultimate reunification. In October 1988, for example, a consortium of West German banks helped bankroll Gorbachev's reform programs by providing a credit line worth $1.6 billion (U.S.), which was to be used by the Soviets to modernize its food and consumer industries. This figure represented the largest extension of credit by a western nation to the Soviets up to that point, although this figure would be eclipsed two years later.[37] While not officially backed by the West German government, it was clearly endorsed by it as Helmut Kohl and Gorbachev conducted a public signing ceremony for the occasion. The value of Bonn's continued economic statecraft became more apparent in 1990 in the period leading up to German reunification, during which West German Chancellor Helmut Kohl agreed to provide the Soviet Union $3 billion (U.S.) (5 billion DM) for financing Gorbachev's reforms in exchange for Soviet support of German reunification efforts. In contrast to the 1988 extension of credit, which can be seen as a broader effort at rapprochement, this represented for the West Germans the ultimate quid pro quo.

It took precisely twenty-one years for the West Germans to achieve their goal of reunification: from Willy Brandt's introduction of his *Ostpolitik* policy in October 1969 until reunification in October 1990. The process was neither quick nor easy and was fraught with a good deal of frustration and criticism along the way. In the final analysis, it was the conflation of several circumstances that led to reunification: poor economic conditions within the Soviet Bloc; Gorbachev's reforms; Poland and Hungary's internal political reforms; and the ousting of longtime German leader Eric Honecker and his cabinet in favor of more moderate leadership. But constructive engagement played an important contributing role in paving the way toward German reunification, helping to slowly erode Cold War barriers. South Korea's *Nordpolitik* was similarly evolutionary in its character, achieving rapprochement with socialist bloc nations and gaining for itself official recognition while further isolating the North Korean regime.

Given the proper conditions, constructive engagement can work. It proved particularly successful with socialist bloc nations because their command economies and the policies that sustained them left them economically weak and vulnerable. Consequently, economic self-interest led them to pursue rapprochement with the West. The economic circumstances that presently exist in North Korea differ from those that existed within the broader socialist bloc of nations perhaps only in degree of severity. The regime as well has signaled its willingness to pursue economic rapprochement, albeit masked in its usual veil of bellicosity. Consider the list of indicators: its expressed willingness to create special economic zones; its ongoing joint ventures with South Korea at the Kaesong Industrial Complex and Pyeonghwa Motors; the Mount Kumgang and Mount Paekche tourist resort projects jointly run with South Korea's Hyundai Asan and open to South Korean tourists; the North-South recently opened, jointly operated graphite mine in North Korea; and the regime's offer to allow South Koreans to own property in North Korea (although this would be financially risky and to date I have heard of no accounts where any South Korean citizen or commercial concern has actually attempted to purchase property). And again, consider the lengths to which the regime has gone during 2006 to get the Bush administration back to the negotiating table to discuss the lifting of sanctions against its assets in Macau. In the aggregate, these points underscore North Korean financial and economic weakness and its willingness to consider alternative economic models.

An important consideration in discussing precursors to North Korean economic rapprochement is how one reconciles such measures with the *Juche* ideology. As pointed out earlier, major characteristics of *Juche* are its eschewal of big-power chauvinism and near obsessive preoccupation with protecting its independence of action. Recall, however, that countervailing factors also exist—the determinant of flexibility and the regime's willingness to pursue pragmatic alliances, both of which have historical precedence. For instance, Kim Jong Il's willingness to assume the initiative in 2000 by dispatching an envoy to meet with Clinton administration officials underscores this point; that he was willing to put the North Korean missile program on the negotiating table for discussion at least highlights the regime's recognition of the value of pragmatic discussions, even if for self-serving reasons.

A growing list of examples through which the regime experiments, at least at the margins, with alternative economic models, coupled with the growth of domestic markets seem to indicate a certain pragmatism on the part of the regime; it is such pragmatism that provides a potential segue for engaging the regime through AES. The key to successful exploitation of circumstances, however, will be the tactics used to engage the regime. If economic engagement through AES is directly linked to CVID rather than broader rapprochement efforts, the results will likely be continued disappointment and frustration. Instead, linking current U.S. financial sanctions on regime assets to AES might yield better initial results, which in turn could be parlayed later down the line into discussions on the regime's ballistic missile programs and later still its nuclear program. (Some might argue that the nuclear weapons program is the priority. I agree, however, past efforts to directly link discussions to the regime's nuclear program have been decidedly unsuccessful. Negotiations over the regime's ballistic missile program potentially hold more promise as the regime has already offered them up once in the past as fodder for negotiation. And if the ballistic missile threat can be eliminated or at least reduced, the by extension so too is the nuclear weapons threat.)

Thus, I believe the requisite "proper conditions" exist in North Korea that make it particularly susceptible to the lure of economic inducements under an aggressive policy of asymmetric economic statecraft (AES). Seoul's program of expanded economic engagement through such means as the South-North Kaesong industrial complex and its various joint venture tourist projects is a major step in the right direction. Where the approach falls short is in its lack of demand for demonstrable quid pro quos. Constructive engagement, as *Ostpolitik* and *Nordpolitik* have illustrated, does work and provides the framework for a new engagement paradigm with the North Korean regime.

9

Asymmetric Economic Statecraft: The Road Ahead

The definition of insanity is doing the same thing over and over again and expecting a different result.

—Einstein

Much of the literature devoted to the transition of the North Korean economy into a form other than its current socialist-styled command structure is based on a scenario under which some form of reunification between North and South Korea occurs, presupposing both political amelioration between them and some measure of voluntary reform of the North Korean economy. Such studies seek to assess the plausibility of infusing market reforms into North Korea or pursuing privatization of the production means. In short, their ultimate goal is predicting how best to capitalize the North while minimizing the potentially adverse economic impacts of such measures on South Korea. This, however, is not the scenario considered here. In fact, the concept of asymmetric economic statecraft (AES) assumes that the North Korean regime will not seek political amelioration nor voluntarily make the extensive economic changes needed to strengthen its economy, for two simple reasons: (1) a lack of knowing how to institute such changes; and (2) fear of losing political and social control within its own borders. Consequently, the theory behind AES is to exploit the known *strategic gap* that exists in the North Korean economic and financial structures: those areas between its present threadbare existence and one that provides for greater self-sufficiency. The fundamental goal of AES differs from an economic reunification model in that rather than seeking economic consonance in order to avoid disruption of the peninsula's two economies, it seeks to deliberately promote greater regime dependence on economic and financial inputs (not humanitarian assistance). These inputs would be provided through the international community of nations, with the goal of gradually laying the foundations for dismantlement of the regime's nuclear weapons program. A secondary goal, to the extent practicable, is to lay the groundwork for future democratization and capitalization. In short, AES seeks to create the conditions necessary to curb the North Korean regime's aberrant behavior while slowly moving it on a path toward normalization.

AES offers several key advantages over the current method of engaging the regime. First, it pursues engagement in an area known to be the soft underbelly of the regime—its economy—offering a greater chance of success than the present tactic of trying to persuade it to negotiate away its only strength—its nuclear weapons program. Seven years into an eight-year administration with little progress toward denuclearization demands a change in the U.S. approach. Under AES, the goal of complete, verifiable, and irreversible dismantlement remains intact, but there is now a strategy for achieving it.

Second, this approach provides necessary confidence building measures (CBM) to begin more broadly engaging the regime on its ballistic missile and nuclear weapons programs. Recall the diplomatic exchanges that took place between the United States and North Korea during the year 2000 as the Clinton administration wound up its last few months in office: reciprocal CBMs are essential to constructive engagement and constructive engagement is the key to successfully denuclearizing the North. This, of course, goes against the current wisdom that the administration not undertake dialogue with morally reprehensible regimes. Both North Korea and Iran fall within the parameters of moral reprehensibility, yet ironically as the United States remains mute, the nuclear threat from both continues to grow according to U.S. officials. Talking only with U.S. allies may be more palatable, but it is not particularly effective. Simply put, without dialogue there is no way forward.[1]

Third, an AES-centered policy approach would help to bring the policy positions of the United States, South Korea, and China into closer alignment, rather than having them work at cross-purposes. Recall the difficulty the United States had in mustering the necessary votes within the UN Security Council to have the desired level of sanctions imposed against North Korea after the July 2006 missile launch and October 2006 nuclear detonation. This was primarily the result of Chinese and Russian reluctance to pursue tougher sanctions. South Korea, through various means discussed earlier, continues to provide economic outreach to the regime, at the expense of U.S. efforts to force its denuclearization. The goal is not to modify U.S. policy solely for the purpose of greater coherence with South Korean and Chinese policies. Rather, it proposes greater accommodation of their positions in order to move the process forward jointly in lieu of the disjointed approach pursued to date. There is greater likelihood of Chinese and South Korean support under such conditions because it reduces the possibility of regional instability, which in turn, brings greater consonance to regional efforts to control North Korea's nuclear weapons program.

Fourth, thoughtful selection and application of AES tools could well lay the economic and financial groundwork and, perhaps to a lesser degree, afford a social safety net that provides for North Korea's soft landing when reunification of the peninsula ultimately occurs. Many unanswered questions remain regarding what the impact of reunification might be on the South Korean economy—the cost of rebuilding the North's infrastructure; massive infusions of capital to bring its economy in line with South Korea's; and the large displacement of North Korean workers and their probable influx into South Korea—are all potentially destabilizing factors. By putting in place mechanisms that could ultimately dampen the sudden impact of reunification works not only to the benefit of South Korea's economy, but to the benefit of other global economies as well.

Finally, perhaps the point that underlies all the preceding points is given the regime's commitment to *Juche* and such policy pursuits as *songun* under its rubric; its historically poor track record on living up to agreements into which it enters; its understanding that nuclear weapons have served as a potent negotiating tool; and its continued distrust of the United States, North Korea is very unlikely to willingly hand over its nuclear weapons program, its single ace in the hole. Once it has fully regained access to frozen assets and has perhaps established more normal relations with the United States, the effectiveness of the *Juche* approach will have been reinforced, not diminished. This is particularly the case given the six years of demands the Bush administration has levied against the regime under CVID. Stated differently, there will be no reason or motivation for the regime to abandon its present course because, from the North Korean perspective, it will have triumphed over the administration. Thus, victory will not come as the result of a singular focus on North Korean nuclear weapons; it will be achieved through application of a broad and comprehensive strategy that requires the regime to reallocate its meager resources into the economy. The strategy for such a course is AES, the primary tool of which is constructive engagement.

For those more comfortable with the traditional engagement paradigm with North Korea, AES can be seen as a continuation of the Cold War through asymmetric economic means.

THE ROAD FORWARD: A BLUEPRINT FOR SUCCESS

The probability of successfully implementing any AES-oriented policy is enhanced by the fact that the regime itself has unintentionally begun laying the groundwork for its success. First, recognizing its own inability to viably function under the strictures of its command economy, the regime has undertaken since 2002, a series of reforms that at least recognize, and in some cases promote, individual or group initiative in the marketplace and the pursuit of profit. Second, through Seoul's economic outreach programs, some segments of North Korean industry are at least inching toward the periphery of market economy operations. Finally, there is fledgling recognition among regime elites that important segments of the population, particularly university students and industry managers, must be "reeducated" in order to create a more viable economic model.

Regime recognition of the need to institute some measure of economic reform can be traced as far back as 1992 when the North Korean constitution was revised and now provides:

> The State shall encourage institutions, enterprises, or associations...to establish and operate equity and contractual joint venture enterprises with corporations or individuals of foreign countries within a special economic zone.[2]

The most substantial movement toward economic reform, however, came with changes instituted in July 2002, in the wake of which important policy shifts could be noted. One such change instituted price and wage increases along with devaluation of North Korean currency, which brought the informal and formal economies more in line with each other. Another important change was the growth of public marketplaces which allow for greater individual commercial activity and the pursuit of profit. By 2004, there existed 350 such markets throughout North Korea offering everything from cigarettes to consumer goods. These commercial venues had become so important to sustaining what little economic vitality the nation enjoys that they provided for approximately 90 percent of the daily average necessities for North Koreans during 2003–2004.[3] Markets, which were legalized in 2003, can be seen then as having reduced the burden on the state for providing for North Korean citizens through the Public Distribution System. There appears to be regime recognition that markets are necessary if widespread starvation and deprivation is to be controlled. To be sure, foreign concepts like "individual initiative" and "profit" remain in a comparatively fledgling status, but their introduction begins to chip away at the outmoded infrastructure of the command economy, particularly when individuals can directly tie improvements in their lives to their own efforts. These lessons are not lost on the individual North Korean. Consider the comments of a street cart vendor: "The more I sell the more money I make." The statement is profound in its simplicity. A female market manager noted: "One of our company's goals is to rake in more money in profits and improve the living standards of its employees."[4] Again, a simple, but compelling argument when viewed through the traditional North Korean prism. Observer accounts also bear this out. Consider the impressions of Ambassador Jack Pritchard, former U.S. envoy to North Korea, during a January 2004 visit to a Pyongyang market:

> ... It was organized, but it was done by the people. It was just jammed full of people doing commerce there. We were being jostled around as other people were. In one case, I'm trying to buy a $2 scroll in one area, and I'm getting bumped out of the way by somebody who just bought an overstuffed chair ... But they had clothes; they had vegetables; they had meat; they had electronics, televisions, furniture—you name it. Now, that's just one tiny piece, but it is a change that is occurring.[5]

Such reforms are not limited to small enterprises. The regime has also exhorted industry to pursue modernization of facilities through its own initiative; in most cases, it will no longer be the responsibility of the state to provide needed investment capital. Consider the comments of Premier Pak Pong Ju to the Supreme People's Assembly in 2004:

> In order to significantly expand and develop foreign trade, it is necessary to concentrate state efforts on such promising fields as the extractive, metal and building materials industries ... All domains and units of the national economy should wage a mass movement to build their own strong export bases, expand and develop foreign trade in a multifaceted manner and encourage equity and contractual joint ventures ... introducing advanced science and technology.[6]

One company, for example, which produces cables, had to replace 1960 circa manufacturing equipment and did so by striking a deal with a Taiwanese firm to import needed equipment into North Korea. This sort of example illustrates the regime's broader recognition that in order to survive, outmoded ways of doing business must be discarded. But it also offers an important window of opportunity to exploit the regime's strategic gaps. To be sure, any such commercial engagement with foreign companies will undoubtedly be closely monitored. Increased exposure, however, to foreigners and their concepts and ideas, their methods of doing business, as well as their ideals and values will, in the end, be quite difficult to eliminate completely, particularly if foreigners are able to communicate with their interlocutors in the Korean language, thus increasing their credibility. Fraternization through commerce could perhaps accomplish what decades of Cold War geopolitics has failed to achieve.

Given North Korea's abysmal record of repaying loans and living up to contractual obligations, the opportunities for joint ventures with foreign

companies have been few. South Korea, however, has successfully undertaken several commercial enterprises with the regime. As mentioned earlier,
there are the Mount Kumgang and Mount Paektu tourist projects with South
Korean tour operator Hyundai Asan and the Kaesong joint industrial complex. Also mentioned earlier is the North-South newly established jointly
operated graphite mine. Another joint venture between the two Koreas
was undertaken through Pyeonghwa (Peace) Motors. The Nampo Industrial Complex, located 40 km west of Pyongyang, began operations in April
2002 producing the "Hwiparam" or Whistle.[7] The complex produces five
models of SUVs and pickups, which comprise 70 percent of its sales and is
in discussions with China to develop a new minibus.[8] Unfortunately, joint
ventures are not immune to the vagaries of the regime's inability to separate
politics from commercial activity. For example, the regime reduced by half
the number of South Korean tourists it permitted to visit Mount Kumgang
in August 2005, as a form of protest against Hyundai Asan when it fired
Kim Yoon Kyu, one of its executives, for embezzlement. Kim headed the
Mt. Kumgang joint venture for the South Korean firm.[9]

That the regime might be on a more serious trajectory toward an economic model that recognizes elements of a market economy can also be
gleaned through its efforts to reeducate officials of the regime and university students. During the period 2000–2004, the regime sent more than 300
officials abroad annually to Europe, China, and Southeast Asia, in order to
learn more about the operation of market economies and other economic
reforms it might institute.[10] This may be more than just a knee-jerk reaction to present economic maladies. Its efforts to train the next generation
of officials and managers indicate the regime might actually view economic
reforms as a long-term remedy. For example, in 2004 the economics faculty
at Kimilsung University undertook revisions of economic textbooks to address changing realities: that the pursuit of profit is a critical and necessary
element of North Korea's emerging economic model.[11]

The importance of such trends should be underscored for two reasons.
First, not unlike the circumstances attendant to implementation of South
Korea's policy of *Nordpolitik* or West Germany's *Ostpolitik*, the North
Korean regime also suffers from flagging conditions under its command
economy. And based on the number of joint and commercial ventures the
regime has undertaken with South Korea, North Korea too is proving itself
amenable, albeit with a bit of truculence, to economic engagement. Second,
these trends also highlight some level of pragmatism in the regime's position, which is not necessarily in contravention of *Juche*, rather its takes a
broader approach to application of the flexibility and pragmatic alliance
determinants.

In order to capitalize on these emerging trends and use them to U.S.
advantage, a fundamental shift in thinking is required that recognizes the
past CVID construct as a goal in need of a workable strategy; AES is just

such a strategy. Recall that North Korea has maintained several foreign policy imperatives, among which was included the lifting of U.S.-imposed financial sanctions against its Macau-based assets and direct negotiations with the United States. Some analysts speculate that the nuclear test was a means of bringing the United States back to the negotiating table to discuss the lifting of financial sanctions.[12] That North Korea agreed to the terms of its own denuclearization within the broader framework of DAP discussions, which themselves called for U.S. commitments to engage in direct dialogue with the regime and to unfreeze its assets, may underscore just how much importance the regime attaches to these issues. Examples like this, along with the regime's inability to fend for itself economically, represent a key strategic gap that the United States and other countries can exploit.

Rather than linking efforts at denuclearizing the regime to punishment, for example sanctions regimes that seek to deny North Korea access to sorely needed funds obtained through the sale of nuclear weapons technology, illicit drugs, counterfeit cigarettes, and counterfeiting ($100 bill supernotes), a more broadly focused process should be applied. The strategy should be to design a framework that cuts off the regime's access to its financial resources while simultaneously increasing regime dependence on controlled international economic and financial inputs, thus beginning the long process of restructuring the North's economic and financial infrastructure. To assist in achieving this end, in addition to applying Chapter VII financial sanctions when and where required, efforts should be redoubled to place broader financial restrictions on the regime on a global scale. This, of course, is in addition to current U.S. efforts to bolster PSI activities to ensure North Korea's ability to buy or sell nuclear technology is hampered. Nations hosting North Korean diplomatic missions should also be called upon to more vigorously prosecute efforts to stifle the regime's illicit drug trade, much of which is handled through diplomatic couriers working at North Korean embassies.

As the regime's access to financial resources dries up, an international coalition of nations, led by the United States through the Six Party Talks venue, could then begin seeking engagement with the North on economic terms. This will likely be one of the more difficult steps for two reasons. First, the regime will likely be less than cooperative in the wake of any sanctions imposed against it, thus timing and continued engagement is vital. Second, is the U.S. administration's own reluctance to engage the North Korean regime. If, however, dismantlement of the regime's nuclear weapons program remains one of its priorities, then the administration must move beyond the playground scenario of "you first; no, you first." The new UN Secretary General Ban Ki Moon, former South Korean minister of foreign affairs and trade, is of such a mind. He has indicated that one of his first acts as Secretary General will be to visit North Korea. A willingness to engage and extend CBMs in order to initiate dialogue beyond the usual demands for denuclearization will be fundamental to any success.

Understanding the regime's own priorities with regard to which sectors it perceives as most important is also crucial; focusing on these may help to make the regime more receptive to CBM overtures. A reasonable conclusion with regard to which areas potentially hold the most promise can be reached through examination of regime proclamations focusing on building heavy industrial capacity and its current joint venture activities with South Korean firms at the Kaesong industrial complex, which are more light industrial operations.[13] The regime's priority areas can thus generally be distilled to the agricultural sector (because of its continued crop failures) and both light and heavy industries. If one considers the possibility of expanding engagement within light or heavy industry, for example, one of the first steps that should be undertaken is negotiation for the creation of new special economic zones (SEZ) in North Korea within which joint manufacturing operations between foreign and North Korean companies could be undertaken. Any joint projects should be based on comparative advantage and follow a model that relies on using North Korean labor and foreign management. Creation of SEZs would provide the regime some level of comfort with regard to its ability to limit the "bad influence" of foreigners on the North Korean population. It also taps into the regime's growing recognition for the need to expand joint ventures. Conversely, the more SEZs that can be created, the greater the likelihood of exposing North Koreans to international norms and values; regardless of how much the regime tries to "control" interaction, it would be nearly impossible to limit the transmission of ideas in day-to-day contact, particularly if managers were trained in the Korean language (and culture, to the extent that there still exists a "Korean" culture untainted by socialist ideals in North Korea). Greater opportunities for North Koreans to work in joint venture operations may also help to reverse the impact of decades of propaganda with which they have been assailed. It also taps into the slowly emerging recognition within certain segments of the North Korean population that there is a link between individual effort and individual well-being. Again, it is critical that any joint ventures remain mindful of avoiding dual-use technologies.

"Coalition" priorities for joint ventures should also focus on secondary consumer goods industries because production and distribution of such goods into the markets of North Korea will likely stimulate market transactions. As Kim Sung Woo points out, secondary goods are not immediately consumed, but rather require the use of the marketplace in order to realize profit: the more secondary goods are available for sale, presumably the greater the number of markets, which increases individual profit motive and market transactions.[14] Recall Ambassador Pritchard's anecdotal accounts of his experience in a Pyongyang market. And that such an economic model is viable even within the North Korean context is borne out by South Korea's experiences with joint ventures.

The goal of AES, of course, is not only to increase the regime's dependence on the international community, but to require some meaningful reciprocal action on its part in exchange for economic CBM. Immediate reciprocity could be sought in the form of demanding that North Korea institute better working conditions for North Korean workers within SEZs that more closely comport with International Labor Organization standards. This approach requires both sides to offer meaningful CBMs without immediately tackling the contentious issues over WMD. Longer term, however, reciprocity would need to be definitively linked to North Korea's nuclear weapons program. One plausible starting point might be to link dismantlement of the regime's nuclear weapons program and reinstitution of an inspections regime to the promise of removing current trade impediments and supporting greater integration into the world economy. For example, under the Smoot-Hawley Tariff Act of 1930, North Korea would be subject to stiff export tariffs on commodities in which it might have a comparative advantage, such as garments.[15] Lifting such impediments to trade in exchange for meaningful progress toward the goal of CVID could prove successful given the rudimentary market-oriented changes presently taking place in North Korea. Similarly, the United States could, if presented with meaningful regime reciprocity, also desist in actively denying the regime access to loans or technical assistance through international financial institutions such as the World Bank or Asian Development Bank. The premise of the preceding ideas is rather straightforward: once the regime becomes accustomed to the economic benefits of expanded engagement, it will not want to forgo them. This transcends political ideology and focuses more on basic human nature, a point borne out by the regime's incessant demands for regaining access to its frozen assets in the Macau bank.

The preceding offers just a few possible scenarios for moving the regime away from its dangerous and abnormal obsession with nuclear weapons as a tool of geopolitics and more toward normalization of its relations with the world community. With the regime's successful test blast of a nuclear weapon and world opinion firmly aligned against it, this may, paradoxically, prove the most opportune time to employ a strategy of AES. Given the lengths to which the regime has gone to engage the United States during 2006, it is clear that financial sanctions imposed against it had an impact. While the current DAP agreement appears to be moving discussions toward a denuclearized North Korea, for reasons outlined in Chapters 1 and 2, I believe, the regime will not, in the end, abandon its nuclear program based on this agreement's provisions. A broader, more comprehensive and long-term policy approach will be required.

But there are important caveats of which the United States must remain mindful under an AES scenario. First, of course, is the need to avoid inadvertently advancing the regime's technological posture by providing dual-use technologies. Second, timing is critical. If the United States is to remain credible in the wake of the regime's most recent nuclear weapons test, it cannot be seen as acquiescing to its demands for engagement. This is, unfortunately, a problem of the administration's own making; its consistent and intractable hard-line approach has painted it into the proverbial corner and now limits its options. This situation was underscored by Tony Snow, White House press secretary, when he pointed out during a press conference regarding the regime's nuclear tests that "China, South Korea and Japan" have more leverage with North Korea than the United States does.[16] Third, that "constructive engagement" should be the strategy for attaining the larger end of CVID; it is not commensurate with weakness or capitulating one's position to the enemy. It is commonsense. With no avenue for dialogue, there simply is no way forward. Finally, an effort must be made to understand the North Korean adversary: how he thinks, why he thinks what he does, and how he will likely react under various scenarios—this has been sorely lacking in the U.S. approach to date. The lessons of *Juche* are not theoretical mumbo-jumbo—they have real-world applications.

The compartmentalized approach of the Bush administration has not served the long-term interests of the United States and its allies—what is needed is a more coherent and comprehensive approach. For any policy to work, to include AES, there must be a long-term commitment to both the strategy and goals, a process that must be protected from the vagaries of Beltway politics; this will not be an overnight success. It will require a long-term commitment and patience that transcends presidential administrations. This, however, is likely the only way to achieve coherence. If the policy is subject to change every four or eight years with the changing of the guard in Washington, the likelihood of success is significantly diminished.

North Korea's nuclear weapons test underscores again just how dangerous the regime is to peninsular and regional stability and global proliferation of nuclear weapons; and it is unlikely to pursue denuclearization on its own. Yet armed conflict on the Korean peninsula is not a viable option; nor is forced regime change. And after almost seven years of a "one size fits all" CVID approach, the United States and its allies are no closer to eliminating the North Korean threat than they were in January 2001. In fact, assessed through the prism of CVID, the approach has been counterproductive. Nor have economic sanctions proven successful. It is time for a paradigmatic shift in U.S. policy toward North Korea and Washington must lead that change.

Appendix 1

Agreed Framework between the United States of America and the Democratic People's Republic of Korea

Geneva, October 21, 1994

Delegations of the governments of the United States of America (U.S.) and the Democratic People's Republic of Korea (DPRK) held talks in Geneva from September 23 to October 21, 1994, to negotiate an overall resolution of the nuclear issue on the Korean Peninsula.

Both sides reaffirmed the importance of attaining the objectives contained in the August 12, 1994 Agreed Statement between the U.S. and the DPRK and upholding the principles of the June 11, 1993 Joint Statement of the U.S. and the DPRK to achieve peace and security on a nuclear-free Korean peninsula. The U.S. and the DPRK decided to take the following actions for the resolution of the nuclear issue:

I. Both sides will cooperate to replace the DPRK's graphite-moderated reactors and related facilities with light-water reactor (LWR) power plants.
   1. In accordance with the October 20, 1994 letter of assurance from the U.S. President, the U.S. will undertake to make arrangements for the provision to the DPRK of a LWR project with a total generating capacity of approximately 2,000 MW(e) by a target date of 2003.
      • The U.S. will organize under its leadership an international consortium to finance and supply the LWR project to be provided to the DPRK. The U.S., representing the international consortium, will

serve as the principal point of contact with the DPRK for the LWR project.

- The U.S., representing the consortium, will make best efforts to secure the conclusion of a supply contract with the DPRK within six months of the date of this Document for the provision of the LWR project. Contract talks will begin as soon as possible after the date of this Document.

- As necessary, the U.S. and the DPRK will conclude a bilateral agreement for cooperation in the field of peaceful uses of nuclear energy.

2. In accordance with the October 20, 1994 letter of assurance from the U.S. President, the U.S., representing the consortium, will make arrangements to offset the energy foregone due to the freeze of the DPRK's graphite-moderated reactors and related facilities, pending completion of the first LWR unit.

- Alternative energy will be provided in the form of heavy oil for heating and electricity production.

- Deliveries of heavy oil will begin within three months of the date of this Document and will reach a rate of 500,000 tons annually, in accordance with an agreed schedule of deliveries.

3. Upon receipt of U.S. assurances for the provision of LWR's and for arrangements for interim energy alternatives, the DPRK will freeze its graphite-moderated reactors and related facilities and will eventually dismantle these reactors and related facilities.

- The freeze on the DPRK's graphite-moderated reactors and related facilities will be fully implemented within one month of the date of this Document. During this one-month period, and throughout the freeze, the International Atomic Energy Agency (IAEA) will be allowed to monitor this freeze, and the DPRK will provide full cooperation to the IAEA for this purpose.

- Dismantlement of the DPRK's graphite-moderated reactors and related facilities will be completed when the LWR project is completed.

- The U.S. and the DPRK will cooperate in finding a method to store safely the spent fuel from the 5 MW(e) experimental reactor during the construction of the LWR project, and to dispose of the fuel in a safe manner that does not involve reprocessing in the DPRK.

4. As soon as possible after the date of this document U.S. and DPRK experts will hold two sets of experts talks.

- At one set of talks, experts will discuss issues related to alternative energy and the replacement of the graphite-moderated reactor program with the LWR project.

- At the other set of talks, experts will discuss specific arrangements for spent fuel storage and ultimate disposition.

II. The two sides will move toward full normalization of political and economic relations.

 1. Within three months of the date of this Document, both sides will reduce barriers to trade and investment, including restrictions on telecommunications services and financial transactions.

 2. Each side will open a liaison office in the other's capital following resolution of consular and other technical issues through expert level discussions.

 3. As progress is made on issues of concern to each side, the U.S. and the DPRK will upgrade bilateral relations to the Ambassadorial level.

III. Both sides will work together for peace and security on a nuclear-free Korean peninsula.

 1. The U.S. will provide formal assurances to the DPRK, against the threat or use of nuclear weapons by the U.S.

 2. The DPRK will consistently take steps to implement the North-South Joint Declaration on the Denuclearization of the Korean Peninsula.

 3. The DPRK will engage in North-South dialogue, as this Agreed Framework will help create an atmosphere that promotes such dialogue.

IV. Both sides will work together to strengthen the international nuclear non-proliferation regime.

 1. The DPRK will remain a party to the Treaty on the Non-Proliferation of Nuclear Weapons (NPT) and will allow implementation of its safeguards agreement under the Treaty.

 2. Upon conclusion of the supply contract for the provision of the LWR project, ad hoc and routine inspections will resume under the DPRK's safeguards agreement with the IAEA with respect to the facilities not subject to the freeze. Pending conclusion of the supply contract, inspections required by the IAEA for the continuity of safeguards will continue at the facilities not subject to the freeze.

 3. When a significant portion of the LWR project is completed, but before delivery of key nuclear components, the DPRK will come into full compliance with its safeguards agreement with the IAEA (INFCIRC/403), including taking all steps that may be deemed necessary by the IAEA, following consultations with the Agency with regard to verifying the accuracy and completeness of the DPRK's initial report on all nuclear material in the DPRK.

Robert L. Gallucci
Head of Delegation of the
United States of America,
Ambassador at Large of the
United States of America

Kang Sok Ju
Head of the Delegation of the
People's Republic of Korea,
First Vice-Minister of Foreign Affairs
of the Democratic People's Republic of Korea

North Korea–Denuclearization Action Plan

The following action plan was released in Beijing on February 13, 2007, following the conclusion of the latest round of Six Party Talks.

Initial Actions for the Implementation of the Joint Statement
13 February 2007

The Third Session of the Fifth Round of the Six-Party Talks was held in Beijing among the People's Republic of China, the Democratic People's Republic of Korea, Japan, the Republic of Korea, the Russian Federation and the United States of America from 8 to 13 February 2007.

Mr. Wu Dawei, Vice Minister of Foreign Affairs of the PRC, Mr. Kim Gye Gwan, Vice Minister of Foreign Affairs of the DPRK; Mr. Kenichiro Sasae, Director-General for Asian and Oceanian Affairs, Ministry of Foreign Affairs of Japan; Mr. Chun Yung-woo, Special Representative for Korean Peninsula Peace and Security Affairs of the ROK Ministry of Foreign Affairs and Trade; Mr. Alexander Losyukov, Deputy Minister of Foreign Affairs of the Russian Federation; and Mr. Christopher Hill, Assistant Secretary for East Asian and Pacific Affairs of the Department of State of the United States attended the talks as heads of their respective delegations.

Vice Foreign Minister Wu Dawei chaired the talks.

I. The Parties held serious and productive discussions on the actions each party will take in the initial phase for the implementation of the Joint Statement of 19 September 2005. The Parties reaffirmed their common goal and will to achieve early denuclearization of the Korean Peninsula in a peaceful manner and reiterated that they would earnestly fulfill their commitments in the Joint Statement. The Parties agreed to take coordinated steps to implement the Joint Statement in a phased manner in line with the principle of "action for action".

II. The Parties agreed to take the following actions in parallel in the initial phase:

1. The DPRK will shut down and seal for the purpose of eventual abandonment the Yongbyon nuclear facility, including the reprocessing facility and invite back IAEA personnel to conduct all necessary monitoring and verifications as agreed between IAEA and the DPRK.

2. The DPRK will discuss with other parties a list of all its nuclear programs as described in the Joint Statement, including plutonium extracted from used fuel rods, that would be abandoned pursuant to the Joint Statement.

3. The DPRK and the US will start bilateral talks aimed at resolving pending bilateral issues and moving toward full diplomatic relations. The US will begin the process of removing the designation of the DPRK as a state-sponsor of terrorism and advance the process of terminating the application of the Trading with the Enemy Act with respect to the DPRK.

4. The DPRK and Japan will start bilateral talks aimed at taking steps to normalize their relations in accordance with the Pyongyang Declaration, on the basis of the settlement of unfortunate past and the outstanding issues of concern.

5. Recalling Section 1 and 3 of the Joint Statement of 19 September 2005, the Parties agreed to cooperate in economic, energy and humanitarian assistance to the DPRK. In this regard, the Parties agreed to the provision of emergency energy assistance to the DPRK in the initial phase. The initial shipment of emergency energy assistance equivalent to 50,000 tons of heavy fuel oil (HFO) will commence within next 60 days.

The Parties agreed that the above-mentioned initial actions will be implemented within next 60 days and that they will take coordinated steps toward this goal.

III. The Parties agreed on the establishment of the following Working Groups (WG) in order to carry out the initial actions and for the purpose of full implementation of the Joint Statement:

1. Denuclearization of the Korean Peninsula
2. Normalization of DPRK-US relations
3. Normalization of DPRK-Japan relations
4. Economy and Energy Cooperation
5. Northeast Asia Peace and Security Mechanism

The WGs will discuss and formulate specific plans for the implementation of the Joint Statement in their respective areas. The WGs shall report to the Six-Party Heads of Delegation Meeting on the progress of their work. In principle, progress in one WG shall not affect progress in other WGs. Plans made by the five WGs will be implemented as a whole in a coordinated manner.

The Parties agreed that all WGs will meet within next 30 days.

IV. During the period of the Initial Actions phase and the next phase - which includes provision by the DPRK of a complete declaration of all nuclear programs and disablement of all existing nuclear facilities, including graphite-moderated reactors and reprocessing plant - economic, energy and humanitarian assistance up to the equivalent of 1 million tons of heavy fuel oil (HFO), including the initial shipment equivalent to 50,000 tons of HFO, will be provided to the DPRK.

The detailed modalities of the said assistance will be determined through consultations and appropriate assessments in the Working Group on Economic and Energy Cooperation.

V. Once the initial actions are implemented, the Six Parties will promptly hold a ministerial meeting to confirm implementation of the Joint Statement and explore ways and means for promoting security cooperation in Northeast Asia.

VI. The Parties reaffirmed that they will take positive steps to increase mutual trust, and will make joint efforts for lasting peace and stability in Northeast Asia. The directly related parties will negotiate a permanent peace regime on the Korean Peninsula at an appropriate separate forum.

VII. The Parties agreed to hold the Sixth Round of the Six-Party Talks on 19 March 2007 to hear reports of WGs and discuss on actions for the next phase.

2007/099

Notes

EPIGRAPH

1. Anna Fifield, "N Korea Demands a Change of Political Heart" *Financial Times* (FT.com) July 7, 2006 http://www.ft.com/cms/s/01e665c6-0dd4-11db-a385-0000779e2340.html

PREFACE

1. Tae-hung Ha, *Maxims and Proverbs of Old Korea, Korean Cultural Series*, Vol. VII (Seoul: Yonsei University Press, 1970) 128.

INTRODUCTION

1. The North Koreans fired one Taepodong-2 missile and six medium range Scud Rodong missiles, which have a range of between 130 and 700 kilometers. (Korea Times, July 9, 2006, "South Korea Seeks to Build Long Range Missile." Jung Sung-ki.

2. Another area of U.S. policy focus with regard to North Korea has been human rights. Since 2001, the Bush Administration has enacted two pieces of legislation to that end: the North Korean Freedom Act of 2003 and its replacement legislation, the North Korean Human Rights Act of 2004; the latter designed to strengthen legal support and provide more tools for improving human rights conditions in North Korea. In accordance with the 2004 legislation, the Administration announced appointment of a special envoy on human rights for North Korea, Jay Lefkowitz, on *August 19, 2005.*

CHAPTER 1

1. "Financial Dispute with N. Korea Resolved," *Korea Times* March 16, 2007.

2. "NK Imports 15,000 Tons of Rice from China in late 2006," *Korea Times* February 9, 2007.

3. Assif Shameen, "South Korea Shifts Up," *Asia, Inc.* February 2006. http://www.asia-inc.com/archives/asiainc_archive_428.html.

4. Senator Joseph Biden and former House Speaker Newt Gingrich, interview, Meet the Press, NBC television, Washington, July 16, 2006.

5. Tim Russert, "Bush North Korea Rhetoric Different," *Russert on Politics.* http://www.msnbc.msn.com/id/13752754/.

6. Barbara Demick, "N. Korea Says It Wants Its Money Back, Then It'll Talk," *Los Angeles Times* July 8, 2006.

7. U.S. State Department, "Background Notes: North Korea." http://www.state.gov/r/pa/ei/bgn/2792.htm. October 2006.

8. Reuben Staines, "Koreans Lean Closer to China," *Korea Times* January 1, 2006.

9. The trend these findings illustrate should be a matter of interest to U.S. policymakers, particularly given our long-term, and one would guess continued, commitment to peninsula security affairs. As the older generation is replaced with the post-1980s born population, such shifts in attitude may likely become more prevalent, impacting U.S. policy. Forward thinking policy pursuits, for example stronger cultural diplomacy, might best serve long-term U.S. interests.

10. "Poll Finds Pragmatic Patriotism among the Young," *Digital Chosunilbo* (English Edition), August 14, 2005. http://english.chosun.com/w21data/html/news/200508/200508140019.html.

11. Ryu Jin, "Japan Hit for Spiking Tension," *Korea Times* July 11, 2006.

12. United Nations, World Food Program, "Food Aid Recipients," 2005 Annual Report, 31.

13. Seo Dong-shin, "Seoul Gives 60,000 Tons of Coal Aid to NK," *Korea Times* January 3, 2006.

14. Jung Sung-ki, "US Plans to Complete Command Transfer by 2009," *Korea Times* August 4, 2006.

15. Madeline Albright, interview, *Frontline*, PBS, "Kim's Nuclear Gamble," March 27, 2003. http://www.pbs.org/wgbh/pages/frontline/shows/kim/interviews/albright.html.

16. In the interest of fairness, adherents to the "no direct negotiations" approach to dealing with rogue regimes can point to the example of Libya, which after renouncing its nuclear, biological, and chemical weapons programs, reestablished formal diplomatic relations with the United States on June 28, 2004. When one compares the stakes and outcomes in the case of Libya to those of North Korea, Iraq, and Iran, however, the differences are stark.

17. Chapter VII of the UN Charter is entitled, "Action with Respect to Threats to the Peace, Breaches of the Peace, and Acts of Aggression." Specifically, the United States and Japan sought to invoke economic sanctions against North Korea via Article 41, which reads in part: " ... partial interruption of economic relations and of rail, sea, air, postal, telegraphic, radio, and other means of communication, and the severance of diplomatic relations."

18. In a 17 July, 2006, article published in the *Korea Times* entitled, "UN Resolution Affects NK Nuke Programs," South Korean officials are quoted as describing the resolution as "meaningful." U.S. ambassador to the UN, John Bolton, referred to it as an "historic" day because the resolution passed unanimously; North Korea rejected the resolution in under an hour. China and Russia (South Korea is not presently a member of the Security Council; Japan, however, is) voted for the resolution because it contained no sanctions and essentially lacks any teeth; the United States and Japan supported it because it was the best they could hope for and helped render a unanimous decision. The resolution calls for North Korea to abandon its nuclear weapons program; for UN member nations to stop dealing with North Korea on material or technology for missiles or nuclear weapons; and for North Korea to immediately return to the Six Party Talks—nothing really new. Much is being made of the resolution's unanimity; my hope is that it will lead to concrete results. Only time will tell how effective the resolution will be, but my own sense is that the "end zone dance" Bolton and others are engaged in may be a bit premature. If history is any guide, what will likely be encountered as a result of the UN resolution is a more recalcitrant North Korea, not one prepared to accede to external pressure.

19. Andrei Lankov, "China Raises its Stake in North Korea," *Asia Times Online* December 17, 2005. http://www.atimes.com/atimes/Korea/GL17Dg01.html.

20. Ibid.

21. It should be noted that neither of these examples offers indisputable evidence of regime intransigence. In the case of the Agreed Framework, the regime contended that the U.S. was not living up to its obligations under the Agreement. And in fact, after the sweep of Congress by the Republicans in 1994, Congress typically delayed appropriating the funds necessary to pay for the 500,000 tons of heavy fuel oil shipments agreed to in the Framework, making shipments erratic. According to Leon V. Sigal, director of the Northeast Asia Cooperative Security Project, the circumstances under which the regime reneged on its September 2005 promise to dismantle its nuclear program are also not so clear cut. During an interview with Marty Moss-Coane on "Radio Times" (October 12, 2006) Sigal indicated that the U.S. administration had empowered Christopher Hill to negotiate with the North Korean representative, which led the regime to agree to dismantle its weapons program in return for provision of nuclear reactors. Secretary of State Rice, however, indicated in a public statement that there would be no discussion of providing nuclear reactors until the regime achieved CVID. Whether the regime would ever have actually dismantled its weapons program is highly suspect; its historical track record does not inspire confidence. Sigal maintains, however, without following through on its end of the agreement, the United States will never know if the regime would have lived up to its promise.

CHAPTER 2

1. Kim il Sung, lecture, "Socialist Construction in the Democratic People's Republic of Korea and the South Korean Revolution," Ali Archam Academy of Social Sciences of Indonesia, April 14, 1965.

2. Herman Franssen and Elaine Morton, "A Review of US Unilateral Sanctions against Iran," *Middle Eastern Economic Survey*, XLV:34 (August 26, 2002). http://www.mafhoum.com/press3/108E16.htm.

3. Franssen and Morton, "A Review of US Unilateral Sanctions Against Iran."

4. United States, Department of the Treasury, Office of Foreign Assets Control, "An Overview of OFAC Regulations Involving Sanctions against Iran" (Washington, March 12, 2003).

5. Benjamin Welles, "North Korean Militancy Linked to 1966 Meeting," *New York Times* February 1, 1968.

6. Charter of the Workers' Party of Korea, 43.

7. Ibid.

8. Democratic People's Republic of Korea, "Democratic People's Republic of Korea Socialist Constitution," preface, 1948.

9. Dae-Ho Byun, *North Korea's Foreign Policy: The Juche Ideology and the Challenge of Gorbachev's New Thinking* (Seoul: Seoul Computer Press, Published for The Research Center for Peace and Unification, 1991) 69.

10. Kim il Sung, *On Eliminating Dogmatism and Formalism and Establishing Juche in Ideological Work* (Pyongyang, North Korea: Foreign Languages Publishing House, 1973) 1–2.

11. Kim il Sung, "Revolution and Socialist Construction in Korea," in *Socialist Construction and Juche and the Mass Line* (News York: International Publishers, 1971) 87.

12. Kim, *Socialist Construction and Juche and the Mass Line*, 87–88.

13. Byung Chul Koh, *The Foreign Policy of North Korea* (New York: FA Praeger, 1969) 54.

14. "North Korean Militancy Linked to 1966 Meeting," *New York Times* February 1, 1968, 15.

15. Kim, *Socialist Construction and Juche and the Mass Line*, 92.

16. Byung Chul Koh, *The Foreign Policy Systems of North and South Korea* (Berkeley, CA: University of California Press, 1984) 74–76.

17. Lee Joo-hee, "President Warns against Great Power Politics," *Korea Herald* September 16, 2005.

18. Koh, *The Foreign Policy Systems of North and South Korea*, 70–77.

19. Ibid.

20. Byun, *North Korea's Foreign Policy*, 71–78.

21. Grace Lee, "The Political Philosophy of Juche," *Stanford Journal of East Asian Affairs* 3(1) (Spring 2003): 105–106.

22. Ibid., 106.

23. Byun, *North Korea's Foreign Policy*, 72.

24. Byun, *North Korea's Foreign Policy*, 72.

25. "North Korea Recalls National Development Movement," *Yonhap News Service* January 12, 2006.

26. United Nations, World Food Program, INTERFAIS. Food Aid Monitor Annual Report (2005), Table 15, June 2006. http://www.wfp.org/interfais/index2.htm#.

27. Kim, *Socialist Construction and Juche and the Mass Line*, 91–92.

28. Byun, *North Korea's Foreign Policy*, 72.

29. Korean Central News Agency, "Great Upsurge of Chollima in Korea," January 10, 2005. http://www.kcna.co.jp/item/2006/200601/news01/11.htm.

30. Brent Choi and Brian Lee, "North is Said to Cut Back Phone Use," *Joongang Daily* (distributed by the Herald Tribune), June 8, 2005. http://joongangdaily.joins.com/200506/07/200506070003592109900090209021.html.

31. While this discussion focuses on the history of foreign incursion into Korea, an equally important point to consider is Korea's own political traditions, which were anything but democratic. The reader will recall that Korea, prior to Japanese annexation in August 1910, was an autocratic monarchy. With the conclusion of WWII and Korea's division into two sphere's of influence—Soviet influence north of the 38th parallel and U.S. influence south of it—each half of the divided peninsula pursued its own style of government. North Korea followed the course of communism; South Korea a centralized and authoritarian form of government that since the establishment of the Republic of Korea in August 1948 has suffered two military coups. In fact, it was the election of Kim Young-sam in February 1993 that ended 32 years of military rule in South Korea. The point here is that although South Korea's present form of government is democratic, its natural inclination after the period of Japanese colonization was to return to a style of governance more in keeping with its political traditions, despite being adorned with institutions of democracy—its first general election and the creation of a national assembly—overseen by the Interim Committee of the United Nations General Assembly. For an in-depth treatment of this topic I recommend Sung Chul Yang's work "The North and South Korean Political Systems: A Comparative Analysis."

32. Sung Chul Yang, *The North and South Korean Political Systems: A Comparative Analysis* (Seoul: Seoul Press, and Boulder, Co: Westview Press, 1994) 41–47.

33. Ibid., 41–42.

34. Much of the historical treatment of Korea through 1300 A.D. was derived from Sung Chul Yang's work, *The North and South Korean Political Systems: A Comparative Analysis*, in which he offers a well documented and highly detailed account of Korea's history and its tumultuous relations with its neighbors. I strongly recommend this book to any reader with an interest in Korea's early foreign relations.

35. Sung, *The North and South Korean Political Systems*, 41–47.

36. Ibid.

37. Ibid., 44–45.

CHAPTER 3

1. The Greater East Asia Co-prosperity Sphere was conceived by the Japanese government during WWII to express the idea of a politically and economically integrated Asia no longer subjugated by Western imperialism—Asia for Asians under Japanese stewardship. The Sphere found its genesis in the "New Order in East Asia" which resulted from the second Sino-Japanese war (1937–1945). Civilian and military leaders feared a protracted war in China would deplete Japan's resources; consequently, some efforts at conciliation were made in China to garner support from the Chinese. These efforts, which included trying to convince the Chinese of Japan's sincerity in creating a new political order of parity in Asia, culminated in the New Order in East Asia. After Japan became a signatory to the Tripartite Pact in 1940, along with Germany and Italy, the idea of the "Order" began to expand both conceptually and geographically to include East Asia and parts of Southeast Asia. It should be noted that geographical boundaries of the Greater East Asia Co-prosperity Sphere were never firmly established; some considered Australia a part of the Sphere. It was generally agreed, however, that Japan, Japanese-occupied China, Korea, Taiwan, Manchuria, Japanese-held Pacific islands and Southeast Asia comprised the grouping.

2. Andrew C. Nahm, *Korea: Tradition and Transformation* (Elizabeth, NJ: Hollym International Corporation, 1991) 329.

3. Ibid.

4. E. Grant Meade, *American Military Government in Korea* (New York: King's Crown Press, Columbia University, 1952) 44.

5. Donald W. Boose, Jr, "Portentous Sideshow: The Korea Occupation Decision," *Parameters: US Army War College Quarterly* (Winter 1995): 113.

6. Operation Downfall, the overall plan for invasion of the Japanese home islands, had two components. The first, Operation Olympic, was the plan to invade Kyushu in November 1945. The second, Operation Coronet, was the plan for the invasion of Honshu, commencing in spring 1946.

7. Boose, "Portentous Sideshow," 113.

8. Ibid., 118.

9. Ibid., 116–117.

10. Ibid., 117.

11. William Franklin Sands, *Undiplomatic Memories* (New York: Whittlesey House, McGraw-Hill Book Company, 1930) 158.

12. Henry C.K. Liu, "China, Part 4: The 38th Parallel Leads Straight to Taiwan," *Asia Times On-Line* January 9, 2004. http://www.atimes.com/atimes/China/FA09Ad03.html.

13. Ibid.

14. "Japs Ordered to Surrender Everywhere," *Washington Post* September 2, 1945, M2.

15. George M. McCune, "Post-War Government and Politics of Korea," *Journal of Politics* 9:4 (November 1947): 607.

16. Bradley K. Martin, *Under the Loving Care of the Fatherly Leader: North Korea and the Kim Dynasty* (New York: Thomas Dunne Books, Imprint of St. Martins' Press, 2004) 54.

17. Bertram D. Sarafan, "Military Government: Korea," *Far Eastern Survey* 15:23 (November 20, 1946): 351–352.

18. McCune, *Post War Government and Politics of Korea*, 606.

19. Ibid., 607.

20. Ibid.

21. Ibid.

22. Nahm, *Korea*, 348.

23. Benjamin Weems, "Behind the Korean Election," *Far Eastern Survey* 17:12 (June 23, 1948): 145.

24. United Nations, 112th Plenary Meeting, General Assembly, "The Problem of the Independence of Korea," November 14, 1947, 16–18. http://www.un.org/documents/ga/res/2/ares2.htm.

25. Weems, "Behind the Korean Election," 142.

26. Andrew J. Grajdanzev, "Korea Divided," *Far Eastern Survey* 14:20 (October 10, 1945): 282–283.

27. Tadao Yanaihara, "Problems of Japanese Administration in Korea," *Pacific Affairs* 11:2 (June 1938): 200.

28. One koku = 5.12 U.S. bushels.

29. Yanaihara, "Problems of Japanese Administration in Korea," 200.

30. Ibid., 201.

31. The Manchurian Incident, also known as the Mukden Incident, occurred in September 1931 and served as the pretext for Japan's occupation of Manchuria, leading to the establishment of Japan's puppet state of Manchukuo. With Japan's victory over Russia in the Russo-Japanese War (1904–1905), it became the dominant power in southern Manchuria, to include the southern Manchurian railway. The railway was bombed at Mukden (present-day Shenyang) and the Japanese army used this as justification to annex Manchuria and create Manchukuo in 1932.

32. Yanaihara, "Problems of Japanese Administration in Korea," 203.

33. Ibid., 202.

34. Meade, *American Military Government in Korea*, 92–93.

35. While the absence of cross-border trade was a leading factor that contributed to the rice shortage, it was one of several reasons. Another important consideration was the influx of Koreans from abroad returning to southern Korea as well as those fleeing the northern zone. Yet another was mismanagement by U.S. military authorities of the rice market. They established price ceilings below market value after the cost of rice rose on the open market, which led farmers to keep their produce off the open market resulting in a zone-wide shortage.

36. Sarafan, "Military Government: Korea," 352.

37. Meade, *American Military Government in Korea*, 93.

CHAPTER 4

1. Kim Il Sung, *On Eliminating Dogmatism and Formalism and Establishing Juche in Ideological Work* (Pyongyang: Foreign Languages Publishing House, 1973) 13.

2. Bradley K. Martin, *Under the Loving Care of the Fatherly Leader: North Korea and the Kim Dynasty* (New York: Thomas Dunne-St. Martin's Press, 2004) 48–49.

3. Ibid.

4. The United Front tactic was a Leninist tactic used by the Soviet regime to authorize communist parties in other countries to collaborate temporarily with non-communist parties. The purpose was theoretically to promote democratic institutions and workers' rights, but in reality it provided opportunities for communists to secure political gains and to seize power without resorting to revolution. This definition is provided courtesy of the "Country Studies Series" by the Federal Research Division of the Library of Congress.

5. Byung Chul Koh, *The Foreign Policy of North Korea* (New York: Frederick A. Praeger Publishers, 1969) 8.

6. Cho Man-sik was a Christian minister located in the Pyongyang area. Christian religious activities had been tolerated by Japanese occupation authorities and Christians were particularly strong in northern Korea as a result of extensive missionary work there in the latter half of the nineteenth century. When the colonial authority mandated worship at Shinto shrines, an order most Christians refused, they suffered harassment. This harassment galvanized the Christians and their subsequent alliance with other nationalists made them, and Cho as their leader, a credible political force. (Politics in North Korea: Pre-Korean War Stage, Chong-sik Lee, *The China Quarterly*, 14, April–June 1963, 4).

7. Martin, *Under the Loving Care of the Fatherly Leader* 52–55.

8. Andrei Lankov, "Death of a Nationalist Leader," *Korea Times* February 19, 2004.

9. Koh, *The Foreign Policy of North Korea*, 8.

10. Ibid., 8.

11. Ibid., 9.

12. Martin, *Under the Loving Care of the Fatherly Leader*, 52.

13. Ibid., 54–55.

14. In the interest of full disclosure, there is some disparity among scholars as to when Kim Il Sung was actually selected as first secretary of the North Korean Central Bureau. For example, Chin O. Chung argues that Kim was selected to the position on October 10, 1945. Conversely, Byung Chul Koh contends that Kim was not initially selected to the position, but rather it was Kim Yong-bom who was selected with Kim Il Sung rising to the position of first secretary in December 1945. Koh's account may be more accurate as the NPP leadership had come to distrust Kim's motives for merging their two parties and were openly uncomfortable when the Soviets pushed for Kim to become first secretary. To allay their fears, Kim Yong-bom was likely elevated to the position, but for a very short time as there is little debate that by December 1945 Kim Il Sung did occupy the position.

15. Andrew C. Nahm, *Korea: Tradition and Transformation* (Seoul: Hollym Corporation, 1988) 369.

16. Ibid., 368.

17. Nikita Sergeyevich Khrushchev served as First Secretary of the Communist Party of the Soviet Union, 1953–1964 and as Chairman of the Council of Ministers (Prime Minister), 1958–1964. During the Twentieth Congress, Khrushchev convened a closed-door session during which he assailed Stalin, his policies, and his cult leadership, ultimately leading to the endorsement of a resolution against cult leaders, which had direct applicability in North Korea; such a resolution could easily have been tied to Kim. It also had direct applicability to Mao in China and was a contributing factor to the ideological schism that occurred between the Soviets and Chinese. For a more in-depth treatment of this topic I recommend reading Byung Chul Koh's *The Foreign Policy of North Korea*.

18. Chin O. Chung, *Pyongyang between Peking and Moscow: North Korea's Involvement in the Sino-Soviet Dispute, 1958–1975* (University of Alabama: University of Alabama Press, 1978) 14–15.

19. Koh, *The Foreign Policy of North Korea*, 13.

20. Ibid.

21. Ibid., 14–15.

22. Chung, *Pyongyang between Peking and Moscow*, 14–15.

23. Koh, *The Foreign Policy of North Korea*, 16–17.

24. Roy U.T. Kim, "Sino-North Korean Relations," *Asian Survey* 8:8 (August 1968) 709.

25. Mineo Nakajima, "The Sino-Soviet Confrontation: Its Roots in the International Background of the Korean War," *Australian Journal of Chinese Affairs* 1 (January 1979) 26.

26. Ibid., 33.

27. Ibid., 34.

28. People's Republic of China, Ministry of Foreign Affairs, "Conclusion of the 'Sino-Soviet Friendship, Alliance and Mutual Assistance'" (November 17, 2000). http://www.fmprc.gov.cn/eng/ziliao/3602/3604/t18011.htm.

29. Nakajima, "The Sino-Soviet Confrontation," 28.

30. Sergei N. Goncharov, John W. Lewis, and Xue Litai, *Uncertain Partners: Stalin, Mao and the Korean War* (Stanford, CA: Stanford University Press, 1993) 159.

31. Ibid.

32. The Domino Theory, first espoused by President Dwight Eisenhower in 1954, was initially applied to Vietnam. Fundamentally, the concept held that if Vietnam fell under the sway of communism, then Thailand, Burma, Indonesia, and Malaya would follow the same course. In the above reference, the fall of North Korea might well precipitate the fall of China, hence ushering in the fall of communism rather than the fall of democracy.

33. United States Government, Statement by the President: Harry S. Truman, June 27, 1950. http://www.trumanlibrary.org/whistlestop/study_collections/korea/large/week1/kw_27_1.htm.

34. Goncharov, Lewis, and Xue, *Uncertain Partners*, 158.

35. Nakajima, "The Sino-Soviet Confrontation," 38–39.

36. Koh, *The Foreign Policy of North Korea*, 46.

37. The full text of Khrushchev's speech can be found at http://home.mira.net/~andy/bs/1956nk.htm.

38. Koh, *The Foreign Policy of North Korea*, 48.

39. Ibid., 57.

40. Li Zhisui, *The Private Life of Chairman Mao* (New York: Random House, 1994) 272–273, 277.

41. Chung, *Pyongyang between Peking and Moscow*, 18.

42. "Economic Aid Pact Signed by Peiping and North Korea," *New York Times* November 24, 1953, 1 and 12.

43. Ibid.

44. Chung, *Pyongyang between Peking and Moscow*, 19.

45. Ibid., 21–22.

46. Koh, *The Foreign Policy of North Korea* 53.

47. "Economic Aid Pact," *New York Times*, 12.

48. The Soviet Union's first forays into collectivization were, by all accounts, failures. Because the quota system upon which Stalin based his collectivization plan hinged on exacting high payments in kind from farmers, they often received less for their labor than during the precollectivization period, leading to a lack of voluntary support of the plan. Farmers were then forced to participate in collectivization. Because of poor implementation policies, famines ensued particularly during 1932–1933.

49. Chung, *Pyongyang between Peking and Moscow*, 31–66.

50. Koh, *The Foreign Policy of North Korea*, 58.

51. Ibid.

52. Sung Chul Yang, *The North and South Korean Political Systems: A Comparative Analysis* (Elizabeth, NJ and Seoul: Hollym, 1999) 192–195.

53. The key policy pillars under Rhee's administration were anticommunism and reunification of the peninsula. Democracy, while also touted as a tenant, received little more than lip service. Rhee often used the threat posed by North Korea as a political expedient to justify his usurpation of power and to dispose of political rivals. One example of such a case was that of Cho Bong-am, head of a rival political party, who Rhee had executed in 1959. Ultimately, Rhee was forced to resign his

post under massive nationwide protests precipitated by disputed election results. He left South Korea and lived the remainder of his life in Hawaii. An excellent source for more information on this topic is Sung Chul Yang, *The North and South Korean Political Systems: A Comparative Analysis* (see Works Cited).

54. B.C. Koh, "North Korea in 1976: Under Stress," *Asian Survey* 17:1 (January 1977) 61.

55. The Cuban missile crisis, October 18–29, 1962, was precipitated by U.S. realization, through intelligence sources, that the Soviets were constructing missile bases on Cuba, only 90 miles away from the U.S. mainland. After considering a range of options to include invasion of Cuba or surgical air strikes to take out the bases, President Kennedy decided on a naval blockade to prevent access to the area by any other Soviet ships, effectively preventing further progress on the project. In response, Khrushchev ordered Soviet commanders in Cuba to launch tactical nuclear weapons in the event of U.S. invasion. The stalemate continued like this for eight days as the world watched its two nuclear superpowers staring each other down. Finally, Khrushchev, perhaps the result of his own policy of peaceful coexistence with the West or realizing his hand had been called, acquiesced to Kennedy's demands for complete removal of the missiles from Cuba.

56. The Rodong Sinmun (Newspaper of the Workers) is the official publication of the KWP and published by the Rodong News Agency. As such, it is considered to be the official mouthpiece of the Party. The publication has been in existence since 1945, but took its current form and name in September 1946.

57. Koh, "North Korea in 1976," 65–66.

58. Ibid., 66.

59. The Asian Economic Bureau, *Second Asian Economic Seminar (Pyongyang) of Delegates of Asian Economic Bureau and Participants from Asia, Africa and Oceania* (Colombo: The Asian Economic Bureau, 1964) 1.

60. Pravda (The Truth) was the official newspaper and mouthpiece of the Centeral Committee of the Soviet Communist Party between 1918 and 1991.

61. Koh offers a comprehensive treatment of articles published in the Rodong Sinmun in his work *The Foreign Policy of North Korea* published by Praeger.

62. The Asian Economic Bureau, *Second Asian Economic Seminar*, 79.

63. Khrushchev was removed from power on October 14, 1964, at a Central Committee meeting; the Party had come to regard his public behavior as an embarrassment to the Soviet image as leader of the Socialist world. He was replaced by Leonid Brezhnev (First Secretary of the Communist Party of the Soviet Union) and Alexei Kosygin (Chairman, Council of Ministers).

64. Koh, *The Foreign Policy of North Korea*, 82.

65. Chung, *Pyongyang between Peking and Moscow*, 112.

66. Ibid., 116.

67. "North Koreans in Moscow Get Pledge of Military Aid," *New York Times* June 1, 1965.

68. Chung, *Pyongyang between Peking and Moscow*, 118–119.

69. Ibid., 109.

70. Ibid.

71. Ibid., 110.

72. "Disorder Termed Aims of Korean Reds," *New York Times* January 24, 1968, 15.

73. Ibid.

74. The USS Pueblo Incident occurred in January 23, 1968. The U.S. naval vessel was on a mission to gather signal and electronic intelligence on Soviet ship activity in the vicinity of the Tsushima Straits. There is dispute over where the ship was actually located: U.S. sources indicate the ship was operating in international waters while North Korean sources indicate it was within North Korean territorial waters. This discrepancy came about because, although international law provides for a 12-nautical-mile maritime boundary, the North Koreans claimed a 50-mile boundary. The ship was captured and its crew taken to North Korea where they were held prisoner and used for propaganda purposes. They were released on December 23, 1968, only after the United States agreed, in writing, that the Pueblo was on a spying mission, apologized, and promised not to undertake such activity in the future. The United States verbally retracted its admission and promises after the safe return of the crew. Given its call for diversionary tactics against the United States in support of North Vietnam, this incident appears to be in keeping with that policy.

75. "North Korean Says Aim was to Assassinate Park," *New York Times* January 23, 1968.

76. "South Korea Calls 'Defection' a Hoax by Northern Spy," *New York Times* February 14, 1969.

77. "North Korean 'Defector' is Indicted by Seoul," *New York Times* March 23, 1969.

78. "North Korea Signs Pact with Soviet," *New York Times* March 6, 1967.

79. "Text of Korean Statement," *New York Times* July 4, 1972, 2.

80. "Washington Hails Korea Plans for Talks," *New York Times* July 5, 1972, 16.

81. "Bid to US Made by North Korea," *New York Times* March 26, 1974, 9.

82. "'Barbarous' Attack on 2 Boats Laid to North Korea by Seoul," *New York Times* February 16, 1974, 3.

83. "North Korea Sinks Seoul Patrol Ship," *New York Times* June 29, 1974, 2.

84. The assassination attempt was undertaken by Mun Segwang, a South Korean living in Japan and a North Korean sympathizer. He was executed in South Korea four months after his failed attempt on Park Chung Hee's life. Ironically, Park was assassinated on October 26, 1979, by Kim Jaegyu, who was chief of the (South) Korean Central Intelligence Agency.

85. On the morning of August 18, 1976 a work detail pruning a poplar tree that obscured the line of sight between two checkpoints; the visibility of one of the checkpoints was limited by the tree's branches and past attempts had been made by North Korean soldiers to grab soldiers manning that position and take them across the Bridge of No Return into North Korea. In the end, the detail came under attack from a contingent of North Korean soldiers and Captain Arthur G. Bonifas and First Lieutenant Mark T. Barrett were killed and nine soldiers injured, four Americans and five South Koreans. Contrary to North Korean claims of self-defense, there are accounts from the United States and South Koreans that an order to "kill" the Americans and South Koreans was overheard. In response, the U.S. Military launched Operation Paul Bunyan to resecure freedom of movement on the allied side of the Joint Security Area. Heavily armed and reinforced, the contingent of U.S. and South Korean soldiers proceeded to prune the tree in question.

86. Sung, *The North and South Korean Political Systems*, 198.

87. Ibid., 199.

88. Ibid., 200.

89. Young C. Kim, "The Democratic People's Republic of Korea in 1975," *Asian Survey* 16:1 (January 1976) 84–86.

90. Ibid., 84–86.

91. The North Koreans suffered major diplomatic setbacks in Scandinavia during October 1976. Amid charges of black market import and sale of drugs, alcohol and cigarettes, the governments of Norway and Denmark declared the North Korean mission persona non grata. A similar fate befell four diplomatic staff members in Finland, while the Ambassador and four staff members in Sweden voluntarily left their posts under a cloud of suspicion as Swedish authorities investigated similar charges. (Koh, "North Korea in 1976," 61).

92. Koh, "North Korea in 1976" 61–70.

93. Young C. Kim, "North Korea in 1979: National Unification and Economic Development," *Asian Survey* 20:1 (January 1980): 53–62.

94. The impetus for improved relations between the United States and China was Nixon's visit to China, the first time for a U.S. president ever to do so, in February 1972, also known as the "Nixon Shock." After his weeklong stay, the two governments issued what is now known as the Shanghai Communiqué, which called for both countries to work for full normalization in Sino-U.S. relations; U.S. recognition of the existence of only one China; and peaceful settlement of the Taiwan issue.

95. Koh, "North Korea in 1976," 66.

96. "Juche [Self-reliance or Self-dependence]," GlobalSecurity.org. http://www.globalsecurity.org/military/world/dprk/juche.htm.

97. B.C. Koh, "North Korea in 1977: A Year of 'Readjustment,'" *Asian Survey* 18:1 (January 1978): 42–43.

98. Koh, "North Korea in 1977," 36–44.

99. Young C. Kim, "The Democratic People's Republic of Korea in 1975," *Asian Survey* 16:1 (January 1976): 92.

100. Ibid., 43.

101. Ibid., 62.

102. Koh, "North Korea in 1976," 67.

103. Ibid.

104. Ibid.

105. Koh, "North Korea in 1977," 36.

106. Ibid., 37.

107. Kim, "North Korea in 1979," 60.

108. Koh, "North Korea in 1977," 39.

109. "US Copter Strayed on North Korea Line," *New York Times* July 15, 1977, 42.

110. "North Korea Says It Will Return Injured G.I. and Copter's Three Dead," *New York Times* July 16, 1977, 1.

111. Team Spirit exercises were conducted from 1976 to 1993. They were scheduled to be held between 1994 and 1996 but were cancelled each year as an inducement for North Korea to work toward better relations.

112. William Chapman, "Burma Says N. Korea Guilty of Bombing that Killed 21; Rangoon Breaks Diplomatic Relations with Pyongyang," *Washington Post*, November 5, 1983.

113. Ibid.

114. John Burgess, "Two Koreas Agree on Relief Plan," *Washington Post* September 27, 1984.

115. "North and South Korea Agree on Family Visits," *New York Times* August 23, 1985, A3.

116. "No Ban on North Korea," *New York Times* January 19, 1988, D27.

117. "North Koreans Propose Reduction of Troops in the North and South," *New York Times* July 24, 1987, A10.

118. From about 1981 when the decision was announced that Seoul would host the 1988 Olympic Games, North Korea attempted in various ways to share the spotlight. In the end, it demanded that Pyongyang be permitted to cohost the games with Seoul. To that end, it sought the support of the socialist bloc and non-aligned nations in order to force the issue, an effort in which it ultimately failed. The Soviet Union, under Gorbachev's new policy pursuits, found it more advantageous to join the games as did other Eastern European nations. North Korea also failed in its attempts to have itself recognized as the sole legitimate government on the peninsula. By the end of the 1980s there was greater support within the socialist bloc for joint admission into the United Nations for both North and South Korea. This, of course, was the direct result of Seoul's increased rapprochement with socialist nations. Although admission into the world body under other circumstances might be considered a diplomatic win for North Korea, given the time and effort its leadership devoted to obviating the concept of "two Koreas" this open global recognition of two distinct states can only be construed as a blow to its international stature. Both nations were admitted to the United Nations on September 17, 1991.

119. B.C. Koh, "North Korea in 1988: The Fortieth Anniversary," *Asian Survey* 29:1 (January 1989) 45.

120. Dae-Ho Byun, *North Korea's Foreign Policy: The Juche Ideology and the Challenge of Gorbachev's New Thinking* (Seoul: Seoul Computer Press; Published for The Research Center for Peace and Unification, 1991) 207.

121. Ibid.

122. Koh, "North Korea in 1988," 43–44.

123. "Seoul Threatens North Korea After Confession on Jet Bomb," *New York Times* January 16, 1988, 2.

124. Rin-sup Shinn, "North Korea in 1981: First Year for De Facto Successor Kim Jong Il," *Asian Survey* 22:1 (January 1982): 99.

125. Dae-Sook Suh, "North Korea in 1986: Strengthening the Soviet Connection," *Asian Survey* 27:1 (January 1987): 59.

126. Young Whan Kihl, "North Korea in 1983: Transforming the 'Hermit Kingdom'?" *Asian Survey* 24:1 (January 1984): 100–101.

127. B.C. Koh, "North Korea in 1987: Launching a New Seven Year Plan," *Asian Survey* 28:1 (January 1988): 64–65.

128. Young C. Kim, "North Korea in 1980: The Son Also Rises," *Asian Survey* 21:1 (January 1981): 112.

129. Young Whan Kihl, "North Korea in 1983: Transforming the 'Hermit Kingdom'?" *Asian Survey* 24:1 (January 1984): 100–101.

130. Koh, "North Korea in 1987," 65.

131. Kong Dan Oh, "North Korea in 1989: Touched by Winds of Change?" *Asian Survey* 30:1 (January 1990): 77.

132. Ibid.

133. Young Whan Kihl, "North Korea in 1984: The 'Hermit Kingdom' turns Outward," *Asian Survey* 25:1 (January 1985): 69–70.

134. Hy-Sang Lee, "North Korea's Closed Economy: The Hidden Opening," *Asian Survey* 28:12 (December 1988): 1264–1265.

135. U.S. Congress, Library of Congress Country Studies: North Korea, Foreign Investment and Joint Ventures (June 1993). http://memory.loc.gov/cgi-bin/query/r?frd/cstdy:@field(DOCID+kp0095).

136. Rhee Sang-woo, "North Korea in 1991: Struggle to Save Chuche Amid Signs of Change," *Asian Survey* 32:1 (January 1992): 59.

137. Sungwoo Kim, "Recent Economic Policies of North Korea: Analysis and Recommendations," *Asian Survey* 33:9 (September 1993): 870.

138. Koh, "North Korea in 1987," 62–70.

CHAPTER 5

1. John Merrill, "North Korea in 1992: Steering Away from the Shoals," *Asian Survey* 33:1 (January 1993): 52.

2. Ibid., 51.

3. Sang-Woo Rhee, "North Korea in 1991: The Struggle to Save Chuch'e Amid Signs of Change." *Asian Survey* 32:1 (January 1992): 59.

4. Ibid.

5. Ibid.

6. Merrill, "North Korea in 1992," 47.

7. Ibid.

8. Samuel S. Kim, "North Korea in 1994: Brinksmanship, Breakdown, and Breakthrough," *Asian Survey* 35:1 (January 1995): 21.

9. Ibid.

10. Roger Dingman, "Atomic Diplomacy during the Korean War," *International Security* 13:3 (Winter 1988–1989): 50–91.

11. For a full analysis of this topic I recommend to the reader Roger Dingman's article, "Atomic Diplomacy during the Korean War," which appeared in *International Security* (Vol. 13, No. 3), Winter 1988–1989, pp. 50–91.

12. Michael J. Mazarr, "Going Just a Little Nuclear: Nonproliferation Lessons from North Korea," *International Security* 20:2 (Autumn 1995): 94.

13. Ibid.

14. Interview with Ambassador Thomas Hubbard (former U.S. ambassador to South Korea), "Illinois International," University of Illinois, October 18, 2006.

15. Interview with William Perry, Frontline, PBS Television, February 26, 2003.

16. Governments of United States and the Democratic People's Republic of Korea, "Agreed Framework between the United States of America and the Democratic People's Republic of Korea," October 21, 1994.

17. Governments of United States and the Democratic People's Republic of Korea, "Agreed Framework between the United States of America and the Democratic People's Republic of Korea," October 21, 1994.

18. David G. Brown, "North Korea in 1998: A Year of Foreboding Developments," *Asian Survey* 39:1 (January–February 1999): 130.

19. During 1998, U.S. intelligence also revealed that North Korea had a secret underground facility of a sort that could well be associated with a nuclear weapons program. This was the first indication that North Korea, in addition to its known plutonium-based weapons program, may also have been developing a uranium-based nuclear weapons program. The 1994 Agreed Framework addressed only the regime's plutonium-based program. Discovery of the underground facility led to an erosion of support for the Framework. Congress, for example, put stipulations on the funding for supplying the heavy fuel oil that required progress first be made on North Korea's missile program and inspection of its underground facility.

20. Ambassador Yang Sung Chul, South Korea's Ambassador to the United States, Speech to the Asia Society in Washington, DC, December 4, 2000. http://www.asiasociety.org/speeches/chul.html.

21. Ibid.

22. Donald Macintyre, "Sunshine Policy: A Very Expensive Affair," *Time Magazine* March 24, 2003.

23. Lee Soo-jeong, "South Korea Proposes Red Cross Talks to Ensure More Family Reunions," *Korea Times* August 27, 2000.

24. Samuel S. Kim, "North Korea in 2000: Surviving through High Hopes of Summit Diplomacy," *Asian Survey* 41:1 (January–February 2001): 17.

25. The ASEAN Regional Forum was created on July 25, 1994, as an informal venue through which Asia-Pacific security issues can be discussed and resolved. There are presently 25 member nations in ARF, which includes all six nations involved in the Six Party Talks over North Korea's nuclear weapons program—United States, China, Russia, Japan, South Korea, and North Korea.

26. For a detailed and informative account of how the Bush administration's North Korea policy developed, I recommend reading Sebastian Harnisch's article, "US-North Korean Relations under the Bush Administration: From 'Slow Go' to 'No Go'." In this article he describes a four-phased process leading to the final iteration of Bush's North Korea Policy. While I don't necessarily subscribe to the concept of the four phases outlined in the article, I do agree with the basic premise that Bush administration policy has gone through an evolutionary process, which I believe continues.

27. Report of Commission to Assess Ballistic Missile Threat to the United States, 104th Congress, July 15, 1998 (Washington, DC: Printing and Production Graphics, 1998): 1.

28. For the full text of the Commission's report, I recommend the reader access it on the Web site of the Federation of American Scientists: http://www.fas.org/irp/threat/bm-threat.htm.

29. Thomas L. Friedman, "Macho on North Korea," *New York Times* March 9, 2001.

30. David E. Sanger, "Bush Tell Seoul Talks with North Won't Resume Now," *New York Times* March 8, 2001.

31. Sebastion Harnisch, "US-North Korean Relations under the Bush Administration: From 'Slow Go' to 'No Go,'" *Asian Survey* 42:6 (November–December 2002): 868.

32. The 11 original countries that agreed to participate in the Initiative included Australia, France, Germany, Italy, Japan, the Netherlands, Poland, Portugal, Spain, the United Kingdom, and the United States. For more on this initiative and details of the principles it produced, visit the U.S. State Department's Web site's "The Proliferation Security Initiative" page at http://www.state.gov/t/np/rls/other/34726. htm. Another helpful site is the Australian government's Web site that can be accessed at http://www.dfat.gov.au/globalissues/psi/.

33. Howard W. French, "In Yet Another Mystery, North Korea has Suddenly Turned Testy," *New York Times* October 26, 2001, A5.

34. Harnisch, "US-North Korean Relations under the Bush Administration," 871.

35. In the interest of full disclosure it should be noted that North Korea maintains the US deliberately misrepresented a key term in translation. North Korean officials contend they were acknowledging their "right" to possess nuclear weapons; they were not admitting to the actual possession of them.

36. "White House Calls Clinton-era North Korea Policy a Failure," *USA Today* July 11, 2006.

37. Fred Kaplan, "Rolling Blunder: How the Bush Administration Let North Korea Get Nukes," *Washington Monthly* May 2004, 3–4.

38. Ibid.

39. Jonathan Marcus, "Bush's Pyongyang Policy 'Futile,'" *BBC News* June 22, 2004.

CHAPTER 6

1. World Food Program activities have, at the request of the North Korean government, been halted effective January 1, 2006, closing all 19 of its food processing facilities in the country. North Korea contends that as the result of a 2005 bumper crop, it has essentially moved beyond the famine conditions of the 1990s and that future international assistance should focus on development assistance.

2. The North Korea issue actually has two facets: the conventional threat it poses to South Korea and its regional nuclear weapons threat. While the focus of this book addresses the broader nuclear issue, it is important for the reader to remain cognizant of the fact that North Korea and South Korea technically remain in a state of war; the 1953 Armistice signed between the United States, China, and North Korea only calls for a cessation of hostilities, it is not a peace treaty. As such, whatever solution is ultimately reached with regard to North Korea's nuclear program should support, or at least not undermine the objective of broader peace on the Korean peninsula.

3. I will use the term "asymmetric warfare" synonymously with "unconventional warfare," to distinguish between conventional combat power—military personnel, armor (tanks and other armored vehicles); artillery, aircraft, ships, etc. The reader should be aware, however, that there is a body of research challenging the widespread and popular use of "asymmetry" as it relates to defining threats to

national security and in warfare, the basic argument of which is twofold: 1) that the term has come to define so many potential threats, it essentially defines nothing; and 2) what it really attempts to define is the "strategy" of avoiding an enemy's strengths while attacking his weaknesses through surprise and deception—in effect, warfare as it has been practiced for centuries. For more information, I recommend reading "Rethinking Asymmetric Threats" by Stephen J. Blank, Strategic Studies Institute, Carlisle Barracks, Carlisle, PA, September 2003; "Reconsidering Asymmetric Warfare" by Steven J. Lambakis, *Joint Force Quarterly*, issue 36: 102–108; and "No More Principles of War?" Russell W. Glenn, Parameters, Spring 1998, 48–66, U.S. Army War College, Carlisle Barracks, PA.

4. The International Institute for Strategic Studies, *The Military Balance, 2004–2005* (London: Oxford University Press, 2004), Table 38, 353–358.

5. Donald S. Zagoria and Young Kun Kim, "North Korea and the Major Powers," *Asia Survey* 15:12 (December 1975): 1026.

6. Republic of Korea, Participatory Government Defense Policy, 2003, 200.

7. "Make a Higher Leap Full of Great Ambition and Confidence" (North Korean 2006 New Year's Message), *North Korea This Week* 378 (Yonhap News).

8. "North Korea's Nuclear New Year's Message," The Australian, January 1, 2007.

9. Chaiki Seong, "A Decade of Economic Crisis in North Korea: Impacts on the Military," *Korea Institute for Defense Analysis Papers* 3 (October 2003): 2.

10. United States, Report to Congress, "Military Situation on the Korean Peninsula," 2000. http://www.defenselink.mil/news/Sep2000/korea09122000.html.

11. Federation of American Scientists, North Korea's Biological Weapons Program, (November 1998). http://www.fas.org/nuke/guide/dprk/bw/.

12. Ibid.

13. Ibid.

14. GlobalSecurity.org, North Korea: Weapons of Mass Destruction: Chemical Weapons. http://www.globalsecurity.org/wmd/world/dprk/cw.htm.April 2005.

15. Federation of American Scientists, North Korea's Chemical Weapons Program (November 1998). http://www.fas.org/nuke/guide/dprk/cw/.

16. Seo Jee-yeon, "NK's Chemical Imports Raise Alarms," *Korea Times* September 28, 2004.

17. "NK Has Plutonium to Make 8 Bombs," *Korea Times* January 3, 2006.

18. GlobalSecurity.org, North Korea: Weapons of Mass Destruction: Uranium Program (April 28, 2005). http://www.globalsecurity.org/wmd/world/dprk/nuke-uranium.htm.

19. Ibid.

20. Center for Defense Information, Fact Sheet: North Korea's Nuclear weapons Program (January 23, 2003). http://www.cdi.org/nuclear/nk-fact-sheet.cfm.

21. GlobalSecurity.org, North Korea: Weapons of Mass Destruction: Uranium Program (April 28, 2005). http://www.globalsecurity.org/wmd/world/dprk/nuke-uranium.htm.

22. Federation of American Scientists, "North Korean Missiles: Taepo'dong 2" (December 1, 2005). http://www.fas.org/nuke/guide/dprk/missile/td-2.htm.

23. Ibid.

24. "US: N. Korea Apparently Tests Missile," *CNN.com* May 1, 2005. http://www.cnn.com/2005/WORLD/asiapcf/05/01/northkorea.missile/.

25. Federation of American Scientists, "WMD Around the World: North Korean Missiles: Taepodong-2" (December 1, 2005). http://www.fas.org/nuke/guide/dprk/missile/td-2.htm.

26. Ibid.

27. "North Korea Agrees to Peace Talks," *CNN Interactive* June 25, 1997. http://www.cnn.com/WORLD/9706/25/korea/.

28. United States, Senate Foreign Relations Committee, 108th Congress, 1st session, "Six Party Talks and the North Korean nuclear Issue: A Staff Trip Report," October 14, 2003. http://www.icasinc.org/2003/2003l/2003lcfr.html.

29. Na Jeong-ju, "NK Opens Mt. Paektu to S. Koreans," *Korea Times* August 10, 2005.

30. Seo Dong-shin, "China Unfreezes NK Bank Accounts," *Korea Times* November 20, 2006.

31. Park Song-wu, "Seoul Will Not Join US-led PSI," *Korea Times* November 13, 2006.

32. "Koizumi Prefers N. Korea Dialogue to Economic Sanctions," *Kyodo News* October 11, 2004.

33. United States, Office of the President of the United States, "Prevent Our Enemies from Threatening Us, Our Allies, and Our Friends with Weapons of Mass Destruction," National Security Strategy 2006. http://www.whitehouse.gov/nsc/nss/2006/nss2006.pdf.

34. "Back to the Brink in Korea," World War 4 Report: Deconstructing the War on Terrorism 66 (December 30, 2002). http://ww4report.com/static/66.html#nuke1.

35. The Robust Nuclear Earth Penetrator, or the nuclear bunker buster, is a low-yield nuclear weapon capable of targeting hard and deeply buried targets (HDBT), funding for the study of which was approved by the U.S. Congress for the Fiscal Year 2006 Defense Authorization Bill. Present technology limits bomb penetration to about 100 feet of loose dirt or 30 feet of rock, falling far short of the anticipated depths of an adversary's underground command and control centers or WMD storage facilities. The controversy over this class of proposed weapons is that a 1-kiloton bomb (about 1/10th the size of the Hiroshima bomb) buried at a depth of 20–50 feet would send about 1 million cubic feet of radioactive debris into the air. In order to avoid such an outcome, the bomb would need to bury itself to a depth of about 850 feet. International response to U.S. plans to study such a weapon has been mixed; while response from NATO countries has been muted (the U.S. deploys nuclear weapons at bases in seven NATO countries: UK, Turkey, Belgium, Greece, Italy, the Netherlands, and Germany), the Russian and Chinese governments have voiced strong opposition to the study, each of which sees potential application of the weapon against its own strategic interests and targets.

36. John Chipman, "North Korea's Weapons Programmes: A Net Assessment," *International Institute for Strategic Studies Dossier* (January 21, 2004): 4. http://www.iiss.org/index.asp?pgid=1241.

37. GlobalSecurity.org, Weapons of Mass Destruction: Special Operations Forces (April 28, 2005). http://www.globalsecurity.org/wmd/library/news/dprk/1996/kpa-guide/part03.htm.

38. Ibid.

39. United Nations, World Food Program, INTERFAIS. Food Aid Monitor Annual Report (2005), Table 1, June 2006. http://www.wfp.org/interfais/index2. htm#.

40. Ibid.

41. Ibid., Table 15.

42. Ibid., Table 4.

43. Mark E. Manyin, Library of Congress, "Foreign Assistance to North Korea," Congressional Research Service Report for Congress, May 26, 2005, 26.

44. Park Song-wu, "Launch Sends Blunt Message to America," *Korea Times* July 5, 2006.

45. Park Song-wu, "Diplomats in N. Korea Believe Underground Nuke Test Highly Probable," *Korea Times* September 10, 2006.

CHAPTER 7

1. Stephan Haggard and Marcus Noland, "Famine, Marketization and Economic Reform in North Korea," Meeting Paper for the Allied Social Sciences Associations (December 6, 2005): 1. http://www.aeaweb.org/annual_mtg_papers/2006/0107_0800_1502.pdf.

2. Ibid., 3.

3. Ibid., 3–5.

4. In congressional testimony provided to the Subcommittee on East Asia and the Pacific of the Committee on International Relations, the regional head of the World Food Program, John Powell, offered that: " . . . we saw farmers preparing land for planting on slopes where it was quite impossible to stand erect. This is land that should be under forest cover, not under cultivation . . . despite the negative impact on the environment that this practice causes—including increased vulnerability to flooding."

5. Sungwoo Kim, "Economic Strategy for Suppression of North Korea's Nuclear Weapons Development," *Vantage Point* 27:7 (July 2004): 42.

6. Daniel Goodkind and Loraine West, "The North Korean Famine and Its Demographic Impact," *Population and Development Review* 27:2 (June 2001): 222.

7. Ibid.

8. Kim, "Economic Strategy for Suppression of North Korea's Nuclear Weapons Development," 42.

9. Goodkind and West, "The North Korean Famine," 221.

10. "North Korea's Foreign Trade Remains Bleak," *Vantage Point: Developments in North Korea* XVIII: 6 (June 1995): 14.

11. Kongdan Oh and Ralph C. Hassig, "North Korea: The Hardest Nut," *The Brookings Institution, Global Politics* (November 2003). http://www.brook.edu/views/articles/fellows/oh20031201.htm.

12. Haggard and Noland, "Famine, Marketization and Economic Reform in North Korea," 4.

13. "North Korea's Foreign Trade Remains Bleak," 14.

14. Ibid.

15. Chong Bong-uk, "Tasks to Meet Three-Pronged Policy Demand," *Vantage Point* 27:2 (February 2004): 6.

CHAPTER 8

1. I recommend reading Fiona Terry's news article, "Food Aid to North Korea Is Propping Up Stalinist a Regime," which appeared in the *Guardian Weekly* (New Zealand) September 6, 2001. Ms. Terry is a researcher for Médecins Sans Frontières.

2. Fiona Terry, "Food Aid to North Korea Is Propping Up a Stalinist Regime," *Guardian Weekly* September 6, 2001, 21. http://www.vuw.ac.nz/~caplabtb/dprk/fiona_terry1.html.

3. The duration of the Cold War is dated in two ways: from 1947 until November 1989 and the fall of the Berlin Wall or, alternatively, the fall of the Soviet Union in December 1991. For the purposes of this book, I recognize the fall of the Berlin Wall as the symbolic end of the Cold War period.

4. The other countries against which the UN has imposed sanctions include: Afghanistan; Angola; Cote d'Ivoire; Democratic Republic of the Congo; Ethiopia and Eritrea; Haiti; Iraq; Liberia; Libya; Rwanda; Sierra Leone; Somalia; Sudan; and the former Yugoslavia.

5. United Nations, Office of the Spokesman for the Secretary-General, Use of Sanctions under Chapter VII of the UN Charter, January 2006. http://www.un.org/News/ossg/sanction.htm.

6. Thomas G. Weiss, "Sanctions as a Foreign Policy Tool: Weighing Humanitarian Impulses," *Journal of Peace Research* 36:5 (September 1999): 499–500.

7. Martin Wolk, "Cost of the War in Iraq Could Surpass $1 Trillion," *MSNBC On-Line* March 17, 2006. http://www.msnbc.msn.com/id/11880954/.

8. Robert Pape, "Why Economic Sanctions Do Not Work," *International Security* 22:2 (Autumn 1997): 92–108.

9. Franklin L.Lavin, "Asphyxiation or Oxygen: The Sanctions Dilemma," *Foreign Policy* 104 (Autumn 1996): 144.

10. Behrooz Ghamari-Tabrizi, "Words, Worries, and Wants: A Glimpse into Life in Iran," *Illinois International Review* 3 (Fall 2006): 2.

11. United Nations, United Nations Foundation, "Oil-for-Food Facts," December 2005. http://www.oilforfoodfacts.org/.

12. Ibid.

13. Lavin, "Asphyxiation or Oxygen," 146.

14. Arne Tostensen and Beate Bull, "Are Smart Sanctions Feasible?" *World Politics* 54 (April 2002): 373–374.

15. United Nations Foundation, "Oil-for-Food Facts" (December 2005). http://www.oilforfoodfacts.org/.

16. Jephraim P. Gundzik, "The Ties that Bind China, Russia and Iran," *Asia Times Online* June 4, 2005. http://www.atimes.com/atimes/China/GF04Ad07.html.

17. "New Sanctions Could Spurt Economic Drive," Economic Focus, *Iran Daily* September 21, 2004. http://www.iran-daily.com/1383/2093/html/focus.htm.

18. Pape, "Why Economic Sanctions Do Not Work," 92.

19. Ibid., 97.

20. Ibid., 93.

21. Named after U.S. Secretary of State George C. Marshall (also U.S. Army Chief of Staff during WWII), the Marshall Plan, formally known as the European Recovery Plan, was implemented in July 1947, and designed to aid in the

reconstruction of those European nations that joined the Organization for Economic Cooperation and Development. The plan extended $13 billion in economic and technical aid.

22. Tom Barry, "U.S. Isn't 'Stingy,' It's Strategic," *International Relations Center* January 7, 2005. http://www.irc-online.org/content/commentary/2005/0501aid. php.

23. John J. Mearsheimer and Stephen M. Walt, "The War Over Israel's Influence," *Foreign Policy* July/August 2006, 57–58.

24. United States, Library of Congress, "South Korea: Relations with the Soviet Union," Country Studies Series by Federal Research Division (June 1990). http://www.country-data.com/cgi-bin/query/r-12358.html.

25. Byung-joon Ahn, "South Korea-Soviet Relations: Contemporary Issues and Prospects," *Asian Survey* 31:9 (September 1991): 819.

26. Two Soviet fighters were responsible for shooting down a Korean Airlines 747, KAL 007, on September 1, 1983, killing all 269 passengers and crew; the aircraft was on a flight from New York's Kennedy Airport to Seoul's Kimpo Airport. The Soviets maintained that the aircraft was on a spy mission as it had strayed over Soviet airspace as it flew over the Kamchatka peninsula heading toward Sakhalin. The Soviets, arriving first at the crash site, secured flight data recorders and refused to turn them over to South Korea. When the flight's tapes were turned over to South Korean officials after Boris Yelstin became president of Russia, it became clear that the flight crew had mistakenly entered in the wrong flight coordinates and had subsequently failed to confirm that their heading was correct, consequently straying into Soviet airspace.

27. Ahn, "South Korea-Soviet Relations," 819–820.

28. Ibid., 821.

29. While *Ostpolitik* moved West Germany away from the Hallstein Doctrine in a practical sense, it wasn't until the signing of the 1972 Basic Treaty that both East and West Germany mutually recognized each other as two separate states.

30. David Binder, "What Bonn Has That East Bloc Wants," *New York Times* December 14, 1969.

31. Clyde H. Farnsworth, "Bonn Is Said to Offer Warsaw a $550-Million Credit in Trade Talks," *New York Times* December 9, 1969.

32. "West Berlin Adds Trade with East," *New York Times* November 9, 1969.

33. Ibid.

34. Ibid.

35. The Renunciation of Force Treaty, formally known as the Moscow Treaty, was signed on August 12, 1970, and provided for the following: both the Soviet Union and West Germany renounced the threat or use of force; both agreed to abide by the UN Charter and ensure the maintenance of peace and stability; and each recognized existing boundaries between European nations. In subsequent agreements, West Germany also agreed to pursue renunciation of force agreements with other eastern bloc nations.

36. Bernard Gwertzman, "Soviet and West Germany Reach Accord on a Treaty to Foster Peace in Europe," *New York Times*, August 6, 1970: 1.

37. Michael Farr, "Bonn Sets Credit Line for Soviets," *New York Times* October 12, 1988.

CHAPTER 9

1. As of this writing, the Bush administration has signaled a slight softening in its position with the North Korean regime, indicating a willingness to favorably consider replacing the existing armistice with a peace treaty if the regime abandons its nuclear weapons program. This is clearly a demonstrable CBM, but continues to fall short in that it is not tied to a comprehensive strategy of engagement and continues to confuse goals and policies. Additionally, much has transpired under the broader rubric of the global war on terror since the inauguration of the first Bush administration in 2001, consequently offering the possibility of a peace treaty as a stand-alone quid pro quo for denuclearization might not be viewed as positively by the regime as the Administration might hope. There are no quick fixes; the likelihood is very slim that this Administration will be able to count resolution of the nuclear crisis with North Korea among its accomplishments. It might, however, yet be able to begin crafting a long-term, de-politicized, comprehensive approach that ultimately leads to CVID.

2. Nam Kwang-sik, "Signs of Expanding Trade with Foreign Countries," *Vantage Point: Developments in North Korea* 27:7 (July 2004): 16–17.

3. Kim Sungwoo, "Economic Strategy for Suppression of North Korea's Nuclear Weapons Development," *Vantage Point: Developments in North Korea* 27:7 (July 2004): 43.

4. Nam Kwang-sik, "North Korea Heading Toward Market Economy," *Vantage Point: Developments in North Korea* 27:2 (February 2004): 10.

5. Ibid.

6. Chong Bong-uk, "All-Out Offensive for Economic Achievements," *Vantage Point: Developments in North Korea* 27:12 (December 2004): 9.

7. Nam, "North Korea Heading Toward Market Economy," 8.

8. Park Hyong-ki, "SUVs, Pickups Hot in N. Korea," *Korea Times* October 15, 2006.

9. Reuben Staines, "NK Cuts Kumgang Tours," *Korea Times* August 29, 2005.

10. Kim Doo-hwan, "A Changing Socialist Country," *Vantage Point: Developments in North Korea* 27:6 (June 2004): 21.

11. Nam Kwang-sik, "North Korea Heading Toward Market Economy," 9.

12. Lee Jin-woo, "US Scholar Calls for Direct Talks between US, N. Korea," *Korea Times* October 2, 2006.

13. Chong Bong-uk "All-Out Offensive for Economic Achievements," 9.

14. Kim, "Economic Strategy for Suppression of North Korea's Nuclear Weapons Development," 47.

15. Marcus Noland, "Legal Framework of US-N. Korea Trade Relations," *Vantage Point: Developments in North Korea* 27:5 (May 2004): 20.

16. Lou Dobbs Tonight, *CNN* October 10, 2006.

Works Cited

MANUSCRIPTS

Borisov, O.B. and Koloskov, B.T. *Soviet-Chinese Relations, 1945–1970*. Blooming-ton: Indiana University Press, 1975.

Byun, Dae-Ho. *North Korea's Foreign Policy: The Juche Ideology and the Challenge of Gorbachev's New Thinking*. Seoul: Seoul Computer Press (published for the Research Center for Peace and Unification), 1991.

Chay, Jongsuk. *Unequal Partners in Peace and War, the Republic of Korea and the United States, 1948–1953*. Westport, CT: Praeger, 2002.

Chin, O. Chung. *Pyongyang between Peking and Moscow: North Korea's Involve-ment in the Sino-Soviet Dispute, 1958–1975*. University of Alabama Press, 1978.

Goncharov, Sergei N., Lewis, John W., and Xue, Litai. *Uncertain Partners*. Stanford, CA: Stanford University Press, 1993.

Goodman, Allan E., ed. *Negotiating While Fighting: The Diary of Admiral C. Turner Joy at the Korean Armistice Conference*. Stanford, CA: Hoover Institution Press, 1978.

Hunter, Helen-Louise. *Kim Il-song's North Korea*. Westport, CT: Praeger, 1999.

Kim, Il Sung. *Revolution and Socialist Construction in Korea*. New York: Interna-tional Publishers, 1971.

———. *On Eliminating Dogmatism and Formalism and Establishing Juche in Ide-ological Work*. Pyongyang: Foreign Languages Publishing House, 1973.

———. *On Juche in Our Revolution*. Pyongyang: Foreign Languages Publishing House, 1982.

Koh, Byung Chul. *The Foreign Policy of North Korea.* New York: Frederick A. Praeger Publishers, 1969.

———. *The Foreign Policy Systems of North and South Korea.* Berkeley: University of California Press, 1984.

Lee, Ki-baik. *A New History of Korea.* Trans. Edward W. Wagner with Edward J. Shultz. Cambridge, MA: Harvard University Press, 1984.

Martin, Bradley K. *Under the Loving Care of the Fatherly Leader: North Korea and the Kim Dynasty.* New York: Thomas Dunne-St. Martin's Press, 2004.

Meade, E. Grant. *American Military Government in Korea.* New York: King's Crown Press, Columbia University, 1952.

Nahm, Andrew C. *Korea: Tradition and Transformation.* Seoul: Hollym Corporation, 1988.

Noland, Marcus. *Avoiding the Apocalypse: The Future of the Two Koreas.* Washington, DC: Institute for International Economics, 2000.

———. *Famine and Reform in North Korea.* Washington, DC: Institute for International Economics, 2003.

Oberdorfer, Don. *The Two Koreas: A Contemporary History.* Basic Books (a member of Perseus Books Group), 2001.

Oh, Kongdan and Hassig, Ralph C. *North Korea through the Looking Glass.* Washington, DC: Brookings Institution Press, 2000.

Park, Jae Kyu, Koh, Byung Chul, and Kwak, Tae-Hwan. *The Foreign Relations of North Korea.* Boulder: Westview Press, 1987.

Shin, Bum Shik, comp. *Major Speeches by Korea's Park Chung Hee.* Seoul: Hollym Corporation Publishers, 1970.

Wit, Joel S., Poneman, Daniel B., and Gallucci, Robert L. *Going Critical: The First North Korean Nuclear Crisis.* Washington, DC: Brookings Institution Press, 2004.

Yang, Sung Chul. *The North and South Korean Political Systems: A Comparative Analysis.* Elizabeth, NJ and Seoul: Hollym, 1999.

JOURNALS

Barna, Brian J. "An Economic Roadmap to Korean Reunification: Pitfalls and Prospects." *Asian Survey* 38(3) (March 1998): 265–290.

Boose, Donald W., Jr. "Portentous Sideshow: The Korea Occupation Decision." *Parameters: US Army War College Quarterly* (Winter 1995): 113–119.

Brown, David G. "North Korea in 1998: A Year of Foreboding Developments." *Asian Survey* 39(1) (January–February 1999): 125–132.

Cha, Victor A. "The Rationale for 'Enhanced' Engagement of North Korea: After the Perry Policy Review." *Asian Survey* 39(6) (November–December 1999): 845–866.

Choi, Chang-yoon. "Korea: Security and Strategic Issues." *Asian Survey* 20(11) (November 1980): 1123–1139.

Choi, Young. "The North Korean Military Buildup and Its Impact on North Korean Military Strategy in the 1980s." *Asian Survey* 25(3) (March 1985): 341–355.

Chong, Bong-uk. "Economic Reforms Underway." *Vantage Point* 27(10) (October 2004): 2–7.

Dingman, Roger. "Atomic Diplomacy during the Korean War." *International Security* 13(3) (Winter 1988–1989): 50–91.

Drury, Cooper A. "Revisiting Economic Sanctions." *Journal of Peace Research* 35(4) (July 1998): 497–509.

Glenn, Russell. "No More Principles of War?" *Parameters* (Spring 1998): 48–66.

Goodkind, Daniel and West, Loraine. "The North Korean Famine and Its Demographic Impact." *Population and Development Review* 27(2) (June 2001): 219–238.

Gordenker, Leon. "The United Nations, United States Occupation, and the 1948 Election in Korea." *Political Science Quarterly* 73(3) (September 1958): 426–450.

Grajdanzev, Andrew J. "Korea Divided." *Far Eastern Survey* 14(20) (October 10, 1945): 281–283.

Harnisch, Sebastian. "US-North Korean Relations under the Bush Administration: From 'Slow Go' to 'No Go'." *Asian Survey* 42(6) (November–December 2002): 856–882.

Kaplan, Fred. "Rolling Blunder: How the Bush Administration Let North Korea Get Nukes." *Washington Monthly* May 2004: 3–4.

Kim, Joungwon Alexander. "Divided Korea in 1969: Consolidating for Transition." *Asian Survey* 10(1) (January 1970): 30–42.

———. "Soviet Policy in North Korea." *World Politics* 22(2) (January 1970): 237–254.

Kim, Samuel S. "North Korea in 1994." *Asian Survey* 35(1) (January 1995): 13–27.

———. "North Korea in 2000: Surviving through the High Hopes of Summit Diplomacy." *Asian Survey* 41(1) (January–February 2001): 12–29.

Kim, Sung-woo. "Economic Strategy for Suppression of North Korea's Nuclear Weapons Development." *Vantage Point* 27(7) (July 2004): 39–50.

Kim, Yongjeung. "The Cold War: Korean Elections." *Far Eastern Survey* 17(9) (May 5, 1948): 101–102.

Kim, Young C. "North Korea in 1974." *Asian Survey* 15(1) (January 1975): 43–52.

———. "The Democratic People's Republic of Korea in 1975." *Asian Survey* 16(1) (January 1976): 82–94.

———. "North Korea 1979: National Unification and Economic Development." *Asian Survey* 20(1) (January 1980): 53–62.

———. "North Korea in 1980: The Son also Rises." *Asian Survey* 21(1) (January 1981): 112–124.

Koh, B.C. "North Korea and Its Quest for Autonomy." *Pacific Affairs* 38 (Fall/Winter 1965/1966): 294–306.

———. "North Korea and the Sino-Soviet Schism." *Western Political Quarterly* 22(4) (December 1969): 940–962.

———. "North Korea in 1976: Under Stress." *Asian Survey* 17(1) (January 1977): 61–70.

———. "North Korea in 1977: Year of 'Readjustment'." *Asian Survey* 18(1) (January 1978): 36–44.

———. "North Korea in 1987: Launching a New Seven Year Plan." *Asian Survey* 28(1) (January 1988): 62–70.

———. "North Korea in 1988: The Fortieth Anniversary." *Asian Survey* 28(1) (January 1989): 39–45.

Lambakis, Steven, J. "Reconsidering Asymmetric Warfare." *Joint Force Quarterly* 36 (First Quarter 2005): 102–108

Lavin, Franklin L. "Asphyxiation or Oxygen." *Foreign Policy* (Autumn 1996): 138–153.

Lee, Chong-Sik. "Korean Communists and Yenan." *China Quarterly* 9 (January–March 1962): 182–192.

——— "Politics in North Korea: Pre-Korean War Stage." *China Quarterly* 14 (April–June 1963): 4

Lee, Chong-Sik and Ki-Wan Oh. "The Russian Faction in North Korea." *Asian Survey* 8(4) (April 1968): 270–288.

Lee, Grace. "The Political Philosophy of Juche." *Stanford Journal of East Asian Affairs* 3(1) (Spring 2003): 105–112.

Lee, Hy-Sang. "North Korea's Closed Economy: The Hidden Opening." *Asian Survey* 28(12) (December 1988): 1264–1279.

Lee, Young Ho. "Military Balance and Peace in the Korean Peninsula." *Asian Survey* 21(8) (August 1981): 852–864.

Liem, Channing. "United States Rule in Korea." *Far Eastern Survey* 18(7) (April 6, 1949): 77–80.

Liu, Hong. "The Sino-South Korean Normalization: A Triangular Explanation." *Asian Survey* 33(11) (November 1993): 1083–1094.

Matray, James I. "Truman's Plan for Victory: National Self-Determination and the Thirty-Eighth Parallel Decision in Korea." *Journal of American History* 66(2) (September 1979): 314–333.

———. "Hodge Podge: American Occupation Policy in Korea, 1945–1948." *Korean Studies* 19 (1995): 17–38.

———. "Korea's Partition: Soviet-American Pursuit of Reunification, 1945–1948." *Parameters, US Army War College Quarterly* 28(1) (Spring 1998): 150–162.

Mazarr, Michael J. "Going Just a Little Nuclear: Nonproliferation Lessons from North Korea." *International Security* 20(2) (Autumn 1995): 92–122.

McCune, George M. "Occupation Politics in Korea." *Far Eastern Survey* 15(3) (February 13, 1946): 33–37.

———. "Korea: The First Year of Liberation." *Pacific Affairs* 20(1) (March 1947): 3–17.

———. "Post-War Government and Politics of Korea." *Journal of Politics* 9(4) (November 1947): 605–623.

———. "The Korean Situation." *Far Eastern Review* 17(17) (September 8, 1948): 197–202.

Mearsheimer, John J. and Walt, Stephen M. "The War Over Israel's Influence." *Foreign Policy* (July/August 2006): 57–58.

Merkl, Peter H. "The German Janus: From Westpolitik to Ostpolitik." *Political Science Quarterly* 89(4) (Winter 1974–1975): 803–824.

Newnham, Randall E. "More Flies with Honey: Positive Economic Linkage in German Ostpolitik from Bismarck to Kohl." *International Studies Quarterly* 44(1) (March 2000): 73–96.

Noland, Marcus. "North Korea in Transition." *Korean Journal of Defense Analysis* XVII(1) (Spring 2005): 7–32.

Oh, John Kie-Chiang. "Role of the United States in South Korea's Democracy." *Pacific Affairs* 42(2) (Summer 1969): 164–177.

Oh, Kong Dan. North Korea in 1989: Touched by Winds of Change?" *Asian Survey* 30(1) (August 1990): 74–80.

Pape, Robert A. "Why Economic Sanctions Do Not Work." *International Security* 22(2) (Autumn 1997): 90–136.

———. "Why Economic Sanctions Still Do Not Work." *International Security* 23(1) (Summer 1998): 66–77.

Rhee, Sang-Woo. "North Korea in 1990: Lonely Struggle to Keep Chuch'e." *Asian Survey* 31(1) (January 1991): 71–78.

———. "North Korea in 1991: The Struggle to Save Chuch'e Amid Signs of Change." *Asian Survey* 32(1) (January 1992): 56–63.

Sarafan, Bertram D. "Military Government: Korea." *Far Eastern Survey* 15(23) (November 20, 1946): 349–352.

Satterwhite, David, H. "North Korea in 1997: New Opportunities in a Time of Crisis." *Asian Survey* 38(1) (January 1998): 11–23.

Scalapino, Robert A. "The Foreign Policy of North Korea." *China Quarterly* 14 (April–June 1963): 30–50.

Seong, Chaiki. "A Decade of Economic Crisis in North Korea: Impacts on the Military." *Korea Institute for Defense Analysis Papers* 3 (October 2003): 2.

Shin, Rin-Sup. "North Korea in 1981: First Year for De Facto Successor Kim Jong Il." *Asian Survey* 22(1) (January 1982): 99–106.

———. "North Korea in 1982: Continuing Revolution under Kim Jong Il." *Asian Survey* 23(1) (January 1983): 102–109.

Suh, Dae-Sook. "North Korea in 1985: A New Era after Forty Years." *Asian Survey* 26(1) (January 1986): 78–85.

———. "North Korea in 1986: Strengthening the Soviet Connection." *Asian Survey* 27(1) (January 1987): 56–63.

Sunoo, Hagwon and Angus, William N. "American Policy in Korea: Two Views." *Far Eastern Survey* 15(15) (July 31, 1946): 228–231.

Tostensen, Arne and Bull, Beate. "Are Smart Sanctions Feasible?" *World Politics* 54 (April 2002): 373–374.

Vinacke, Harold M. "United States Far Eastern Policy." *Pacific Affairs* 19(4) (December 1946): 351–363.

Wales, Nym. "Rebel Korea." *Pacific Affairs* 15(1) (March 1942): 25–43.

Washburn, John N. "Russia Looks at Northern Korea." *Pacific Affairs* 20(2) (June 1947): 152–160.

Weems, Benjamin. "Behind the Korean Elections." *Far Eastern Survey* 17(12) (June 23, 1948): 142–147.

Weiss, Thomas G. "Sanctions as a Foreign Policy Tool: Weighing Humanitarian Impulses." *Journal of Peace Research* 36(5) (September 1999): 499–509.

Yanaihara, Tadao. "Problems of Japanese Administration in Korea." *Pacific Affairs* 11(2) (June 1938): 198–207.

Young, Whan Kihl. "North Korea: A Reevaluation." *Current History* 81 (April 1982): 155–-182.

———. "North Korea in 1983: Transforming the 'Hermit Kingdom'?" *Asian Survey* 24(1) (January 1984): 100–111.

————. "North Korea in 1984: 'The Hermit Kingdom' Turns Outward!" *Asian Survey* 25(1) (January 1985): 65–79.

Zagoria, Donald S. and Young, Kun Kim. "North Korea and the Major Powers." *Asian Survey* 15(12) (December 1975): 1017–1035.

GOVERNMENT SOURCES

Republic of Korea and the Democratic People's Republic of Korea. Joint Communiqué, July 7, 1972.

Republic of Korea, Ministry of National Defense. Participatory Government Defense Policy 2003.

United Nations, General Assembly. 112th Plenary Session. The Problem of the Independence of Korea, November 14, 1947. Resolution (1947).

United Nations, Security Council. 473rd Meeting. Resolution on the Korean Question, June 25, 1950. Resolution (1950).

United States Government and the Democratic People's Republic of Korea. Agreed Framework between the United States of America and the Democratic People's Republic of Korea, October 21, 1994.

United States, Commission to Assess the Ballistic Missile Threat to the United States. Report of the Commission to Assess the Ballistic Missile Threat to the United States. 104th Congress, July 15, 1998. Washington, DC: Printing and Production Graphics, 1998.

United States, 2000 Report to Congress. Military Situation on the Korean Peninsula, September 12, 2000.

WEB SOURCES

Internet Databases

The Avalon Project at Yale Law School: Yalta (Crimea) Conference. This document is located at the following URL: http://www.yale.edu/lawweb/avalon/wwii/yalta.htm. October 2006.

The Avalon Project at Yale Law School: Interim Meeting of Foreign Ministers of the United States, the United Kingdom, and the Union of Soviet Socialist Republics, Moscow, December 16–26, 1945. This document is located at the following URL: http://www.yale.edu/lawweb/avalon/decade/decade19.htm. April 2006.

Reports

Pyongyang, Second Asian Economic Seminar (Pyongyang) of Delegates of Asian Economic Bureau and Participants from Asia, Africa and Oceania (Colombo: The Asian Economic Bureau, 1964): 1.

United States, CRS Report for Congress. US Assistance to North Korea: Fact Sheet. By Mark E. Manyin, February 11, 2005. http://fpc.state.gov/documents/organization/62647.pdf.

United States, CRS Report for Congress. Foreign Assistance to North Korea. By Mark E. Manyin, May 26, 2005. http://www.nautilus.org/napsnet/sr/2005/0550ACRS.pdf.

United States, 2000 Report to Congress on the Military Situation on the Korean Peninsula, September 12, 2000. http://defenselink.mil/news/Sep2000/korea09122000.html.

United Nations, World Food Programme. World Food Programme Annual Report 2004. http://www.wfp.org/policies/Annual_Reports/index.asp?section=6&sub_section=3.

United Nations, World Food Programme. World Food Programme Annual Report 2005. http://www.wfp.org/policies/Annual_Reports/index.asp?section=6&sub_section=3.

NEWSPAPERS AND MAGAZINES

Korea Times

"Financial Dispute with N. Korea Resolved." *Korea Times* March 16, 2007.

Jung, Sung-ki. "US Plans to Complete Command Transfer by 2009." *Korea Times* August 4, 2006.

Lee, Jin-woo. "US Scholar Calls for Direct Talks between US, N. Korea." *Korea Times* October 2, 2006.

Lee, Soo-jeong. "South Korea Proposes Red Cross Talks to Ensure More Family Reunions." *Korea Times* August 27, 2000.

Na, Jeong-ju. "NK Opens Mt. Paektu to S. Koreans." *Korea Times* August 10, 2005.

"NK Has Plutonium to Make 8 Bombs." *Korea Times* January 3, 2006.

"NK Imports 15,000 Tons of Rice from China in late 2006." *Korea Times* February 9, 2007.

Park, Hyong-ki. "SUVs, Pickups Hot in N. Korea." *Korea Times* October 15, 2006.

Park, Song-wu. "Launch Sends Blunt Message to America." *Korea Times* July 5, 2006.

———."Diplomats in N. Korea Believe Underground Nuke Test Highly Probable." *Korea Times* September 10, 2006.

———. "Seoul Will Not Join US-led PSI." *Korea Times* November 13, 2006.

Ryu, Jin. "Japan Hit for Spiking Tension." *Korea Times* July 11, 2006.

Seo, Dong-shin. "China Unfreezes NK Bank Accounts." *Korea Times* November 20, 2006.

———. "Seoul Gives 60,000 Tons of Coal Aid to NK." *Korea Times* January 3, 2006.

———. "NK's Chemical Imports Raise Alarms." *Korea Times* September 28, 2004.

Staines, Reuben. "NK Cuts Kumgang Tours." *Korea Times* August 29, 2005.

———. "Koreans Lean Closer to China." *Korea Times* January 1, 2006.

"UN Resolution Affects NK Nuke Programs." *Korea Times* July 17, 2006.

Korea Herald

Lee, Joo-hee. "President Warns against Great Power Politics." *Korea Herald* September 16, 2005.

New York Times

"'Barbarous' Attack on 2 Boats Laid to North Korea by Seoul." *New York Times* February 16, 1974, 3.

"Bid to US Made by North Korea." *New York Times* March 26, 1974, 9.

Binder, David. "What Bonn Has That East Bloc Wants." *New York Times* December 14, 1969, E4.

"Disorder Termed Aims of Korean Reds." *New York Times* January 24, 1968, 15.

"Economic Aid Pact Signed by Peiping and North Korea." *New York Times* November 24, 1953, 1 and 12.

Farnsworth, Clyde H. "Bonn Is Said to Offer Warsaw a $550-Million Credit in Trade Talks." *New York Times* December 9, 1969, 6.

Farr, Michael. "Bonn Sets Credit Line for Soviets: Some of $1.6 Billion to go for Upgrading of Consumer Goods German Deal with Soviets." *New York Times* October 12, 1988, D1.

French, Howard W. "In Yet Another Mystery, North Korea has Suddenly Turned Testy." *New York Times* October 26, 2001, A5.

Friedman, Thomas L. "Macho on North Korea." *New York Times* March 9, 2001, A19.

Gwertzman, Bernard. "Soviet and West Germany Reach Accord on a Treaty to Foster Peace in Europe." *New York Times* August 6, 1970, 1.

"No Ban on North Korea." *New York Times* January 19, 1988, D27.

"North Korean 'Defector' Is Indicted by Seoul." *New York Times* March 23, 1969, 5.

"North Korean Says Aim was to Assassinate Park." *New York Times* January 23, 1968, 6.

"North Koreans in Moscow Get Pledge of Military Aid." *New York Times* June 1, 1965, 7.

"North Koreans Propose Reduction of Troops in the North and South." *New York Times* July 24, 1987, A10.

"North Korea Says It Will Return Injured G.I. and Copter's Three Dead." *New York Times* July 16, 1977, 1.

"North Korea Signs Pact with Soviet." *New York Times* March 6, 1967, 3.

"North Korea Sinks Seoul Patrol Ship." *New York Times* June 29, 1974, 2.

"North and South Korea Agree on Family Visits." *New York Times* August 23, 1985, A3.

Sanger, David E. "Bush Tells Seoul Talks with North Won't Resume Now: Lays Clinton Plan Aside." *New York Times* March 8, 2001, A1.

"Seoul Threatens North Korea after Confession on Jet Bomb." *New York Times* January 16, 1988, 2.

"South Korea Calls 'Defection' a Hoax by Northern Spy." *New York Times* February 14, 1969, 1.

"Text of Korean Statement." *New York Times* July 4, 1972, 2.

"US Copter Strayed on North Korea Line." *New York Times* July 15, 1977, 42.
"Washington Hails Korea Plans for Talks." *New York Times* July 5, 1972, 16.
Welles, Benjamin. "North Korean Militancy Linked to 1966 Meeting." *New York Times* February 1, 1968, 15.
"West Berlin Adds Trade with East." *New York Times* November 9, 1969, 17.

International Herald Tribune

Choi, Brent and Lee, Brian. "North is Said to Cut Back Phone Use." *Joongang Daily* (distributed by the Herald Tribune), June 7, 2005. (Website: http://joongangdaily.joins.com/article/view.asp?aid=2577677)

Los Angeles Times

Demick, Barbara. "N. Korea Says It Wants Its Money Back, Then It'll Talk." *Los Angeles Times (LATimes.com)* July 8, 2006.

Time Magazine

Macintyre, Donald. "Sunshine Policy: A Very Expensive Affair." *Time Magazine* March 24, 2003. Vol. 161, No. 11.

Yonhap News Service

"Make a Higher Leap Full of Great Ambition and Confidence" (North Korean 2006 New Year's Message). *Yonhap News Service* , North Korea This Week 378, January 2006.
"North Korea Recalls National Development Movement." *Yonhap News Service* January 12, 2006.

Washington Post

Burgess, John. "Two Koreas Agree on Relief Plan." *Washington Post* September 27, 1984, A23.
Chapman, William. "Burma Says N. Korea Guilty of Bombing that Killed 21; Rangoon Breaks Diplomatic Relations with Pyongyang." *Washington Post* November 5, 1983, A24.
"Japs Ordered to Surrender Everywhere." *Washington Post* September 2, 1945, M2.

Miscellaneous

Ghamari-Tabrizi, Behrooz. "Words, Worries, and Wants: A Glimpse into Life in Iran." *Illinois International Review* 3 (Fall 2006): 2.
"Koizumi Prefers N. Korea Dialogue to Economic Sanctions." *Kyodo News Service* October 11, 2004.

"North Korea's Nuclear New Year's Message." *Australian*, January 1, 2007.

Terry, Fiona. "Food Aid to North Korea Is Propping Up Stalinist a Regime." *Guardian Weekly* (New Zealand) September 6, 2001.

"White House Calls Clinton-era North Korea Policy a Failure." *USA Today* July 11, 2006.

Index

About the Author

JACQUES FUQUA, a retired U.S. Army officer, presently serves as Director of International Engagement and Communications at the University of Illinois (Urbana-Champaign). He has authored numerous journal and newspaper articles on Korean peninsula and U.S.-Japan security issues and has participated in various television and radio interviews discussing the North Korean nuclear issue. He also researches and teaches courses on East Asian security and the diplomatic/security history of Korea. Prior to his current posting, Fuqua served as Associate Director of the East Asian Studies Center at Indiana University (Bloomington). He retired from the U.S. Army in February 2000 as a Lieutenant Colonel (Northeast Asia Foreign Area Officer) after 21 years of active duty service.